The Works of
Alice Dunbar-Nelson

THE SCHOMBURG LIBRARY OF
NINETEENTH-CENTURY BLACK WOMEN WRITERS

General Editor, Henry Louis Gates, Jr.

Titles are listed chronologically; collections that include works published over a span of years are listed according to the publication date of their initial work.

The Works

of

Alice Dunbar-Nelson

Volume 3

Edited by
GLORIA T. HULL

ᔰ ᔰ ᔰ

ᔰ ᔰ ᔰ

New York   Oxford
OXFORD UNIVERSITY PRESS
1988

Oxford University Press

Oxford   New York   Toronto
Delhi   Bombay   Calcutta   Madras   Karachi
Petaling Jaya   Singapore   Hong Kong   Tokyo
Nairobi   Dar es Salaam   Cape Town
Melbourne   Auckland

and associated companies in
Beirut   Berlin   Ibadan   Nicosia

Library of Congress Cataloging-in-Publication Data

Dunbar-Nelson, Alice Moore, 1875–1935.
The works of Alice Dunbar-Nelson.
(The Schomburg library on nineteenth-century black women writers)
Bibliography: v. 3, p.
1. Afro-Americans—literary collections.
I. Hull, Gloria T.   II. Title.   III. Series.
PS3507.U6228   1988   818'.5209   87-14118
ISBN 0-19-505252-8 (v. 3)
ISBN 0-19-505267-6 (set)

6 8 10 9 7

Printed in the United States of America
on acid-free paper

The
Schomburg Library
of
Nineteenth-Century
Black Women Writers
is
Dedicated
in Memory
of
PAULINE AUGUSTA COLEMAN GATES

1916–1987

PUBLISHER'S NOTE

FOREWORD
In Her Own Write

Henry Louis Gates, Jr.

One muffled strain in the Silent South, a jarring chord and a vague and uncomprehended cadenza has been and still is the Negro. And of that muffled chord, the one mute and voiceless note has been the sadly expectant Black Woman, ...

The "other side" has not been represented by one who "lives there." And not many can more sensibly realize and more accurately tell the weight and the fret of the "long dull pain" than the open-eyed but hitherto voiceless Black Woman of America.

. . . as our Caucasian barristers are not to blame if they cannot *quite* put themselves in the dark man's place, neither should the dark man be wholly expected fully and adequately to reproduce the exact Voice of the Black Woman.

—ANNA JULIA COOPER, *A Voice From the South* (1892)

The birth of the Afro-American literary tradition occurred in 1773, when Phillis Wheatley published a book of poetry. Despite the fact that her book garnered for her a remarkable amount of attention, Wheatley's journey to the printer had been a most arduous one. Sometime in 1772, a young African girl walked demurely into a room in Boston to undergo an oral examination, the results of which would determine the direction of her life and work. Perhaps she was shocked upon entering the appointed room. For there, perhaps gathered in a semicircle, sat eighteen of Boston's most notable citizens. Among them were John Erving, a prominent Boston merchant; the Reverend Charles Chauncy, pastor of the Tenth Congregational Church; and John Hancock, who would later gain fame for his signature on the Declaration of Independence. At the center of this group was His Excellency, Thomas Hutchinson, governor of Massachusetts, with Andrew Oliver, his lieutenant governor, close by his side.

Why had this august group been assembled? Why had it seen fit to summon this young African girl, scarcely eighteen years old, before it? This group of "the most respectable Characters in *Boston*," as it would later define itself, had assembled to question closely the African adolescent on the slender sheaf of poems that she claimed to have "written by herself." We can only speculate on the nature of the questions posed to the fledgling poet. Perhaps they asked her to identify and explain—for all to hear—exactly who were the Greek and Latin gods and poets alluded to so frequently in her work. Perhaps they asked her to conjugate a verb in Latin or even to translate randomly selected passages from the Latin, which she and her master, John Wheatley, claimed that she "had made some Progress in." Or perhaps they asked her to recite from memory key passages from the texts of John Milton and Alexander Pope, the two poets by whom the African claimed to be most directly influenced. We do not know.

We do know, however, that the African poet's responses were more than sufficient to prompt the eighteen august gentlemen to compose, sign, and publish a two-paragraph "Attestation," an open letter "To the Publick" that prefaces Phillis Wheatley's book and that reads in part:

> We whose Names are under-written, do assure the World, that the Poems specified in the following Page, were (as we

verily believe) written by Phillis, a young Negro Girl, who
was but a few Years since, brought an uncultivated Barbarian
from *Africa*, and has ever since been, and now is, under the
Disadvantage of serving as a Slave in a Family in this Town.
She has been examined by some of the best Judges, and is
thought qualified to write them.

So important was this document in securing a publisher for
Wheatley's poems that it forms the signal element in the
prefatory matter preceding her *Poems on Various Subjects, Religious and Moral*, published in London in 1773.

Without the published "Attestation," Wheatley's publisher
claimed, few would believe that an African could possibly
have written poetry all by herself. As the eighteen put the
matter clearly in their letter, "Numbers would be ready to
suspect they were not really the Writings of Phillis." Wheatley and her master, John Wheatley, had attempted to publish
a similar volume in 1772 in Boston, but Boston publishers
had been incredulous. One year later, "Attestation" in hand,
Phillis Wheatley and her master's son, Nathaniel Wheatley,
sailed for England, where they completed arrangements for
the publication of a volume of her poems with the aid of the
Countess of Huntington and the Earl of Dartmouth.

This curious anecdote, surely one of the oddest oral ex-
aminations on record, is only a tiny part of a larger, and
even more curious, episode in the Enlightenment. Since the
beginning of the sixteenth century, Europeans had wondered aloud whether or not the African "species of men," as
they were most commonly called, *could* ever create formal
literature, could ever master "the arts and sciences." If they
could, the argument ran, then the African variety of humanity was fundamentally related to the European variety. If not,
then it seemed clear that the African was destined by nature

to be a slave. This was the burden shouldered by Phillis
Wheatley when she successfully defended herself and the authorship of her book against counterclaims and doubts.

Indeed, with her successful defense, Wheatley launched
two traditions at once—the black American literary tradition
and the black woman's literary tradition. If it is extraordinary
that not just one but both of these traditions were founded
simultaneously by a black woman—certainly an event unique
in the history of literature—it is also ironic that this important fact of common, coterminous literary origins seems to
have escaped most scholars.

That the progenitor of the black literary tradition was a
woman means, in the most strictly literal sense, that all sub-
sequent black writers have evolved in a matrilinear line of
descent, and that each, consciously or unconsciously, has extended and revised a canon whose foundation was the poetry
of a black woman. Early black writers seem to have been
keenly aware of Wheatley's founding role, even if most of
her white reviewers were more concerned with the implica-
tions of her race than her gender. Jupiter Hammon, for example, whose 1760 broadside "An Evening Thought. Salvation by Christ, With Penitential Cries" was the first
individual poem published by a black American, acknowledged Wheatley's influence by selecting her as the subject of
his second broadside, "An Address to Miss Phillis Wheatly
[*sic*], Ethiopian Poetess, in Boston," which was published at
Hartford in 1778. And George Moses Horton, the second
Afro-American to publish a book of poetry in English (1829),
brought out in 1838 an edition of his *Poems By A Slave*
bound together with Wheatley's work. Indeed, for fifty-six
years, between 1773 and 1829, when Horton published *The
Hope of Liberty*, Wheatley was the *only* black person to have
published a book of imaginative literature in English. So

central was this black woman's role in the shaping of the
Afro-American literary tradition that, as one historian has
maintained, the history of the reception of Phillis Wheatley's
poetry *is* the history of Afro-American literary criticism. Well
into the nineteenth century, Wheatley and the black literary
tradition were the same entity.

But Wheatley is not the only black woman writer who
stands as a pioneering figure in Afro-American literature.
Just as Wheatley gave birth to the genre of black poetry, Ann
Plato was the first Afro-American to publish a book of essays
(1841) and Harriet E. Wilson was the first black person to
publish a novel in the United States (1859).

Despite this pioneering role of black women in the tradition, however, many of their contributions before this century have been all but lost or unrecognized. As Hortense
Spillers observed as recently as 1983,

> With the exception of a handful of autobiographical narratives
> from the nineteenth century, the black woman's realities are
> virtually suppressed until the period of the Harlem Renais-
> sance and later. Essentially the black woman as artist, as
> intellectual spokesperson for her own cultural apprenticeship,
> has not existed before, for anyone. At the source of [their]
> own symbol-making task, [the community of black women
> writers] confronts, therefore, a tradition of work that is quite
> recent, its continuities, broken and sporadic.

Until now, it has been extraordinarily difficult to establish
the formal connections between early black women's writing
and that of the present, precisely because our knowledge of
their work has been broken and sporadic. Phillis Wheatley,
for example, while certainly the most reprinted and discussed
poet in the tradition, is also one of the least understood. Ann
Plato's seminal work, *Essays* (which includes biographies and
poems), has not been reprinted since it was published a cen-

tury and a half ago. And Harriet Wilson's *Our Nig,* her
compelling novel of a black woman's expanding consciousness in a racist Northern antebellum environment, never received even *one* review or comment at a time when virtually
all works written by black people were heralded by abolition-
ists as salient arguments against the existence of human slavery. Many of the books reprinted in this set experienced a
similar fate, the most dreadful fate for an author: that of
being ignored then relegated to the obscurity of the rare book
section of a university library. We can only wonder how
many other texts in the black woman's tradition have been
lost to this generation of readers or remain unclassified or
uncatalogued and, hence, unread.

This was not always so, however. Black women writers
dominated the final decade of the nineteenth century, perhaps
spurred to publish by an 1886 essay entitled "The Coming
American Novelist," which was published in *Lippincott's
Monthly Magazine* and written by "A Lady From Philadelphia." This pseudonymous essay argued that the "Great
American Novel" would be written by a black person. Her
argument is so curious that it deserves to be repeated:

> When we come to formulate our demands of the Coming
> American Novelist, we will agree that he must be native-
> born. His ancestors may come from where they will, but we
> must give him a birthplace and have the raising of him. Still,
> the longer his family has been here the better he will represent
> us. Suppose he should have no country but ours, no traditions
> but those he has learned here, no longings apart from us, no
> future except in our future—the orphan of the world, he
> finds with us his home. And with all this, suppose he refuses
> to be fused into that grand conglomerate we call the "Amer-
> ican type." With us, he is not of us. He is original, he has
> humor, he is tender, he is passive and fiery, he has been

taught what we call justice, and he has his own opinion about
it. He has suffered everything a poet, a dramatist, a novelist
need suffer before he comes to have his lips anointed. And
with it all he is in one sense a spectator, a little out of the
race. How would these conditions go towards forming an
original development? In a word, suppose the coming novelist
is of African origin? When one comes to consider the subject,
there is no improbability in it. One thing is certain,—our
great novel will not be written by the typical American.

An atypical American, indeed. Not only would the great
American novel be written by an African-American, it would
be written by an African-American *woman:*

> Yet farther: I have used the generic masculine pronoun
> because it is convenient; but Fate keeps revenge in store. It
> was a woman who, taking the wrongs of the African as her
> theme, wrote the novel that awakened the world to their
> reality, and why should not the coming novelist be a woman
> as well as an African? She—the woman of that race—has
> some claims on Fate which are not yet paid up.

It is these claims on fate that we seek to pay by publishing
The Schomburg Library of Nineteenth-Century Black Women
Writers.

This theme would be repeated by several black women
authors, most notably by Anna Julia Cooper, a prototypical
black feminist whose 1892 *A Voice From the South* can be
considered to be one of the original texts of the black feminist movement. It was Cooper who first analyzed the fal-
lacy of referring to "the Black man" when speaking of black
people and who argued that just as white men cannot speak
through the consciousness of black men, neither can black
men "fully and adequately . . . reproduce the exact Voice of
the Black Woman." Gender and race, she argues, cannot be

conflated, except in the instance of a black woman's voice, and it is this voice which must be uttered and to which we must listen. As Cooper puts the matter so compellingly:

> It is not the intelligent woman vs. the ignorant woman; nor the white woman vs. the black, the brown, and the red,—it is not even the cause of woman vs. man. Nay, 'tis woman's strongest vindication for speaking that *the world needs to hear her voice*. It would be subversive of every human interest that the cry of one-half the human family be stifled. Woman in stepping from the pedestal of statue-like inactivity in the domestic shrine, and daring to think and move and speak,— to undertake to help shape, mold, and direct the thought of her age, is merely completing the circle of the world's vision. Hers is every interest that has lacked an interpreter and a defender. Her cause is linked with that of every agony that has been dumb—every wrong that needs a voice.
>
> It is no fault of man's that he has not been able to see truth from her standpoint. It does credit both to his head and heart that no greater mistakes have been committed or even wrongs perpetrated while she sat making tatting and snipping paper flowers. Man's own innate chivalry and the mutual interdependence of their interests have insured his treating her cause, in the main at least, as his own. And he is pardonably surprised and even a little chagrined, perhaps, to find his legislation not considered "perfectly lovely" in every respect. But in any case his work is only impoverished by her remaining dumb. The world has had to limp along with the wobbling gait and one-sided hesitancy of a man with one eye. Suddenly the bandage is removed from the other eye and the whole body is filled with light. It sees a circle where before it saw a segment. The darkened eye restored, every member rejoices with it.

The myopic sight of the darkened eye can only be restored when the full range of the black woman's voice, with its own special timbres and shadings, remains mute no longer.

Similarly, Victoria Earle Matthews, an author of short stories and essays, and a cofounder in 1896 of the National Association of Colored Women, wrote in her stunning essay, "The Value of Race Literature" (1895), that "when the literature of our race is developed, it will of necessity be different in all essential points of greatness, true heroism and real Christianity from what we may at the present time, for convenience, call American literature." Matthews argued that this great tradition of Afro-American literature would be the textual outlet "for the unnaturally suppressed inner lives which our people have been compelled to lead." Once these "unnaturally suppressed inner lives" of black people are unveiled, no "grander diffusion of mental light" will shine more brightly, she concludes, than that of the articulate Afro-American woman:

And now comes the question, What part shall we women play in the Race Literature of the future? . . . within the compass of one small journal ["Woman's Era"] we have struck out a new line of departure—a journal, a record of Race interests gathered from all parts of the United States, carefully selected, moistened, winnowed and garnered by the ablest intellects of educated colored women, shrinking at no lofty theme, shirking no serious duty, aiming at every possible excellence, and determined to do their part in the future uplifting of the race.

If twenty women, by their concentrated efforts in one literary movement, can meet with such success as has engendered, planned out, and so successfully consummated this convention, what much more glorious results, what wider spread success, what grander diffusion of mental light will not come forth at the bidding of the enlarged hosts of women writers, already called into being by the stimulus of your efforts?

And here let me speak one word for my journalistic sisters

who have already entered the broad arena of journalism. Before the "Woman's Era" had come into existence, no one except themselves can appreciate the bitter experience and sore disappointments under which they have at all times been compelled to pursue their chosen vocations.

If their brothers of the press have had their difficulties to contend with, I am here as a sister journalist to state, from the fullness of knowledge, that their task has been an easy one compared with that of the colored woman in journalism.

Woman's part in Race Literature, as in Race building, is the most important part and has been so in all ages. . . . All through the most remote epochs she has done her share in literature. . . .

One of the most important aspects of this set is the republication of the salient texts from 1890 to 1910, which literary historians could well call "The Black Woman's Era." In addition to Mary Helen Washington's definitive edition of Cooper's *A Voice From the South*, we have reprinted two novels by Amelia Johnson, Frances Harper's *Iola Leroy*, two novels by Emma Dunham Kelley, Alice Dunbar-Nelson's two impressive collections of short stories, and Pauline Hopkins's three serialized novels as well as her monumental novel, *Contending Forces*—all published between 1890 and 1910. Indeed, black women published more works of fiction in these two decades than black men had published in the previous half century. Nevertheless, this great achievement has been ignored.

Moreover, the writings of nineteenth-century Afro-American women in general have remained buried in obscurity, accessible only in research libraries or in overpriced and poorly edited reprints. Many of these books have never been reprinted at all; in some instances only one or two copies are extant. In these works of fiction, poetry, autobiography, biography, essays, and journalism resides the mind of the nineteenth-century Afro-American woman. Until these works are made readily available to teachers and their students, a significant segment of the black tradition will remain silent.

Oxford University Press, in collaboration with the Schomburg Center for Research in Black Culture, is publishing thirty volumes of these compelling works, each of which contains an introduction by an expert in the field. The set includes such rare texts as Johnson's *The Hazeley Family* and *Clarence and Corinne*, Plato's *Essays*, the most complete edition of Phillis Wheatley's poems and letters, Emma Dunham Kelley's pioneering novel *Megda*, several previously unpublished stories and a novel by Alice Dunbar-Nelson, and the first collected volumes of Pauline Hopkins's three serialized novels and Frances Harper's poetry. We also present four volumes of poetry by such women as Mary Eliza Tucker Lambert, Adah Menken, Josephine Heard, and Maggie Johnson. Numerous slave and spiritual narratives, a newly discovered novel—*Four Girls at Cottage City*—by Emma Dunham Kelley (-Hawkins), and the first American edition of *Wonderful Adventures of Mrs. Seacole in Many Lands* are also among the texts included.

In addition to resurrecting the works of black women authors, it is our hope that this set will facilitate the resurrection of the Afro-American woman's literary tradition itself by unearthing its nineteenth-century roots. In the works of Nella Larsen and Jessie Fauset, Zora Neale Hurston and Ann Petry, Lorraine Hansberry and Gwendolyn Brooks, Paule Marshall and Toni Cade Bambara, Audre Lorde and Rita Dove, Toni Morrison and Alice Walker, Gloria Naylor and Jamaica Kincaid, these roots have branched luxuriantly. The eighteenth- and nineteenth-century authors whose works are presented in this set founded and nurtured the black women's literary tradition, which must be revived, explicated, analyzed, and debated before we can understand more completely the formal shaping of this tradition within a tradition, a coded literary universe through which, regrettably, we are only just beginning to navigate our way. As Anna Cooper said nearly one hundred years ago, we have been blinded by the loss of sight in one eye and have therefore been unable to detect the full *shape* of the Afro-American literary tradition.

Literary works configure into a tradition not because of some mystical collective unconscious determined by the biology of race or gender, but because writers read other writers and *ground* their representations of experience in models of language provided largely by other writers to whom they feel akin. It is through this mode of literary revision, amply evident in the *texts* themselves—in formal echoes, recast metaphors, even in parody—that a "tradition" emerges and defines itself.

This is formal bonding, and it is only through formal bonding that we can know a literary tradition. The collective publication of these works by black women now, for the first time, makes it possible for scholars and critics, male and female, black and white, to *demonstrate* that black women writers read, and revised, other black women writers. To demonstrate this set of formal literary relations is to demonstrate that sexuality, race, and gender are both the condition and the basis of *tradition*—but tradition as found in discrete acts of language use.

A word is in order about the history of this set. For the past decade, I have taught a course, first at Yale and then at Cornell, entitled "Black Women and Their Fictions," a course that I inherited from Toni Morrison, who developed it in the mid-1970s for Yale's Program in Afro-American Studies. Although the course was inspired by the remarkable accomplishments of black women novelists since 1970, I gradually extended its beginning date to the late nineteenth century, studying Frances Harper's *Iola Leroy* and Anna Julia Cooper's *A Voice From the South*, both published in 1892. With the discovery of Harriet E. Wilson's seminal novel, *Our Nig* (1859), and Jean Yellin's authentication of Harriet Jacobs's brilliant slave narrative, *Incidents in the Life of a Slave Girl* (1861), a survey course spanning over a century and a quarter emerged.

But the discovery of *Our Nig*, as well as the interest in nineteenth-century black women's writing that this discovery generated, convinced me that even the most curious and diligent scholars knew very little of the extensive history of the creative writings of Afro-American women before 1900. Indeed, most scholars of Afro-American literature had never even read most of the books published by black women, simply because these books—of poetry, novels, short stories, essays, and autobiography—were mostly accessible only in rare book sections of university libraries. For reasons unclear to me even today, few of these marvelous renderings of the Afro-American woman's consciousness were reprinted in the late 1960s and early 1970s, when so many other texts of the Afro-American literary tradition were resurrected from the dark and silent graveyard of the out-of-print and were reissued in facsimile editions aimed at the hungry readership for canonical texts in the nascent field of black studies.

So, with the help of several superb research assistants—including David Curtis, Nicola Shilliam, Wendy Jones, Sam Otter, Janadas Devan, Suvir Kaul, Cynthia Bond, Elizabeth Alexander, and Adele Alexander—and with the expert advice of scholars such as William Robinson, William Andrews, Mary Helen Washington, Maryemma Graham, Jean Yellin, Houston A. Baker, Jr., Richard Yarborough, Hazel Carby, Joan R. Sherman, Frances Foster, and William French, dozens of bibliographies were used to compile a list of books written or narrated by black women mostly before 1910. Without the assistance provided through this shared experience of scholarship, the scholar's true legacy, this project could not have been conceived. As the list grew, I was struck by how very many of these titles that I, for example, had never even heard of, let alone read, such as Ann Plato's *Essays*, Louisa Picquet's slave narrative, or Amelia Johnson's two novels, *Clarence and Corinne* and *The Hazeley Family*. Through our research with the Black Periodical Fiction and Poetry Project (funded by NEH and the Ford Foundation), I also realized that several novels by black women, including three works of fiction by Pauline Hopkins, had been serialized in black periodicals, but had never been collected and published as books. Nor had the several books of poetry published by black women, such as the prolific Frances E. W. Harper, been collected and edited. When I discovered still another "lost" novel by an Afro-American woman (*Four Girls at Cottage City*, published in 1898 by Emma Dunham Kelley-Hawkins), I decided to attempt to edit a collection of reprints of these works and to publish them as a "library" of black women's writings, in part so that I could read them myself.

Convincing university and trade publishers to undertake this project proved to be a difficult task. Despite the commercial success of *Our Nig* and of the several reprint series of women's works (such as Virago, the Beacon Black Women Writers Series, and Rutgers' American Women Writers Series), several presses rejected the project as "too large," "too limited," or as "commercially unviable." Only two publishers recognized the viability and the import of the project and, of these, Oxford's commitment to publish the titles simultaneously as a set made the press's offer irresistible.

While attempting to locate original copies of these exceedingly rare books, I discovered that most of the texts were housed at the Schomburg Center for Research in Black Culture, a branch of The New York Public Library, under the direction of Howard Dodson. Dodson's infectious enthusiasm for the project and his generous collaboration, as well as that of his stellar staff (especially Diana Lachatanere, Sharon Howard, Ellis Haizip, Richard Newman, and Betty Gubert), led to a joint publishing initiative that produced this set as part of the Schomburg's major fund-raising campaign. Without Dodson's foresight and generosity of spirit, the set would not have materialized. Without William P. Sisler's masterful editorship at Oxford and his staff's careful attention to detail, the set would have remained just another grand idea that tends to languish in a scholar's file cabinet.

I would also like to thank Dr. Michael Winston and Dr. Thomas C. Battle, Vice-President of Academic Affairs and the Director of the Moorland-Spingarn Research Center (respectively) at Howard University, for their unending encouragement, support, and collaboration in this project, and Esme E. Bhan at Howard for her meticulous research and bibliographical skills. In addition, I would like to acknowledge the aid of the staff at the libraries of Duke University, Cornell University (especially Tom Weissinger and Donald Eddy), the Boston Public Library, the Western Reserve Historical Society, the Library of Congress, and Yale University. Linda Robbins, Marion Osmun, Sarah Flanagan, and Gerard Case, all members of the staff at Oxford, were extraordinarily effective at coordinating, editing, and producing the various segments of each text in the set. Candy Ruck, Nina de Tar, and Phillis Molock expertly typed reams of correspondence and manuscripts connected to the project.

I would also like to express my gratitude to my colleagues who edited and introduced the individual titles in the set. Without their attention to detail, their willingness to meet strict deadlines, and their sheer enthusiasm for this project, the set could not have been published. But finally and ultimately, I would hope that the publication of the set would help to generate even more scholarly interest in the black women authors whose work is presented here. Struggling against the seemingly insurmountable barriers of racism *and* sexism, while often raising families and fulfilling full-time professional obligations, these women managed nevertheless to record their thoughts and feelings and to *testify* to all who dare read them that the will to harness the power of collective endurance and survival is the will to write.

The Schomburg Library of Nineteenth-Century Black Women Writers is dedicated in memory of Pauline Augusta Coleman Gates, who died in the spring of 1987. It was she who inspired in me the love of learning and the love of literature. I have encountered in the books of this set no will more determined, no courage more noble, no mind more sublime, no self more celebratory of the achievements of all Afro-American women, and indeed of life itself, than her own.

A NOTE FROM
THE SCHOMBURG CENTER

Howard Dodson

The Schomburg Center for Research in Black Culture, The New York Public Library, is pleased to join with Dr. Henry Louis Gates and Oxford University Press in presenting The Schomburg Library of Nineteenth-Century Black Women Writers. This thirty-volume set includes the work of a generation of black women whose writing has only been available previously in rare book collections. The materials reprinted in twenty-four of the thirty volumes are drawn from the unique holdings of the Schomburg Center.

A research unit of The New York Public Library, the Schomburg Center has been in the forefront of those institutions dedicated to collecting, preserving, and providing access to the records of the black past. In the course of its two generations of acquisition and conservation activity, the Center has amassed collections totaling more than 5 million items. They include over 100,000 bound volumes, 85,000 reels and sets of microforms, 300 manuscript collections containing some 3.5 million items, 300,000 photographs and extensive holdings of prints, sound recordings, film and videotape, newspapers, artworks, artifacts, and other book and nonbook materials. Together they vividly document the history and cultural heritages of people of African descent worldwide.

Though established some sixty-two years ago, the Center's book collections date from the sixteenth century. Its oldest item, an Ethiopian Coptic Tunic, dates from the eighth or ninth century. Rare materials, however, are most available for the nineteenth-century African-American experience. It is from these holdings that the majority of the titles selected for inclusion in this set are drawn.

The nineteenth century was a formative period in African-American literary and cultural history. Prior to the Civil War, the majority of black Americans living in the United States were held in bondage. Law and practice forbade teaching them to read or write. Even after the war, many of the impediments to learning and literary productivity remained. Nevertheless, black men and women of the nineteenth century persevered in both areas. Moreover, more African-Americans than we yet realize turned their observations, feelings, social viewpoints, and creative impulses into published works. In time, this nineteenth-century printed record included poetry, short stories, histories, novels, autobiographies, social criticism, and theology, as well as economic and philosophical treatises. Unfortunately, much of this body of literature remained, until very recently, relatively inaccessible to twentieth-century scholars, teachers, creative artists, and others interested in black life. Prior to the late 1960s, most Americans (black as well as white) had never heard of these nineteenth-century authors, much less read their works.

The civil rights and black power movements created unprecedented interest in the thought, behavior, and achievements of black people. Publishers responded by revising traditional texts, introducing the American public to a new generation of African-American writers, publishing a variety of thematic anthologies, and reprinting a plethora of "classic texts" in African-American history, literature, and art. The reprints usually appeared as individual titles or in a series of bound volumes or microform formats.

The Schomburg Center, which has a long history of supporting publishing that deals with the history and culture of Africans in diaspora, became an active participant in many of the reprint revivals of the 1960s. Since hard copies of original printed works are the preferred formats for producing facsimile reproductions, publishers frequently turned to the Schomburg Center for copies of these original titles. In addition to providing such material, Schomburg Center staff members offered advice and consultation, wrote introductions, and occasionally entered into formal copublishing arrangements in some projects.

Most of the nineteenth-century titles reprinted during the 1960s, however, were by and about black men. A few black women were included in the longer series, but works by lesser known black women were generally overlooked. The Schomburg Library of Nineteenth-Century Black Women Writers is both a corrective to these previous omissions and an important contribution to Afro-American literary history in its own right. Through this collection of volumes, the thoughts, perspectives, and creative abilities of nineteenth-century African-American women, as captured in books and pamphlets published in large part before 1910, are again being made available to the general public. The Schomburg Center is pleased to be a part of this historic endeavor.

I would like to thank Professor Gates for initiating this project. Thanks are due both to him and Mr. William P. Sisler of Oxford University Press for giving the Schomburg Center an opportunity to play such a prominent role in the set. Thanks are also due to my colleagues at The New York Public Library and the Schomburg Center, especially Dr. Vartan Gregorian, Richard De Gennaro, Paul Fasana, Betsy

Pinover, Richard Newman, Diana Lachatanere, Glenderlyn Johnson, and Harold Anderson for their assistance and support. I can think of no better way of demonstrating than in this set the role the Schomburg Center plays in assuring that the black heritage will be available for future generations.

CONTENTS

INTRODUCTION

Gloria T. Hull

One senses in practically everything that Alice Dunbar-Nelson wrote a driving desire to pull together the multiple strands of her complex personality and poetics. Yet this desire seems to be undercut or subverted by an opposing—and perhaps ultimately more powerful—ambivalence (I want to say schizophrenia) that makes W. E. B. Du Bois's racially "warring bloods" and Virginia Woolf's female "contrary instincts" look simple. Dunbar-Nelson spent her life assiduously writing herself both into and out of her literary "fictions," using conventional concepts of form, genre, and propriety that (given her lack of creative genius) bound her to divisiveness and inarticulation. This scenario becomes all the more complicated when one remembers that it was played in a late-nineteenth-, early-twentieth-century world where social conditions and the literary establishment made authentic self-definition (as persons and artists) extremely difficult for black women writers.

Dunbar-Nelson began her life as Alice Ruth Moore on July 19, 1875, in New Orleans, Louisiana—marked from the beginning by the mixed white, black, and Indian of her Creole ancestral strains.[1] This mixture endowed her with reddish-blonde baby curls and a fair enough complexion to pass occasionally for white when she was an adult intent on imbibing the high culture (operas, bathing spas, art museums) of the Jim Crow United States society, which was just as committed to her exclusion. Evidence suggests that—a feeling of shame about some circumstance(s) of her birth notwithstanding—she preferred her mixed racial appearance and sometimes looked down on darker skinned blacks, especially if they were also less educated and refined. (Skin color and status were often connected in those early postbellum times. Many progressive colored people believed that the best way to prove their worth was to be as little black as possible, black being equated with narrowness and limitation.) Nevertheless, Dunbar-Nelson fought for the rights of black people in a variety of individual and organizational ways ranging from the women's club movement, to the Dyer Anti-Lynching Bill, to financially aiding, from her own shallow pocket, young charges at the Industrial School for Colored Girls, which she helped to found. She was generally active on behalf of women, motivated by genuine feminist instincts and the available avenues for sociopolitical work. Making a living also occupied and preoccupied her. She was a teacher, stenographer, executive secretary, editor, newspaper columnist, platform speaker, and campaign manager.

All of this reminds us that Dunbar-Nelson perforce wrote in the interstices of a busy existence unsupported (except for one brief period) by any of the money or leisure traditionally associated with people of letters. Doggedly determined to be an author, she plied her trade, often too facilely, hastily, opportunistically, and without revision—carried forward on the flow of words that came quite easily for her. Interestingly enough, she called all of her writing "producing literature," in a humorously ironic leveling of forms and types. But just as ironically, her status is lowered since the more belletristic genres of poetry and fiction are more valued than the noncanonical forms—notably the diary and journalistic essay—that claimed so much of her attention.

Dunbar-Nelson began her career early. As a daring young

author "just on the threshold of life," she published *Violets and Other Tales** in 1895 when she was barely twenty years old. A potpourri of short stories, sketches, essays, reviews, and poetry, this volume is interesting and promising juvenilia wherein the budding writer tries out many voices. Even this early, some of her lifelong characteristics are evident: wide reading and love of books ("Salammbo"); catholicity of intellect ("Unknown Life of Jesus Christ," "Anarchy Alley," "Ten Minutes' Musing"); alienation from her own autobiography and mundane experience; Creole materials and themes ("Titee," "A Carnival Jangle," "Little Miss Sophie"); competence in many genres; use of standard lyric themes; a leaning toward the romantic; ambivalence about woman's concept of self and proper role in the emerging modern world ("Violets," "The Woman," "At Eventide," etc.); a felicitous prose style; and a tendency to pay obeisance to literary and social proprieties. Summarizing the work in this way suggests that it is most profitably read as a precursor of later work, or consulted in retrospect for its revelations of Dunbar-Nelson's roots.

Dunbar-Nelson's second book, *The Goodness of St. Rocque and Other Stories* (Vol. 1, WADN), appeared four years later. Thus, the only two volumes of her own work published during her lifetime (which have kept her writings marginally accessible to later generations of scholars and readers) were printed at the very beginning of her career—before the turn of the century and before books by black writers ceased to be novelties during the "New Negro" era. Therefore, Dunbar-Nelson, in her way, helped to create a black short-story

---

*Included in Volume 1, *The Works of Alice Dunbar-Nelson*, hereafter cited as WADN.

tradition for a reading public conditioned to expect only plantation and minstrel stereotypes. Her strategy for escaping these odious expectations was to eschew black characters and culture and to write, instead, charming, aracial, Creole sketches that solidified her in the then-popular, "female-suitable" local color mode. In the words of one contemporary reviewer, these are

> delightful Creole stories, all bright and full of the true Creole air of easy-going . . . brief and pleasing, instinct with the passion and romance of the people who will ever be associated with such names as Bayou Teche and Lake Pontchartrain.[2]

In part, this sprightly description of the book is accurate. One thinks, for example, of "Titee" (a story that was printed first in *Violets* and then here, with a revised, happy ending). The colorful young hero with a tender heart is eventually rewarded for his self-sacrificing faithfulness to an old derelict as he roams the bayous and canals. Further, the surfaces of all the stories so coruscate with South Louisiana flavor that they give an impression of superficial charm and pleasantness. Yet the truth of the matter is that this apparent brightness is belied by situations of sadness, loss, death, and oppression.

In a story not found in *St. Rocque* ("On the Bayou Bridge," Vol. 3, WADN), Dunbar-Nelson describes the Bayou St. John:

> In its dark bosom many secrets lie buried. It is like some beautiful serpent, langurous, sinister. It ripples in the sunshine, sparkles in the moonlight, glooms in the dusk and broods in the dark. But it thinks unceasingly, and below its brightest sparkle you feel its unknown soul.

Her stories work in this way. Looking upon them (too) closely, "you would shudder because you feel what lies beneath

the brown waters." In *St. Rocque*, the dark Manuela resorts
to a voodoo madam to vanquish her blonde rival in romance;
Tony's wife is beaten and kicked out on the street; Annette
gives up her operatic ambitions after being misled by the
fisherman of Pass Christian; dire economic want forces M'sieu
Fortier to sell his beloved violin; Athanasia's story becomes
yet another "broken-hearted romance" by the Bayou St. John;
Sylves', a young Cajun man, is brought back to his fond
Maman and fiancé Louisette dead in his coffin after working
a winter in Chicago; and thus one could continue.

Beyond these plots, one notes that Dunbar-Nelson is inclined to write about difference—for example, Catholic versus
Protestant, Anglo versus Creole. Grandpère Colomes is shamed
when "his petite Juanita, his Spanish blossom, his hope of a
family that had held itself proudly aloof from 'dose Americain'
from time immemorial," smiles "upon this Mercer, this pale-
eyed youth." More deeply still, one encounters disturbing
tropes of enclosure (the veil, the closing door) which subtly
critique female confinement and lack of options. Polysemous
texts like "Sister Josepha" (Vol. 1, WADN) and "The Locket"
(published outside of *St. Rocque*; Vol. 3, WADN), quasicon-
ventional convent stories, further indict the patriarchal
oppression of young girls. Obviously, for the readers of these
tales, suffering was romantic—as it has often been taken to
be, especially when the sufferer is someone other than oneself.

After *The Goodness of St. Rocque*, Dunbar-Nelson continued
to mine Creole materials, but went far beyond the ostensibly
safe mode of that volume. The undercurrent of "dark-blooded
passion" hinted at in *St. Rocque* erupts into the murderous
heroine of "On the Bayou Bridge," whose "long fingers"
wind themselves around her abandoning lover's neck "like
steel cords." Anglo prejudice becomes overt racism in "Nat-

alie" when Olivia's mother opposes the friendship of her white daughter and the brown maiden Natalie, who has been treated before this incident with "supercilious indifference" or "contemptuous patronage." Most significantly of all, Dunbar-Nelson stops dealing with the Creole as a racial monolith and addresses the specific dilemma of the black Creole who has immediate or identifiable Negro ancestry.

"The Pearl in the Oyster" is one such story, but "The Stones of the Village" is weightier (both stories appear in Vol. 3, WADN). Young Victor Grabért's childhood has been blighted by his ambiguous racial identity. His loving, but stern, old West Indian grandmother forbids him social interaction with the youngsters on his street (whom she vehemently calls "dose niggers").

> It had been loneliness ever since. For the parents of the little black and yellow boys resenting the insult Grandmére had offered their offspring, sternly bade them have nothing more to do with Victor. Then when he toddled after some other little boys, whose faces were white like his own, they ran him away with derisive hoots of "Nigger! Nigger!" And again, he could not understand. . . . [A]ll the boys, white and black and yellow hooted at him and called him "White nigger! White nigger!"

Furthermore, Grandmére forces him to cease speaking "the soft, Creole patois that they chattered together" and learn English, the result being "a confused jumble which was no language at all." This "confused jumble," this silence—linguistic, racial, psychic, and emotional—determines his entire life.

A chain of circumstances cuts off Victor from his past, and he becomes a highly successful lawyer and judge, marries into a leading (white) family, and fathers a fine son. Yet the fear of racial exposure torments him and eventually ends in psychosis, madness, and death. He dies apoplectically, about to address a political banquet, imagining that the men who crowd around to help him are "all boys with stones to pelt him because he wanted to play with them."

In this story, Dunbar-Nelson handles complexities she never touched any place else. Certainly, she is treating the popular Afro-American literary themes of the "color line"— that is, passing—and the "tragic mulatto" from the unique vantage of the Louisiana black Creole. That this troubled subject has autobiographical resonance is clear when it is compared with an essay she wrote around 1929. Entitled "Brass Ankles Speaks" (Vol. 2, WADN), it is an outspoken denunciation of darker skinned black people's prejudice against light-skinned blacks told by a "brass ankles," a black person "white enough to pass for white, but with a darker family back-ground, a real love for the mother race, and no desire to be numbered among the white race." This brass ankles recalls her "miserable" childhood in "a far Southern city" where other schoolchildren taunted and plagued her because she was a "light nigger, with straight hair!" This kind of rebuff and persecution continued into a Northern college and her first teaching job:

> Small wonder, then, that the few lighter persons in the community drew together; we were literally thrown upon each other, whether we liked or not. But when we began going about together and spending time in each other's society, a howl went up. We were organizing a "blue vein" society. We were mistresses of white men. We were Lesbians. We hated black folk and plotted against them. As a matter of fact, we had no other recourse but to cling together.

And she states further that "To complain would be only to bring upon themselves another storm of abuse and fury."

This essay was as close as Dunbar-Nelson ever got to revealing feelings about her own racial status as a "yaller nigger." She tried to publish it, but would not or could not do so under her own name, and the magazine editor refused to print it pseudonymously. "The Stones of the Village" is, likewise, as close as she ever got to turning this kind of personal and cultural confusion into art. One notes, though, that in the story, she uses a male rather than a female protagonist, thereby making it easier to write and keep at a safer distance from herself.

Uncollected stories such as this one are serious, potentially threatening. Consequently, they did not sell easily and many were never published. During the years (1898–1902) of professional authorship when she was the lesser known, female half of the Dunbar writing duo, one of the concrete perquisites of her position was sharing the literary agent Paul Reynolds. Her letters to him show that she kept him supplied with a steady stream of material, much of which came back to her. Those stories of hers that "some of the leading magazines of the country regularly print[ed]"[3] tended to be fluffy romances, often with local color backdrops. To Bliss Perry of *The Atlantic Monthly*, she proposed expanding "The Stones of the Village" into a novel. In an August 22, 1900, reply, he offered his opinion that at present the American public had a "dislike" for treatment of "the color-line." And "Stones" remained in manuscript. Knowing more of these previously unpublished stories would certainly have modified our simple generalizations about Alice Dunbar-Nelson.

This becomes even truer when two other of her stories are considered—"Elisabeth" and "Ellen Fenton" (both appear in

Vol. 3, WADN). With ten additional works, they were to be included in a volume, *Women and Men*, which Dunbar-Nelson projected sometime around 1902. Elisabeth is a thirty-year-old single woman who abruptly finds herself alone in New York City needing to make a living: "I am too old to think about marrying, and too young to go to the poorhouse. . . . Too ugly to be attractive, and not ugly enough to make a living in a sideshow." Her efforts to find a job prove "a lonely struggle, lonely and hard" and the one she finally secures "paid little." Here Dunbar-Nelson begins to explore the psyche and life of an ordinary, post-Victorian working woman. Elisabeth is not rich. She is not a Creole exotic. She is not exemplary in any way.

Ellen Fenton, likewise, wakes up one morning and finds herself unaccountably dissatisfied with her forty years of living: "Something was whirling within her, an indefinable feeling that she too, wanted to say aloud . . . 'I don't want to do the same thing; I want to do something different.' " She has been a model wife and mother, a civic inspiration, but now she begins to brood and change until she makes a startling discovery:

> She had always been a woman, who in addition to the multiple cares of her household and public philanthropy, to use the cant phrase, "lived her own life." She was discovering now that the term was a misnomer. The average woman, she found, who "lives her own life," in reality, lives others', and has no life of her own.

Today, this reads like an early formulation of "the feminine mystique"—and indeed would have been had Dunbar-Nelson stuck with her gender analysis and not "universalized" the issue by also giving Ellen's husband Herbert a parallel midlife crisis. Similarly, she sidesteps original exploration of Elisabeth's dilemma by turning her story into a happily-ever-after romance. In both cases, her "modern feminist realism" (a phrase Alain Locke used in commenting upon Georgia Douglas Johnson, Edna St. Vincent Millay, and Sara Teasdale)[4] is wrenched into submission and never fully realized.

This realism burgeons into urban naturalism in *The Annals of 'Steenth Street* (Vol. 3, WADN), another projected volume of short stories. These stories build on the experience Dunbar-Nelson gained doing settlement work and teaching on New York City's East Side in 1897–1898. 'Steenth Street is her "Main Street," located around 87th between Second and Third Avenues, underneath the El with the East River in view. The protagonists of these tales are Irish ghetto youth whom the reader comes to know as they appear throughout the collection—Abe Powers, James Brown, Scrappy Franks, Dobson, Hattie Gurton, Della Mott, Lizzie Williams, Gus Schwartz. Perhaps Dunbar-Nelson saw these narratives as juvenile fiction, a possibility that is suggested by the fact that one of the two stories from this set that were published, "The Revenge of James Brown," appeared as a Methodist Episcopal Church young people's story in 1929. Again perhaps, this fictional vehicle may have been chosen because it helped to present the harsh social criticism inherent in the selections in a more harmless guise.

The denizens of this neighborhood live hard lives. Money is short or nonexistent, the next meal is a daily problem, parents are alcoholics, and drunken fathers beat their step-daughters. In the midst of all this, a guy must save face with the gang, a girl needs a dress for the ball of a lifetime, a rival wins favor for peanuts, and women like Mrs. McMahon pick up the pieces when the makeshift foundations crumble. Dunbar-Nelson sees with analytical clarity the female lot. When Belle finally kills her deserving husband ("Witness for the Defense," Vol. 3, WADN), 'Steenth Street celebrates:

> For so long had woman-kind in this particular section of the world quietly taken its beatings, gone without food or fire or light, while its better half found all three with amusement and jollity thrown in at McEneny's on the corner; . . . for so long had the survival of the strongest been the implacable law that now when one woman had broken the bonds of custom and established the right to live and to kill too, there was great rejoicing. The women stood about in doorways and halls and discussed the event with avidity. Emancipation was in the air.

Dunbar-Nelson is also sensitive to the plight of the children. Abe Powers ("The Downfall of Abe Powers," Vol. 3, WADN) writes to the mission matron:

> "Dere Miss Morton, I beat Mr. coller an put him out becos he talked too much an i dont see why we has to be bothered when our mothers is drunk an if you will plese forgive me an let me come to the [Christmas] tree i will be gode. . ."

The stories are about oppression. The idea of difference, which always interested Dunbar-Nelson, becomes here class difference. This she uses, I am sure, as a signifier for race. The vocabulary of racism is unmistakable in Miss Tillman's language ("Miss Tillman's Protege," Vol. 3, WADN) when she breathes raptures about adopting little Hattie: "Such a dear, sweet, patient face. She'd look lovely in a dear white apron with her hair smooth sitting at my feet in my study." When Mrs. Morton reminds her that Hattie may have "family ties, and a mother," she counters, "it's absurd. These people are very different from us. I thought you knew that from your long experience with them."

The kind of transmutations occurring in these stories is further suggested when they are compared with Dunbar-Nelson's comments in a January 23, 1898, letter to her fiancé Paul. She reported a visit to the home of one of her students, where she found a German woman married to a "shiftless, dirty Negro" who drank, beat, and neglected her and the children. They were about to be evicted from two smelly, squalid rooms, had no coal, no food, a nursing baby, a toddler with chicken pox, etc. The scene gets shifted straight into the 'Steenth Street fiction, with only the "shiftless, dirty Negro" bleached out. Why? One reason is that Dunbar-Nelson did not wish to portray this type of black person. Other reasons may relate to marketing conditions, her authorial psychology, and the tricky *whys* and *wherefores* of her literary passing game. ("Hope Deferred" [Vol. 3, WADN] is an exception in her fictional corpus.)

Nowhere is the sense of passing greater than in her specifically autobiographical stories, those few pieces where she takes herself and the details of her experience as material. It could also be said that nowhere would the need for camouflage be as crucial. Yet one wonders what Dunbar-Nelson thought she could have been concealing. Any of these stories published under her own name would have functioned like public monologues to a voyeuristic analyst. This accounts for her use of a pseudonym and also for the fact that at least one of them reads more like a therapeutic piece of personal catharsis than a work she intended to publish.

Three stories (Vol. 3, WADN) fall into this category—"Mrs. Newly-wed and Her Servants," "The Decision," and

"No Sacrifice." Interestingly, all of them reflect her relationship with Paul Laurence Dunbar. "Mrs. Newly-wed" does so in an innocuous manner, since it is a doleful tale of a freshly married young wife reciting to her amused but sympathetic friend the problems she has had with a long roll of unsatisfactory female servants. She is Alice as Mrs. Paul Laurence Dunbar, after the couple set up housekeeping in Washington, D.C., casting herself into yet another role. "The Decision" and "No Sacrifice" are barely veiled accounts of Alice's courtship and marriage with Paul. Here is a trove of accurate information about their meeting through a magazine, becoming impulsively engaged before Paul sails overseas, Alice's mother's disapproval, their romantic passion and stormy public fights, his bouts with alcohol, her refusal to visit him on his sick bed, and all the rest that made their union romantic copy for scandalmongers. A reader familiar with the relationship peruses these stories for clues to answer the questions of what went wrong and why Alice so obdurately refused to be reconciled.

This aspect of the works aside, their next most striking feature is the way that Dunbar-Nelson has made the narratives racially white. Mrs. Newly-wed recruits her help from the "camp," "that disreputable part of the town just below the Sixth Street hill where a lot of colored folks have congregated." When he is intoxicated, Burt Courtland's eyes are "red-streaked across their blue." Gerald Kennedy is a "Greek God" with "chestnut hair" whose emotional face "flares crimson." Furthermore, wealth abounds. Burt has built Marion a "great, dreary new mansion," the couples "jet-set" like Scott and Zelda Fitzgerald, rich uncles die leaving behind their millions. This lavish flow of dollars calls to mind Dunbar-Nelson saying that play money figured so prominently on stage in black drama because the real thing was such a scarce commodity in actual life (a circumstance that was true for her until the end of her days). Seemingly, too, for Dunbar-Nelson, white equalled rich (or was it that rich equalled white?)—unless fate landed one on 'Steenth Street.

So much of these stories is fact-based fantasy ("No Sacrifice" was written as a "True Story") that it is hard to think through (and beyond) this component—and in the works themselves, images of falseness and illusion are prevalent. Ultimately, these texts reveal the author's attempt to write about herself— but from deep within limiting psychic and formal structures.

Dunbar-Nelson rounded out her short-story career with snappily written pieces in the newly emerging American detective genre. It is not surprising that she would find this "hard-boiled" tradition attractive since the no-nonsense, rational "tough guy" was one of her private personae—and also because she often tried her hand at whatever was new and modern and promised financial reward. A vacationing private detective lays the foundation for the surprise ending of "His Great Career," while "Summer Session" shows us Mr. Terence McShane nabbing the criminal (a white slavery perpetrator) and then winning the girl, to boot. Both stories are slick, well-made; but there is no evidence that they were ever published (Vol. 3, WADN).

Dunbar-Nelson wrote many stories not included here in *The Works of Alice Dunbar-Nelson* and, at her death, left behind both typescripts and holograph drafts. From the publication of *Violets* through the early 1900s, short stories received her most concentrated attention. And as late as 1928, a newspaper article reported that she "considers her short stories her most representative work."[5] Certainly, taken as a whole, this fiction is impressively various and surprisingly complex.

Dunbar-Nelson also tried longer fiction, writing (or partially writing) at least four novels—*The Confessions of a Lazy Woman* (ca. 1899, cast in diary form); *A Modern Undine* (ca. 1901–1903; Vol. 2, WADN); *Uplift* (1930–1931, intended as a satire of an insincere black woman who professionally represents the race; Dunbar-Nelson destroyed the manuscript because of dissatisfaction with it); and *This Lofty Oak* (1932–1933, the extremely long, fictionalized biography of her friend, Delaware educator Edwina B. Kruse). While she was writing *Uplift*, she derisively referred to it as "the Great American Novel," indicating, I think, both her desire to pen that national classic and her knowledge that she was incapable of doing so.[6]

Of these works, *A Modern Undine* is the most satisfactory and most fully realized. It exists as a seventy-nine-page, typed manuscript that can be justifiably considered an organic novelette since it is Dunbar-Nelson's first, complete draft (stretching plots to standard novel length was always one of her problems). We know that she added some now-lost pages because a professional opinion she received in 1903 objected to the ease with which the heroine finds her lost husband.[7] *Undine* tells the story of Marion, a decorous, self-centered, introverted, prickly-sensitive, twenty-four-year-old Southern woman. From a home made lively by her mother and hoydenish sister, she marries Howard, a Northern businessman who falls in love with her despite her aloofness. Mistakenly thinking that Howard is having an affair with a poor girl in the town, Marion retreats even further into paranoia and obsessive mothering of their crippled son. Everything climaxes at once. The truth about the affair comes out; Howard's business fails in the general crash and he has to flee charges of embezzlement; he and Marion for the first time in their lives speak frankly about their feelings, with Howard openly criticizing her narrowness and self-centeredness. Reading this, one is somehow drawn into the rather strange tale, becoming irritated with Marion's almost-total withdrawal from feelings and the world, sympathizing with Howard, and so on. The psychological dimensions are strong (reflecting Dunbar-Nelson's lifelong fascination with this field).

However, the key to understanding this novelette lies in its title. In folklore, an *undine* is a "female water sprite who could acquire a soul by marrying a human being." But if her lover proved unfaithful, she would have to return to the sea.[8] Marion is this spirit. When we first glimpse her on the night she meets Howard, she is standing on the edge of a breakwater with the sea surging at her feet "in a low monotone of life and death." The second time we see her, she gazes "out at the sea," seeming more than ever "in her curious detachment from her surroundings" to remind Howard of "a vestal set apart from the rest of mankind, awaiting mysterious voices from heaven." Water references and the sea motif continue, especially at critical points in the plot. When she first discovers what she thinks is her husband's infidelity, Marion's fainting is imaged as "the darkness and roaring of the sea clos[ing] over her head." After her baby dies, she directs her mother to "bury him by the sea . . . perhaps it will sing to him the same songs it has sung to me."

Further, in these folkloric terms, Marion's "becoming human" through the vicissitudes of love and marriage is emphatically focused. That she is warped is symbolized in the deformity of her child, who was maimed in her womb when she fainted, and of whom she is jealously possessive. During their climactic argument, Howard rebukes her for fancying herself "too superior to come out of the clouds long enough to touch the vital human things of this world," and tells her that getting involved with charity work "would have made [her] seem more like a human being." Humanity first flares in her when she waits to accuse Howard of visiting his paramour: "A cold, deadly fury was stirring at her heart, becoming more passionate and human at every instant that Howard stayed in the house." At the end of their encounter, "for an instant she felt again strangely aloof from the whole scene, apart and out of the disaster which threatened her whole life, but only for an instant." She has entered the realm of human love and sorrow, in a novel which affirms both.

A Modern Undine reflects the fact that Dunbar-Nelson, an astrological Cancer, loved the sea—and rhapsodized about it in her diary:

> But the water! . . . Weeks I dreamed of it. . . . No
> inconvenience too great for the love of it. . . Lovely, luxu-
> rious, voluptuous water.[9]

Deeper still, the work reveals her connection with myth, the mystical, and the spiritual. Her daily living envinced an awareness of meta-realms of experience beyond the visible world which was rooted in her mother's Obeah beliefs and enhanced by her own attention to the spiritual arts. This seems to be the level of reality she is adumbrating here—and is the only time this mystical consciousness is specifically developed in her literary work.

On a completely different plane, it can be noted that, more than once, Dunbar-Nelson wrote about an uninvolved female. *The Confessions of a Lazy Woman*—ultimately a rather silly work—features a heroine who strives (and she really has to work at it) to do absolutely nothing. Dunbar-Nelson was just the opposite, what she herself once described as "another too-busy woman." Might this imaging of idleness and withdrawal

be wish fulfillment of a more significant kind than that
represented by the material wealth of her romances? It may
be that these figures represent—simultaneously—a longing
for and a critique of female passivity/inactivity/worldly iso-
lation (they don't even read the newspaper). As a critique,
they present the feminine ideal elevated to the satiric nth
degree of foolishness.

Thinking in this way raises the comparison between
Dunbar-Nelson and her female protagonists. Not one of them
is even remotely like her. Unfortunately, when she tried to
transcribe her own self/body in the autobiographical romances, the attempts were unsuccessful at best and disastrous
at worst. None of her heroines are black—no Iola Leroy or
Megda or some other figure to carry us forward to Helga
Crane or Janie Starks. One wonders, if they had been black,
could Dunbar-Nelson have done a better, or different, job
with them? A black woman like herself on the printed page
in 1915 would have been a sight to behold. What she did
(and did not do) with *Uplift* and *This Lofty Oak* suggests that
black women's lives (her own and others') were too real to be
fiction—as she understood fiction to be in those largely pre-
modernist days. And there was simply too much that she did
not want to say about herself. All of this is, of course,
speculation; Dunbar-Nelson did what she could and we can
try to understand and appreciate that, even as we wish for
more.

What she was able to achieve in prose outweighs her poetic
accomplishments although, ironically, being taken as a poet
has helped immensely to keep her reputation alive. Dunbar-
Nelson was not driven to write poems and did not focus on
the genre. When asked by an editor for a poem in 1900, she
confessed to being short on poetic inspiration and added,

"Mr. Dunbar tells me that I average one poem in six months, and that there will be none due for several weeks to come."[10] If anything, Paul's estimate is a bit high when spread over her lifetime of writing.

By and large, Dunbar-Nelson's poetry (included in Vol. 2, WADN) is what it appears to be—competent treatments of conventional lyric themes in traditional forms and styles. Her signature poem, "Violets," is the apogee of this type. A few others stand out for various reasons. "I Sit and Sew," wherein a woman chafes at her domestic role during wartime, seems feminist in spirit. "You! Inez!" appears to be a rare eruption in verse of Dunbar-Nelson's lesbian feelings. "Communion" and "Music" were probably (like "Violets") selections in a no longer extant *Dream Book* commemorating her illicit affair with Emmett J. Scott, Jr. "To Madame Curie" and "Cano—I Sing" are strikingly well executed. "April Is On the Way" is a confusingly complicated work about a rape (or attempted rape) and lynching. "Forest Fire" shows Dunbar-Nelson trying to modernize her technique during the Harlem Renaissance years of experimentation. "The Proletariat Speaks" reminds one of her consciousness about difference and class contrasts. "Little Roads" contains a pun on "Fay," the name of the woman with whom she was romantically involved when she wrote it in 1930–1931. "Harlem John Henry Views the Airmada" is an "epic of Negro Peace" complete with a black protagonist and slave spirituals.

Though Dunbar-Nelson's poetry improves markedly from her juvenile verse to the mature work of the 1920s, her gifts—which were more discursive than poetic—were not geared in that direction. Furthermore, her essentially romantic conception of poetry caused her to reserve it for intense emotion and other special occasions. Yet it was one more way that she proved herself a writer and solidified her stature as such.

This same statement can be made about her drama, with the clarification that her interest in this genre may have been keener. From her girlhood in New Orleans, Dunbar-Nelson participated in amateur theater. She was also an avid play (and movie) goer, and she wrote and directed plays and pageants for school and community groups. In the Afro-American community, skits and plays for class night programs, for Christmas and Easter church celebrations, and for club fundraising attractions have always been important. Thus, this form was very much a part of Dunbar-Nelson's personal and cultural background. It also suited her often dramatic (not to say theatrical) temperament.

Furthermore, the early twentieth-century black cultural debates often eddied around the drama. The explosion of dark faces on Broadway (notably in the musicals of the 1920s) was paralleled by the development of serious drama in predominantly black colleges (Howard University in Washington, D.C., was a major center) and the proliferation of plays about blacks by famous white playwrights (Eugene O'Neill's *Emperor Jones* was perhaps the most celebrated). At the same time, Oscar Michaeux and a few others were pioneering the race film and black movie making. Something of this ferment can be picked up in Dunbar-Nelson's newspaper columns. It was a time of intense pronouncements about the proper portrayal of the Negro on stage. A 1928 newspaper article uncovers Dunbar-Nelson adding her bit to the current dialogue:

> [Dunbar-Nelson] believes that the stage is the best medium
> for exploiting ourselves; that we must break away from

propaganda per se and the conventional musical comedy that
starts on a plantation and ends in a cabaret, and present to
the American public all phases of Negro life and culture.[11]

This contextual grounding of her plays in black life probably helps account for Dunbar-Nelson's use in them of iden-
tifiably black characters, settings, and situations (which is
unlike her fiction). Then, too, this would have to be the case
if she had any intention at all of seeing them performed. The
same 1928 article also mentioned that she "preferred" writing
plays (though one cannot fathom what that really means,
given her literary record) and had done "a number" of them
for "amateur producers." Her extant works for her Howard
High School groups are obviously designed for the educational and moral edification of the students. Something like
the *Club Ritz-Carlton*, a cabaret show that she staged for the
Wilmington, Delaware, Elk Daughters, can only be conjec-
tured about. Her most well-known and probably most acted
play was *Mine Eyes Have Seen* (Vol. 3, WADN; publication
in the *Crisis* helped its visibility). There is no evidence that
the others included here (Vol. 3, WADN) were ever mounted.

Question: What kind of black folk does Dunbar-Nelson
present in her racial plays? On the whole, they are all
recognizable types—as dramatic characters are traditionally
wont to be. In *Mine Eyes*, Lucy is the gentle, patient sister
who takes care of her two motherless brothers; Cornelia Lewis
is a conscientious settlement worker; Dan is the older brother
literally crippled by racial prejudice. *Gone White* (Vol. 3,
WADN) highlights Allan Franklin Cordell, a light-skinned,
young, educated black man determined to compel potential
employers "to admit that a Negro can be as good or better
an engineer than a white man," to "ram their damn prejudice

down their throats." Granny Wimbish moans spirituals, and
Anna Martin is as long-serving as Lucy. Blanche Parker,
Allan's aunt, strikes a more original note. Frankly (even
immorally) pragmatic, she puts Allan through college (by
dressing hair in her own beauty shop), then counsels him to
pass for white and maintain his white wife, family, and
position, and—if he must—"love" his brown-skinned Anna
on the side. Though mostly poor, the characters are decent,
respectable, and above all, well-spoken. There is no dialect
here, no comedy, as Dunbar-Nelson tries to live up to her
call for a broader, more realistic Afro-American drama.

The fact that these plays treat controversial topics helped
Dunbar-Nelson achieve more intense effects. *Mine Eyes* argues for blacks to support World War I, but presents the
glaring contradictions. When Chris is drafted, he asks, "Must
I go and fight for the nation that let my father's murder [by
whites] go unpunished? That killed my mother—that took
away my chances for making a man out of myself?" And in
Gone White when Anna comprehends what Allan wants, she
"speaks through clenched teeth":

> You are offering me the position of your mistress. . . . You
> would keep your white wife, and all that that means, for
> respectability's sake—but you would have a romance, a liaison
> with the brown woman whom you love, after dark. No Negro
> could stoop so low as to take on such degraded ideals of so-
> called racial purity. And this is the moral deterioration to
> which you have brought your whole race. White Man! Go
> on back to your white gods! Lowest and vilest of scum. White
> Man! Go Back!

The Author's Evening at Home and *Love's Disguise*, a silent
film scenario (both in Vol. 3, WADN), round out the view
of Dunbar-Nelson in the dramatic media. The first work,

really a 1900 playlet, is a slick piece that capitalizes on her relationship with Paul. The credit line in *Smart Set* read "By Alice Dunbar (Mrs. Paul Laurence Dunbar)" and suggested a real-life genesis for this comedy about an author in his library who cannot write because of his disruptive wife and mother. *Love's Disguise*—with its extreme portrayal of duality—is simply an instance of Dunbar-Nelson's flirtation with silent filmscripts. Eventually, she gave up the notion and concentrated her talent in forms more feasible for her.

This completes the survey of Dunbar-Nelson's work in the canonical genres. She also did a large amount of other writing that is just as important. In it (her essays, for example), she is as relentlessly racial as she is nonracial in the fine genres, suggesting, of course, that her concepts of genre-reality-race were rigidly stratified. Furthermore, it is in this nonbelletristic work that she truly inscribes herself. Nowhere is this more evident than in her diary, which she kept during 1921 and 1926–1931. Here she allows herself to star, center stage in all her complexity and beauty. Even though no excerpts are included in this collection because this journal is easily available, it is an indispensable portion of her works.[12]

The "real" Dunbar-Nelson also "stands up" in her newspaper columns, playing the role of the urbane journalist—a pose that superbly suited her as individual and artist. This liberating stance permitted her to be as contrary and self-contradictory as she wished. A mobile, moody thinker, she could say one thing on Saturday and something completely different the next week. The column form likewise allowed for variation in length and emphasis ranging from one-liners and snippets to full-scale, expository essays. In any case, Dunbar-Nelson consistently spoke out "from a (black) woman's point of view" (as she did, too, in essays such as "Facing Life Squarely" [Vol. 2, WADN] with its memorable obser-

vation that "the spectacle of two or three ordinary Southern
white women sitting down to talk with several very high class
black women" does not represent racial progress worth "sobbing with joy" about). However, what she wrote was definitely not a typical "woman's" column devoted to narrowly
defined feminine concerns.

Even after sixty years, her weekly pieces are very readable
and engaging—which is praise indeed for writing produced
as ephemera. The intellect, wit, protest, sassiness, iconoclasm,
racial pride, feminism, and humor that one yearns for in her
fictional heroines can all be found here. These columns have
to be read to be appreciated, and some of their impact is
cumulative (like the diary). In her April 10, 1926 "Une
Femme Dit" (Vol. 2, WADN), Dunbar-Nelson repeats an
accolade:

> Mrs. Myrtle Foster Cook, the charming and gracile editor
> of the National Notes, the official organ of the National
> Association of Colored Women, says that this column is "as
> delectable and refreshing as a cool lemonade after a hectic
> day."
>
> That is delightful praise. Should one be too modest to
> reproduce it? Not so. Modesty went out with the corset, the
> pompadour, long skirts, lined dresses, the knitted petticoat,
> the merry widow hat, the lisle stocking, the chatelaine bag,
> and the fleur de lys watch pin. Indeed, so much is modesty a
> lost art, that one is almost tempted to repeat the entire
> paragraph from the National Notes. But lingering phases of
> reluctance, delicate and obscure, forbid. We rise and make
> our best bow in the direction of Kansas City

—while "we" blow our nails and polish them on the bodice
of our dress, in that stage business of self-satisfied modesty
whose verbal approximation is "ahem." Mrs. Cook is backed

up—though in sexist fashion—by Eugene Gordon, who wrote this of Dunbar-Nelson in a 1927 *Opportunity* magazine "Survey of the Negro Press": "In my estimation there are few better column conductors of her sex on any newspaper. I should like to see her on some influential daily where her unmistakable talents would be allowed full exercise." [13]

"Une Femme Dit"—which began as "From A Woman's Point of View," and which shows Dunbar-Nelson at her best—was written for the Pittsburgh *Courier* from February 20, 1926, to September 18, 1926. "As In a Looking Glass" (Vol. 2, WADN) appeared in the Washington *Eagle* from 1926 to 1930. (Dunbar-Nelson also wrote another column, "So It Seems—to Alice Dunbar-Nelson," for the *Courier* from January to May 1930, but this series betrays some diminution of verve and interest.) In these columns (of which the selection in Vol. 2 represents only a small part), Dunbar-Nelson shines as literary critic, political analyst, social commentator, race theorist, humorist, and stage and film critic. During this age of print journalism and rising syndicated chains, when newspaper work was a man's profession, Dunbar-Nelson felt that pressure but excelled nonetheless.

It is unfortunate that this writing, which contains so much of her creative energy, is so underrated as art. Valorizing these texts is the most radical example of the re-reading of Alice Dunbar-Nelson which I hope this edition of her works will foster.

NOTES

1. For a fuller treatment of Alice Dunbar-Nelson's life and more information about her writings, see the chapter devoted to her in

Gloria T. Hull, *Color, Sex, and Poetry: Three Women Writers of the Harlem Renaissance* (Bloomington: Indiana University Press, 1987). Some material in this introduction is taken from this source.

2. Pittsburgh *Christian Advocate*, December 21, 1899.

3. "Mrs. Paul Laurence Dunbar, Wife of the Colored Poet and Novelist," Chicago *Recorder*, August 4, 1902.

4. Alain Locke, "Foreword" to Georgia Douglas Johnson, *An Autumn Love Cycle* (New York: Harold Vinal, Ltd., 1928), p. xviii.

5. Newspaper clipping, no name, July 4, 1928. From the vertical file of the Schomburg Center for Research in Black Culture, New York City.

6. Dunbar-Nelson's diary for 1930–1931 charts her writing of *Uplift*. See Gloria T. Hull (ed.), *Give Us Each Day: The Diary of Alice Dunbar-Nelson* (New York: W. W. Norton, 1984).

7. J. N. M. (?) to Alice Dunbar-Nelson, July 16, 1903. For this "expert opinion," Dunbar-Nelson paid five dollars.

8. Information taken from William H. Harris and Judith S. Levey (eds.), *The New Columbia Encyclopedia* (New York: Columbia University Press, 1975), p. 2822.

9. Hull (ed.), *Give Us Each Day*, p. 325.

10. The New York City *Chute* (?), May 1900.

11. Unidentified July 4, 1928 clipping from the Schomburg Center vertical file.

12. Bibliographical data cited in note 6 above.

13. Quoted as an epigraph to Dunbar-Nelson's February 25, 1927, "As In a Looking Glass" column.

EDITORIAL NOTE

Bibliographic information for Alice Dunbar-Nelson's published work, when known, is noted at the beginning of each text. Unpublished manuscripts can be found in the Special Collections of the Morris Library, University of Delaware, Newark, Delaware. Prior to this present edition, R. Ora Williams helped to make Dunbar-Nelson's work somewhat more available in her *An Alice Dunbar-Nelson Reader* (Washington, D.C.: University Press of America, Inc., 1979). She also published "Works By and About Alice Ruth (Moore) Dunbar-Nelson: A Bibliography" in the *CLA Journal*, XIX, No. 3 (March, 1976). Both of these are useful references.

For this edition of Dunbar-Nelson's works, it was clear that her two published books should be reprinted. In selecting the other works, I used the criteria of autobiographical and literary interest, artistic merit, and representativeness, while keeping in mind the space available. Including the 595 typed manuscript pages of *This Lofty Oak* did not seem compellingly feasible or worthwhile. Nor did I choose to collect a greater number of her slighter romantic stories. Likewise, high school plays and pageants were not considered important enough for publication, but all of her apparently finished, available poetry is here.

Her articles and essays for outlets like *The Southern Workman*, *The Messenger*, and the *Journal of Negro History* are least represented. Though valuable, they are standard expository and argumentative pieces written in an objective style, which makes them not as vital as Dunbar-Nelson's other

noncanonical work for understanding her life and art. However, what they do sharpen is the dichotomy between the
nonracialness of her belletristic genres and the racialness of
her other writings. The inclusions from her newspaper columns were probably made most impressionistically (and were
also influenced by whether the originals were crumbling or
had been photocopied). Given what they are, reading through
any runs of them provides very similar materials and insights.

   The selections are presented here as Dunbar-Nelson wrote
them, with only obvious typographical and spelling errors
corrected.

ALICE DUNBAR-NELSON

A CHRONOLOGY

1875	July 19, born in New Orleans, Louisiana.
1892	Graduated from Straight College, New Orleans; subsequently studied at Cornell, Columbia, the Pennsylvania School of Industrial Art, and the University of Pennsylvania, specializing in English educational measurements and psychology.
1892–1896	Taught school in New Orleans.
1895	Published *Violets and Other Tales* (Boston: The Monthly Review Press)—short stories and poems.
1897–1898	Taught in Brooklyn, New York; helped to found the White Rose Mission, which became the White Rose Home for Girls in Harlem.
1898	March 8, married poet Paul Laurence Dunbar and began living in Washington, D.C.
1899	Published *The Goodness of St. Rocque and Other Stories* (New York: Dodd, Mead, and Co.)—short stories.
1902	Separated from Paul Laurence Dunbar and moved to Wilmington, Delaware (he died February 6, 1906).
1902–1920	Taught and administered at the Howard High School, Wilmington; for seven of these years, also directed the summer sessions for in-

This chronology appeared in Gloria T. Hull (ed.), *Give Us Each Day: The Diary of Alice Dunbar-Nelson*. New York: W. W. Norton, 1984.

service teachers at State College for Colored Students (now Delaware State College), Dover; and taught two years in the summer session at Hampton Institute.

1909   April, published "Wordsworth's Use of Milton's Description of Pandemonium" in *Modern Language Notes*.

1910   January 19, married teacher Henry Arthur Callis secretly in Wilmington. He left the next year for medical school in Chicago. (They were later divorced at some unknown time.)

1913–1914 Wrote for and helped edit the *A.M.E. Church Review*.

1914   Edited and published *Masterpieces of Negro Eloquence* (Harrisburg, Pennsylvania: The Douglass Publishing Company).

1915   Was field organizer for the Middle Atlantic States in the campaign for women's suffrage.

1916   April 20, married Robert J. Nelson, a journalist.

1916–1917 Published a two-part article, "People of Color in Louisiana," in *The Journal of Negro History*.

1917–1928 Published poems in *Crisis, Ebony and Topaz, Opportunity, Negro Poets and Their Poems, Caroling Dusk, The Dunbar Speaker and Entertainer, Harlem: A Forum of Negro Life,* etc.

1918   Toured the South as a field representative of the Woman's Committee of the Council of National Defense.

1920   Served on the State Republican Committee of
                Delaware and directed political activities
                among black women; edited and published
                The Dunbar Speaker and Entertainer (Naper-
                ville, Illinois: J. L. Nichols and Co.);
                drawing on her interests in juvenile delin-
                quency and "abnormal psychology," worked
                with women from the State Federation of
                Colored Women to found the Industrial
                School for Colored Girls in Marshalltown,
                Delaware.

1920–1922   Coedited and published the Wilmington *Ad-
                vocate* newspaper.

1921   August, began her *Diary* and kept an extant
                portion of it for the remainder of the year.

1922   Headed the Anti-Lynching Crusaders in Del-
                aware fighting for the Dyer Anti-Lynching
                Bill.

1924   Directed the Democratic political campaign
                among black women from New York head-
                quarters; August and September, published
                a two-part article on Delaware in "These
                'Colored' United States" in *The Messenger*.

1924–1928   Was teacher and parole officer at the Industrial
                School for Colored Girls.

1926   January 2–September 18, wrote column "From
                A Woman's Point of View" (later changed
                to "Une Femme Dit") in the Pittsburgh
                Courier.

1926–1930   Wrote column "As In a Looking Glass" in the
                Washington *Eagle* (her columns and/or ver-
                sions of them were also syndicated for the
                Associated Negro Press).

1926–1931   Resumed and kept the remaining extant por-
             tions of her *Diary*.

1928–1931   Was executive secretary of the American Friends
             Inter-Racial Peace Committee, which en-
             tailed much travel and public speaking.

1930   January–May, wrote column "So It Seems to
             Alice Dunbar-Nelson" in the Pittsburgh
             Courier.

1931   Included in James Weldon Johnson's *The Book
             of American Negro Poetry*.

1932   Moved to Philadelphia, after Robert was ap-
             pointed to the Pennsylvania Athletic (Box-
             ing) Commission in January.

1935   September 18, died of heart trouble at the
             University of Pennsylvania Hospital. She was
             cremated in Wilmington and her ashes
             eventually scattered over the Delaware River.

SHORT STORIES

STORIES OF
*WOMEN AND MEN**

THE STONES OF THE VILLAGE†

Victor Grabért strode down the one, wide, tree-shaded street
of the village, his heart throbbing with a bitterness and anger
that seemed too great to bear. So often had he gone home in
the same spirit, however, that it had grown nearly second
nature to him—this dull, sullen resentment, flaming out now
and then into almost murderous vindictiveness. Behind him
there floated derisive laughs and shouts, the taunts of little
brutes, boys of his own age.

He reached the tumble down cottage at the farther end of
the street and flung himself on the battered step. Grandmére
Grabért sat rocking herself to and fro, crooning a bit of song
brought over from the West Indies years ago; but when the
boy sat silent, his head bowed in his hands she paused in the
midst of a line and regarded him with keen, piercing eyes.

"Eh, Victor?" she asked. That was all, but he understood.
He raised his head and waved a hand angrily down the street
towards the lighted square that marked the village center.

"Dose boy," he gulped.

Grandmére Grabért laid a sympathetic hand on his black
curls, but withdrew it the next instant.

"Bien," she said angrily, "Fo' what you go by dem, eh?
W'y not keep to yo'self? Dey don' want you, dey don' care
fo' you. H'ain' you got no sense?"

---

*A manuscript volume that Dunbar-Nelson probably worked on between
1900 and 1910.
†Typescript.

"Oh, but Grandmére," he wailed piteously, "I wan' fo' to play."

The old woman stood up in the doorway, her tall, spare form towering menacingly over him.

"You wan' fo' to play, eh? Fo' w'y? You don' need no play. Dose boy," she swept a magnificent gesture down the street, "Dey fools!"

"Eef I could play wid—" began Victor, but his grand-mother caught him by the wrist, and held him as in a vise.

"Hush," she cried, "You mus' be goin' crazy," and still holding him by the wrist, she pulled him indoors.

It was a two room house, bare and poor and miserable but never had it seemed so meagre before to Victor as it did this night. The supper was frugal almost to the starvation point. They ate in silence, and afterwards Victor threw himself on his cot in the corner of the kitchen and closed his eyes. Grandmére Grabért thought him asleep, and closed the door noiselessly as she went into her own room. But he was awake, and his mind was like a shifting kaleidoscope of miserable incidents and heartaches. He had lived fourteen years, and he could remember most of them as years of misery. He had never known a mother's love, for his mother had died, so he was told, when he was but a few months old. No one ever spoke to him of a father, and Grandmére Grabért had been all to him. She was kind, after a stern, unloving fashion, and she provided for him as best she could. He had picked up some sort of an education at the parish school. It was a good one after its way, but his life there had been such a succession of miseries, that he rebelled one day and refused to go any more.

His earliest memories were clustered about this poor little cottage. He could see himself toddling about its broken steps, playing alone with a few broken pieces of china which his fancy magnified into glorious toys. He remembered his first whipping too. Tired one day of the loneliness which even the broken china could not mitigate, he had toddled out the side gate after a merry group of little black and yellow boys of his own age. When Grandmére Grabért, missing him from his accustomed garden corner, came to look for him, she found him sitting contentedly in the center of the group in the dusty street, all of them gravely scooping up handsful of the gravelly dirt and trickling it down their chubby bare legs. Grandmére snatched at him fiercely, and he whimpered, for he was learning for the first time what fear was.

"What you mean?" she hissed at him, "What you mean playin' in de strit wid dose niggers?" And she struck at him wildly with her open hand.

He looked up into her brown face surmounted by a wealth of curly black hair faintly streaked with gray, but he was too frightened to question.

It had been loneliness ever since. For the parents of the little black and yellow boys resenting the insult Grandmére had offered their offspring, sternly bade them have nothing more to do with Victor. Then when he toddled after some other little boys, whose faces were white like his own, they ran him away with derisive hoots of "Nigger! Nigger!" And again, he could not understand.

Hardest of all, though, was when Grandmére sternly bade him cease speaking the soft, Creole patois that they chattered together, and forced him to learn English. The result was a confused jumble which was no language at all; that when he spoke it in the streets or in the school, all the boys, white and black and yellow hooted at him and called him "White nigger! White nigger!"

He writhed on his cot that night and lived over all the anguish of his years until hot tears scalded their way down a burning face, and he fell into a troubled sleep wherein he sobbed over some dreamland miseries.

The next morning, Grandmére eyed his heavy swollen eyes sharply, and a momentary thrill of compassion passed over her and found expression in a new tenderness of manner toward him as she served his breakfast. She too, had thought over the matter in the night, and it bore fruit in an unexpected way.

Some few weeks after, Victor found himself timidly ringing the door-bell of a house on Hospital Street in New Orleans. His heart throbbed in painful unison to the jangle of the bell. How was he to know that old Madame Guichard, Grandmére's one friend in the city, to whom she had confided him, would be kind? He had walked from the river landing to the house, timidly inquiring the way of busy pedestrians. He was hungry and frightened. Never in all his life had he seen so many people before, and in all the busy streets there was not one eye which would light up with recognition when it met his own. Moreover, it had been a weary journey down the Red River, thence into the Mississippi, and finally here. Perhaps it had not been devoid of interest, after its fashion, but Victor did not know. He was too heartsick at leaving home.

However, Mme. Guichard was kind. She welcomed him with a volubility and overflow of tenderness that acted like balm to the boy's sore spirit. Thence they were firm friends, even confidants.

Victor must find work to do. Grandmére Grabért's idea in sending him to New Orleans was that he might "mek one man of himse'f" as she phrased it. And Victor, grown suddenly old in the sense that he had a responsibility to bear, set about his search valiantly.

It chanced one day that he saw a sign in an old bookstore on Royal Street that stated in both French and English the need of a boy. Almost before he knew it, he had entered the shop and was gasping out some choked words to the little old man who sat behind the counter.

The old man looked keenly over his glasses at the boy and rubbed his bald head reflectively. In order to do this, he had to take off an old black silk cap which he looked at with apparent regret.

"Eh, what you say?" he asked sharply, when Victor had finished.

"I—I—want a place to work," stammered the boy again.

"Eh, you do? Well, can you read?"

"Yes sir," replied Victor.

The old man got down from his stool, came from behind the counter, and putting his finger under the boy's chin, stared hard into his eyes. They met his own unflinchingly, though there was the suspicion of pathos and timidity in their brown depths.

"Do you know where you live, eh?"

"On Hospital Street," said Victor. It did not occur to him to give the number, and the old man did not ask.

"Trés bien," grunted the book-seller, and his interest relaxed. He gave a few curt directions about the manner of work Victor was to do, and settled himself again upon his stool, poring into his dingy book with renewed ardor.

Thus began Victor's commercial life. It was an easy one. At seven, he opened the shutters of the little shop and swept and dusted. At eight, the book-seller came down stairs, and passed out to get his coffee at the restaurant across the street.

At eight in the evening, the shop was closed again. That was all.

Occasionally, there came a customer, but not often, for there were only odd books and rare ones in the shop, and those who came were usually old, yellow, querulous bookworms, who nosed about for hours, and went away leaving many bank notes behind them. Sometimes there was an errand to do, and sometimes there came a customer when the proprietor was out. It was an easy matter to wait on them. He had but to point to the shelves and say, "Monsieur will be in directly," and all was settled, for those who came here to buy had plenty of leisure and did not mind waiting.

So a year went by, then two and three, and the stream of Victor's life flowed smoothly on its uneventful way. He had grown tall and thin, and often Mme. Guichard would look at him and chuckle to herself, "Ha, he is lak one bean-pole, yaas, *mais*—" and there would be a world of unfinished reflection in that last word.

Victor had grown pale from much reading. Like a shadow of the old book-seller he sat day after day poring into some dusty yellow-paged book, and his mind was a queer jumble of ideas. History and philosophy and old-fashioned social economy were tangled with French romance and classic mythology and astrology and mysticism. He had made few friends, for his experience in the village had made him chary of strangers. Every week, he wrote to Grandmére Grabért and sent her part of his earnings. In his way he was happy, and if he was lonely, he had ceased to care about it, for his world was peopled with images of his own fancying.

Then all at once, the world he had built about him tumbled down, and he was left, staring helplessly at its ruins. The little book-seller died one day, and his shop and its books were sold by an unscrupulous nephew who cared not for bindings nor precious yellowed pages, but only for the grossly material things that money can buy. Victor ground his teeth as the auctioneer's strident voice sounded through the shop where all once had been hushed quiet, and wept as he saw some of his favorite books carried away by men and women, whom he was sure could not appreciate their value.

He dried his tears however, the next day when a grave faced lawyer came to the little house on Hospital Street, and informed him that he had been left a sum of money by the book-seller.

Victor sat staring at him helplessly. Money meant little to him. He never needed it, never used it. After he had sent Grandmére her sum each week, Mme. Guichard kept the rest and doled it out to him as he needed it for carfare and clothes.

"The interest of the money," continued the lawyer clearing his throat, "is sufficient to keep you very handsomely without touching the principal. It was my client's wish that you should enter Tulane College, and there fit yourself for your profession. He had great confidence in your ability."

"Tulane College!" cried Victor. "Why—why—why—" then he stopped suddenly, and the hot blood mounted to his face. He glanced furtively about the room. Mme. Guichard was not near; the lawyer had seen no one but him. Then why tell him? His heart leaped wildly at the thought. Well, Grandmére would have willed it so.

The lawyer was waiting politely for him to finish his sentence.

"Why—why—I should have to study in order to enter there," finished Victor lamely.

"Exactly so," said Mr. Buckley, "and as I have, in a way, been appointed your guardian, I will see to that."

Victor found himself murmuring confused thanks and

good-byes to Mr. Buckley. After he had gone, the boy sat down and gazed blankly at the wall. Then he wrote a long letter to Grandmére.

A week later, he changed boarding places at Mr. Buckley's advice, and entered a preparatory school for Tulane. And still, Mme. Guichard and Mr. Buckley had not met.

* * *

It was a handsomely furnished office on Carondelet Street in which Lawyer Grabért sat some years later. His day's work done, he was leaning back in his chair and smiling pleasantly out of the window. Within, was warmth and light and cheer; without, the wind howled and gusty rains beat against the window pane. Lawyer Grabért smiled again as he looked about at the comfort, and found himself half pitying those without who were forced to buffet the storm afoot. He rose finally, and donning his overcoat, called a cab and was driven to his rooms in the most fashionable part of the city. There he found his old-time college friend, awaiting him with some impatience.

"Thought you never were coming, old man," was his greeting.

Grabért smiled pleasantly, "Well, I was a bit tired, you know," he answered, "and I have been sitting idle for an hour or more, just relaxing, as it were."

Vannier laid his hand affectionately on the other's shoulder. "That was a mighty effort you made to-day," he said earnestly, "I, for one, am proud of you."

"Thank you," replied Grabért simply, and the two sat silent for a minute.

"Going to the Charles' dance to-night?" asked Vannier finally.

"I don't believe I am. I am tired and lazy."

"It will do you good. Come on."

"No, I want to read and ruminate."

"Ruminate over your good fortune of to-day?"

"If you will have it so, yes."

But it must not simply over his good fortune of that day over which Grabért pondered. It was over the good fortune of the past fifteen years. From school to college, and from college to law school he had gone, and thence into practice, and he was now accredited a successful young lawyer. His small fortune, which Mr. Buckley, with generous kindness, had invested wisely, had almost doubled, and his school career, while not of the brilliant, meteoric kind, had been pleasant and profitable. He had made friends, at first, with the boys he met and they in turn, had taken him into their homes. Now and then, the Buckleys asked him to dinner, and he was seen occasionally in their box at the opera. He was rapidly becoming a social favorite, and girls vied with each other to dance with him. No one had asked any questions, and he had volunteered no information concerning himself. Vannier, who had known him in preparatory school days, had said that he was a young country fellow with some money, no connections, and a ward of Mr. Buckley's, and somehow, contrary to the usual social custom of the South, this meagre account had passed muster. But Vannier's family had been a social arbiter for many years, and Grabért's personality was pleasing, without being aggressive, so he had passed through the portals of the social world and was in the inner circle.

One year, when he and Vannier were in Switzerland, pretending to climb impossible mountains and in reality smoking many cigars a day on hotel porches, a letter came to Grabért from the priest of his old-time town, telling him that Grandmére Grabért had been laid away in the parish church-

yard. There was no more to tell. The little old hut had been
sold to pay funeral expenses.

"Poor Grandmére," sighed Victor, "She did care for me
after her fashion. I'll go take a look at her grave when I go
back."

But he did not go, for when he returned to Louisiana, he
was too busy, then he decided that it would be useless,
sentimental folly. Moreover, he had no love for the old
village. Its very name suggested things that made him turn
and look about him nervously. He had long since eliminated
Mme. Guichard from his list of acquaintances.

And yet, as he sat there in his cozy study that night, and
smiled as he went over in his mind triumph after triumph
which he had made since the old bookstore days in Royal
Street, he was conscious of a subtle undercurrent of annoyance;
a sort of mental reservation that placed itself on every pleasant
memory.

"I wonder what's the matter with me?" he asked himself
as he rose and paced the floor impatiently. Then he tried to
recall his other triumph, the one of the day. The case of Tate
vs. Tate, a famous will contest, had been dragging through
the courts for seven years and his speech had decided it that
day. He could hear the applause of the courtroom as he sat
down, but it rang hollow in his ears, for he remembered
another scene. The day before he had been in another court,
and found himself interested in the prisoner before the bar.
The offence was a slight one, a mere technicality. Grabért
was conscious of a something pleasant in the man's face; a
scrupulous neatness in his dress, an unostentatious conforming
to the prevailing style. The Recorder, however, was short
and brusque.

"Wilson—Wilson—" he growled, "Oh, yes, I know you,

always kicking up some sort of a row about theatre seats and cars. Hum-um. What do you mean by coming before me with a flower in your buttonhole?"

The prisoner looked down indifferently at the bud on his coat, and made no reply.

"Hey?" growled the Recorder. "You niggers are putting yourselves up too much for me."

At the forbidden word, the blood rushed to Grabért's face, and he started from his seat angrily. The next instant, he had recovered himself and buried his face in a paper. After Wilson had paid his fine, Grabért looked at him furtively as he passed out. His face was perfectly impassive, but his eyes flashed defiantly. The lawyer was tingling with rage and indignation, although the affront had not been given him.

"If Recorder Grant had any reason to think that I was in any way like Wilson, I would stand no better show," he mused bitterly.

However, as he thought it over to-night, he decided that he was a sentimental fool. "What have I to do with them?" he asked himself, "I must be careful."

The next week, he discharged the man who cared for his office. He was a Negro, and Grabért had no fault to find with him generally, but he found himself with a growing sympathy toward the man, and since the episode in the courtroom, he was morbidly nervous lest a something in his manner would betray him. Thereafter, a round-eyed Irish boy cared for his rooms.

The Vanniers were wont to smile indulgently at his every move. Elise Vannier particularly, was more than interested in his work. He had a way of dropping in of evenings and talking over his cases and speeches with her in a cosy corner of the library. She had a gracious sympathetic manner that was soothing and a cheery fund of repartee to whet her conversation. Victor found himself drifting into sentimental bits of talk now and then. He found himself carrying around in his pocketbook, a faded rose which she had once worn, and when he laughed at it one day and started to throw it in the wastebasket, he suddenly kissed it instead, and replaced it in the pocketbook. That Elise was not indifferent to him he could easily see. She had not learned yet how to veil her eyes and mask her face under a cool assumption of superiority. She would give him her hand when they met with a girlish impulsiveness, and her color came and went under his gaze. Sometimes, when he held her hand a bit longer than necessary, he could feel it flutter in his own, and she would sigh a quick little gasp that made his heart leap and choked his utterance.

They were tucked away in their usual cosy corner one evening, and the conversation had drifted to the problem of where they would spend the summer.

"Papa wants to go to the country house," pouted Elise, "and mama and I don't want to go. It isn't fair, of course, because when we go so far away, Papa can be with us only for a few weeks when he can get away from his office, while if we go to the country place, he can run up every few days. But it is so dull there, don't you think so?"

Victor recalled some pleasant vacation days at the plantation home and laughed, "Not if you are there."

"Yes, but you see, I can't take myself for a companion. Now if you'll promise to come up sometimes, it will be better."

"If I may, I shall be delighted to come."

Elise laughed intimately, "If you may—" she replied, "as if such a word had to enter into our plans. Oh, but Victor, haven't you some sort of plantation somewhere? It seems to

me that I heard Steven years ago speak of your home in the
country, and I wondered sometimes that you never spoke of
it, or ever mentioned having visited it."

The girl's artless words were bringing cold sweat to Victor's
brow, his tongue felt heavy and useless, but he managed to
answer quietly, "I have no home in the country."

"Well, didn't you ever own one, or your family?"

"It was old quite a good many years ago," he replied, and
a vision of the little old hut with its tumble down steps and
weed-grown garden came into his mind.

"Where was it?" pursued Elise innocently.

"Oh, away up in St. Landry parish, too far away from
civilization to mention." He tried to laugh, but it was a
hollow forced attempt that rang false. But Elise was too
absorbed in her own thoughts of the summer to notice.

"And you haven't a relative living?" she continued.

"Not one."

"How strange. Why it seems to me if I did not have a
half a hundred cousins and uncles and aunts that I should
feel somehow out of touch with the world."

He did not reply, and she chattered away on another topic.

When he was alone in his room that night, he paced the
floor again, chewing wildly at a cigar that he had forgotten
to light.

"What did she mean? What did she mean?" he asked
himself over and over. Could she have heard or suspected
anything that she was trying to find out about? Could any
action, any unguarded expression of his have set the family
thinking? But he soon dismissed the thought as unworthy of
him. Elise was too frank and transparent a girl to stoop to
subterfuge. If she wished to know anything, she was wont to
ask out at once, and if she had once thought anyone was

sailing under false colors, she would say so frankly, and dismiss them from her presence.

Well, he must be prepared to answer questions if he were going to marry her. The family would want to know all about him, and Elise, herself, would be curious for more than her brother, Steve Vannier's meagre account. But was he going to marry Elise? That was the question.

He sat down and buried his head in his hands. Would it be right for him to take a wife, especially such a woman as Elise, and from such a family as the Vanniers? Would it be fair? Would it be just? If they knew and were willing, it would be different. But they did not know, and they would not consent if they did. In fancy, he saw the dainty girl whom he loved, shrinking from him as he told her of Grandmére Grabért and the village boys. This last thought made him set his teeth hard, and the hot blood rushed to his face.

Well, why not, after all, why not? What was the difference between him and the hosts of other suitors who hovered about Elise? They had money; so had he. They had education, polite training, culture, social position; so had he. But they had family traditions, and he had none. Most of them could point to a long line of family portraits with justifiable pride; while if he had had a picture of Grandmére Grabért, he would have destroyed it fearfully, lest it fall into the hands of some too curious person. This was the subtle barrier that separated them. He recalled with a sting how often he had had to sit silent and constrained when the conversation turned to ancestors and family traditions. He might be one with his companions and friends in everything but this. He must ever be on the outside, hovering at the gates, as it were. Into the inner life of his social world, he might never enter. The charming impoliteness of an intercourse begun by their fathers and grandfathers, was not for him. There must always be a certain formality with him, even though they were his most intimate friends. He had not fifty cousins, therefore, as Elise phrased it, he was "out of touch with the world."

"If ever I have a son or a daughter," he found himself saying unconsciously, "I would try to save him from this."

Then he laughed bitterly as he realized the irony of the thought. Well, anyway, Elise loved him. There was a sweet consolation in that. He had but to look into her frank eyes and read her soul. Perhaps she wondered why he had not spoken. Should he speak? There he was back at the old question again.

"According to the standard of the world," he mused reflectively, "my blood is tainted in two ways. Who knows it? No one but myself, and I shall not tell. Otherwise, I am quite as good as the rest, and Elise loves me."

But even this thought failed of its sweetness in a moment. Elise loved him because she did not know. He found a sickening anger and disgust rising in himself at a people whose prejudices made him live a life of deception. He would cater to their traditions no longer; he would be honest. Then he found himself shrinking from the alternative with a dread that made him wonder. It was the old problem of his life in the village; and the boys, both white and black and yellow, stood as before, with stones in their hands to hurl at him.

He went to bed worn out with the struggle, but still with no definite idea what to do. Sleep was impossible. He rolled and tossed miserably, and cursed the fate that had thrown him in such a position. He had never thought very seriously over the subject before. He had rather drifted with the tide and accepted what came to him as a sort of recompense the world owed him for his unhappy childhood. He had known fear, yes, and qualms now and then, and a hot resentment occasionally when the outsideness of his situation was inborne to him; but that was all. Elise had awakened a disagreeable conscientiousness within him, which he decided was as unpleasant as it was unnecessary.

He could not sleep, so he arose, and dressing, walked out and stood on the banquette. The low hum of the city came to him like the droning of some sleepy insect, and ever and anon, the quick flash and fire of the gas houses like a huge winking fiery eye lit up the south of the city. It was inexpressingly soothing to Victor; the great unknowing city, teeming with life and with lives whose sadness mocked his own teacup tempest. He smiled and shook himself as a dog shakes off the water from his coat.

"I think a walk will help me out," he said absently, and presently he was striding down St. Charles Avenue, around Lee Circle and down to Canal Street, where the lights and glare absorbed him for a while. He walked out the wide boulevard towards Claiborne Street, hardly thinking, hardly realizing that he was walking. When he was thoroughly worn out, he retraced his steps and dropped wearily into a restaurant near Bourbon Street.

"Hullo!" said a familiar voice from a table as he entered. Victor turned and recognized Frank Ward, a little oculist, whose office was in the same building as his own.

"Another night owl besides myself," laughed Ward, making room for him at his table. "Can't you sleep too, old fellow?"

"Not very well," said Victor taking the proferred seat, "I believe I'm getting nerves. Think I need toning up."

"Well, you'd have been toned up if you had been in here a few minutes ago. Why—why—" and Ward went off into peals of laughter at the memory of the scene.

"What was it?" asked Victor.

"Why—a fellow came in here, nice sort of fellow, apparently, and wanted to have supper. Well, would you believe it, when they wouldn't serve him, he wanted to fight everything in sight. It was positively exciting for a time."

"Why wouldn't the waiter serve him?" Victor tried to make his tone indifferent, but he felt the quaver in his voice.

"Why? Why, he was a darkey, you know."

"Well, what of it?" demanded Grabért fiercely, "Wasn't he quiet, well-dressed, polite? Didn't he have money?"

"My dear fellow," began Ward mockingly, "Upon my word, I believe you are losing your mind. You do need toning up or something. Would you—could you—?"

"Oh, pshaw," broke in Grabért, "I—I—believe I am losing my mind. Really, Ward, I need something to make me sleep. My head aches."

Ward was at once all sympathy and advice, and chiding to the waiter for his slowness in filling their order. Victor toyed with his food, and made an excuse to leave the restaurant as soon as he could decently.

"Good heavens," he said when he was alone, "What will I do next?" His outburst of indignation at Ward's narrative had come from his lips almost before he knew it, and he was frightened, frightened at his own unguardedness. He did not know what had come over him.

"I must be careful, I must be careful," he muttered to himself. "I must go to the other extreme, if necessary." He was pacing his rooms again, and suddenly, he faced the mirror.

"You wouldn't fare any better than the rest, if they knew," he told the reflection, "You poor wretch, what are you?"

When he thought of Elise, he smiled. He loved her, but he hated the traditions which she represented. He was conscious of a blind fury which bade him wreak vengeance on those traditions, and of a cowardly fear which cried out to him to retain his position in the world's and Elise's eyes at any cost.

* * *

Mrs. Grabért was delighted to have visiting her her old school friend from Virginia, and the two spent hours laughing over their girlish escapades, and comparing notes about their little ones. Each was confident that her darling had said the cutest things, and their polite deference to each other's opinions on the matter was a sham through which each saw without resentment.

"But Elise," remonstrated Mrs. Allen, "I think it so strange you don't have a mammy for Baby Vannier. He would be so much better cared for than by that harum-scarum young white girl you have."

"I think so too, Adelaide," sighed Mrs. Grabért, "It seems strange for me not to have a darkey maid about, but Victor can't bear them. I cried and cried for my old mammy, but he was stern. He doesn't like darkies, you know, and he says old mammies just frighten children, and ruin their childhood. I don't see how he could say that, do you?" She looked wistfully to Mrs. Allen for sympathy.

"I don't know," mused that lady, "We were all looked after by our mammies, and I think they are the best kind of nurses."

"And Victor won't have any kind of darkey servant either here or at the office. He says they're shiftless and worthless and generally no-account. Of course, he knows, he's had lots of experience with them in his business."

Mrs. Allen folded her hands behind her head and stared hard at the ceiling. "Oh, well, men don't know everything," she said, "and Victor may come around to our way of thinking after all."

It was late that evening when the lawyer came in for dinner. His eyes had acquired a habit of veiling themselves under their lashes as if they were constantly concealing something which they feared might be wrenched from them by a stare. He was nervous and restless, with a habit of glancing about him furtively, and a twitching compressing of his lips when he had finished a sentence, which somehow reminded you of a kindhearted judge, who is forced to give a death sentence.

Elise met him at the door as was her wont, and she knew from the first glance into his eyes that something had disturbed him more than usual that day, but she forbore asking questions, for she knew he would tell her when the time had come.

They were in their room that night when the rest of the household lay in slumber. He sat for a long while gazing at the open fire, then he passed his hand over his forehead wearily.

"I have had a rather unpleasant experience to-day," he began.

"Yes."

"Pavageau, again."

His wife was brushing her hair before the mirror. At the name she turned hastily with the brush in her uplifted hand.

"I can't understand, Victor, why you must have dealings with that man. He is constantly irritating you. I simply wouldn't associate with him."

"I don't," and he laughed at her feminine argument. "It isn't a question of association, cherie, it's a purely business and unsocial relation, if relation it may be called, that throws us together."

She threw down the brush petulantly, and came to his side, "Victor," she began hesitatingly, her arms about his neck, her face close to his, "Won't you—won't you give up politics for me? It was ever so much nicer when you were just a lawyer and wanted only to be the best lawyer in the state, without all this worry about corruption and votes and such things. You've changed, oh, Victor, you've changed so. Baby and I won't know you after a while."

He put her gently on his knee. "You musn't blame the poor politics, darling. Don't you think, perhaps, it's the inevitable hardening and embittering that must come to us all as we grow older?"

"No, I don't," she replied emphatically, "Why do you go into this struggle, anyhow? You have nothing to gain but an empty honor. It won't bring you more money, or make you more loved or respected. Why must you be mixed up with such—such—awful people?"

"I don't know." he said wearily.

And in truth, he did not know. He had gone on after his marriage with Elise making one success after another. It seemed that a beneficent Providence had singled him out as the one man in the state upon whom to heap the most lavish attentions. He was popular after the fashion of those who are high in the esteem of the world; and this very fact made him tremble the more, for he feared that should some disclosure come, he could not stand the shock of public opinion that must overwhelm him.

"What disclosure?" he would say impatiently when such a thought would come to him, "Where could it come from, and then, what is there to disclose?"

Thus he would deceive himself for as much as a month at a time.

He was surprised to find awaiting him in his office one day the man Wilson, whom he remembered in the courtroom before Recorder Grant. He was surprised and annoyed. Why had the man come to his office? Had he seen the telltale flush on his face that day?

But it was soon evident that Wilson did not even remember having seen him before.

"I came to see if I could retain you in a case of mine," he began, after the usual formalities of greeting were over.

"I am afraid, my good man," said Grabért brusquely, "that you have mistaken the office."

Wilson's face flushed at the appellation, but he went on bravely, "I have not mistaken the office. I know you are the best civil lawyer in the city, and I want your services."

"An impossible thing."

"Why? Are you too busy? My case is a simple thing, a mere point in law, but I want the best authority and the best opinion brought to bear on it."

"I could not give you any help—and—I fear, we do not understand each other—I do not wish to." He turned to his desk abruptly.

"What could he have meant by coming to me?" he questioned himself fearfully, as Wilson left the office. "Do I look like a man likely to take up his impossible contentions?"

He did not look like it, nor was he. When it came to a question involving the Negro, Victor Grabért was noted for his stern, unrelenting attitude; it was simply impossible to convince him that there was anything but sheerest incapacity in that race. For him, no good could come out of this Nazareth. He was liked and respected by men of his political belief, because, even when he was a candidate for a judgeship, neither money nor the possible chance of a deluge of votes from the First and Fourth Wards could cause him to swerve one hair's breadth from his opinion of the black inhabitants of those wards.

Pavageau, however, was his *bête noir*. Pavageau was a lawyer, a coolheaded, calculating man with steely eyes set in a grim brown face. They had first met in the courtroom in a case which involved the question whether a man may set aside the will of his father, who disregarding the legal offspring of another race than himself, chooses to leave his property to educational institutions which would not have granted admission to that son. Pavageau represented the son. He lost, of course. The judge, the jury, the people and Grabért were against him; but he fought his fight with a grim determination which commanded Victor's admiration and respect.

"Fools," he said between his teeth to himself, when they were crowding about him with congratulations, "Fools, can't they see who is the abler man of the two?"

He wanted to go up to Pavageau and give him his hand; to tell him that he was proud of him and that he had really won the case, but public opinion was against him; but he dared not. Another one of his colleagues might; but he was afraid. Pavageau and the world might misunderstand, or would it be understanding?

Thereafter they met often. Either by some freak of nature, or because there was a shrewd sense of the possibilities in his position, Pavageau was of the same political side of the fence as Grabért. Secretly, he admired the man; he respected him; he liked him, and because of this he was always ready with sneer and invective for him. He fought him bitterly when there was no occasion for fighting, and Pavageau became his enemy, and his name a very synonym of horror to Elise, who learned to trace her husband's fits of moodiness and depression to the one source.

Meanwhile, Vannier Grabért was growing up, a handsome lad, with his father's and mother's physical beauty, and a strength and force of character that belonged to neither. In him, Grabért saw the reparation of all his childhood's wrongs and sufferings. The boy realized all his own longings. He had family traditions, and a social position which was his from birth and an inalienable right to hold up his head without an unknown fear gripping at his heart. Grabért felt that he could forgive all; the village boys of long ago, and the imaginary village boys of to-day when he looked at his son. He had bought and paid for Vannier's freedom and happiness. The coins may have been each a drop of his heart's blood, but he had reckoned the cost before he had given it.

It was a source of great pride for him to take the boy to court with him,* and one Saturday morning when he was starting out, Vannier asked if he might go.

"There is nothing that would interest you to-day, mon fils," he said tenderly, "but you may go."

In fact, there was nothing interesting that day; merely a troublesome old woman, who instead of taking her fair-skinned grandchild out of the school where it had been found it did not belong, had preferred to bring the matter to court. She was represented by Pavageau. Of course, there was not the ghost of a show for her. Pavageau had told her that. The law was very explicit about the matter. The only question lay in proving the child's affinity to the Negro race, which was not such a difficult matter to do, so the case was quickly

* Editor's note: Grabért is now a judge.

settled, since the child's grandmother accompanied him. The judge, however, was irritated. It was a hot day and he was provoked that such a trivial matter should have taken up his time. He lost his temper as he looked at his watch.

"I don't see why these people want to force their children into the white schools," he declared, "There should be a rigid inspection to prevent it, and all the suspected children put out and made to go where they belong."

Pavageau, too, was irritated that day. He looked up from some papers which he was folding, and his gaze met Grabért's with a keen, cold, penetrating flash.

"Perhaps Your Honor would like to set the example by taking your son from the schools."

There was an instant silence in the courtroom, a hush intense and eager. Every eye turned upon the judge who sat still, a figure carven in stone with livid face and fear-stricken eyes. After the first flash of his eyes, Pavageau had gone on cooly sorting the papers.

The courtroom waited, waited, for the judge to rise and thunder forth a fine against the daring Negro lawyer for contempt. A minute passed, which seemed like an hour. Why did not Grabért speak? Pavageau's implied accusation was too absurd for denial; but he should be punished. Was His Honor ill, or did he merely hold the man in too much contempt to notice him or his remark?

Finally Grabért spoke; he moistened his lips, for they were dry and parched, and his voice was weak and sounded far away in his own ears. "My son—does—not—attend the public schools."

Someone in the rear of the room laughed, and the atmosphere lightened at once. Plainly Pavageau was an idiot, and His Honor too far above him; too much of a gentleman to notice him. Grabért continued calmly; "The gentleman," there was an unmistakable sneer in this word, habit if nothing else, and not even fear could restrain him, "The gentleman doubtless intended a little pleasantry, but I shall have to fine him for contempt of court."

"As you will," replied Pavageau, and he flashed another look at Grabért. It was a look of insolent triumph and derision. His Honor's eyes dropped beneath it.

"What did that man mean, father, by saying you should take me out of school?" asked Vannier on his way home.

"He was provoked, my son, because he had lost his case, and when a man is provoked he is likely to say silly things. By the way, Vannier, I hope you won't say anything to your mother about the incident. It would only annoy her."

For the public, the incident was forgotten as soon as it had closed, but for Grabért, it was indelibly stamped on his memory; a scene that shrieked in his mind and stood out before him at every footstep he took. Again and again as he tossed on a sleepless bed did he see the cold flash of Pavageau's eyes, and hear his quiet accusation. How did he know? Where had he gotten his information? For he spoke, not as one who makes a random shot in anger; but as one who knows, who has known a long while, and who is betrayed by irritation into playing his trump card too early in the game.

He passed a wretched week, wherein it seemed that his every footstep was dogged, his every gesture watched and recorded. He fancied that Elise, even, was suspecting him. When he took his judicial seat each morning, it seemed that every eye in the courtroom was fastened upon him in derision; every one who spoke, it seemed were but biding their time to shout the old village street refrain which had haunted him all his life, "Nigger!—Nigger!—White nigger!"

Finally, he could stand it no longer, and with leaden feet and furtive glances to the right and left for fear he might be seen; he went up a flight of dusty stairs in an Exchange Alley building, which led to Pavageau's office.

The latter was frankly surprised to see him. He made a polite attempt to conceal it, however. It was the first time in his legal life that Grabért had ever sought out a Negro; the first time that he had ever voluntarily opened conversation with one.

He mopped his forehead nervously as he took the chair Pavageau offered him; he stared about the room for an instant; then with a sudden, almost brutal directness, he turned on the lawyer.

"See here, what did you mean by that remark you made in court the other day?"

"I meant just what I said," was the cool reply.

Grabért paused, "Why did you say it?" he asked slowly.

"Because I was a fool. I should have kept my mouth shut until another time, should I not?"

"Pavageau," said Grabért softly, "let's not fence. Where did you get your information?"

Pavageau paused for an instant. He put his fingertips together and closed his eyes as one who meditates. Then he said with provoking calmness,

"You seem anxious—well, I don't mind letting you know. It doesn't really matter."

"Yes, yes," broke in Grabért impatiently.

"Did you ever hear of a Mme. Guichard of Hospital Street?"

The sweat broke out on the judge's brow as he replied weakly, "Yes."

"Well, I am her nephew."

"And she?"

"Is dead. She told me about you once—with pride, let me say. No one else knows."

Grabért sat dazed. He had forgotten about Mme. Guichard. She had never entered into his calculations at all. Pavageau turned to his desk with a sigh as if he wished the interview were ended. Grabért rose.

"If—if—this were known—to—to—my—my wife," he said thickly, "it would hurt her very much."

His head was swimming. He had had to appeal to this man, and to appeal in his wife's name. His wife, whose name he scarcely spoke to men whom he considered his social equals.

Pavageau looked up quickly. "It happens that I often have cases in your court," he spoke deliberately, "I am willing, if I lose fairly, to give up; but I do not like to have a decision made against me because my opponent is of a different complexion from mine, or because the decision against me would please a certain class of people. I only ask what I have never had from you—fair play."

"I understand," said Grabért.

He admired Pavageau more than ever as he went out of his office, yet this admiration was tempered by the knowledge that this man was the only person in the whole world who possessed positive knowledge of his secret. He groveled in a self-abasement at his position; and yet he could not but feel a certain relief that the vague formless fear which had hitherto dogged his life and haunted it, had taken on a definite shape. He knew where it was now; he could lay his hands on it, and fight it.

But with what weapons? There were none offered him save a substantial backing down from his position on certain

questions; the position that had been his for so long that he
was almost known by it. For in the quiet deliberate sentence
of Pavageau's, he read that he must cease all the oppression,
all the little injustices which he had offered Pavageau's clientele. He must act now as his convictions and secret sympathies
and affiliations had bidden him act; not as prudence and fear
and cowardice had made him act.

Then what would be the result? he asked himself. Would
not the suspicions of the people be aroused by this sudden
change in his manner? Would not they begin to question and
to wonder? Would not someone remember Pavageau's remark
that morning, and putting two and two together, start some
rumor flying? His heart sickened again at the thought.

There was a banquet that night. It was in his honor, and
he was to speak, and the thought was distasteful to him
beyond measure. He knew how it all would be. He would
be hailed with shouts and acclamations, as the finest flower of
civilization. He would be listened to deferentially, and younger
men would go away holding him in their hearts as a truly
worthy model. When all the while—

He threw back his head and laughed. Oh, what a glorious
revenge he had on those little white village boys! How he
had made a race atone for Wilson's insult in the courtroom;
for the man in the restaurant at whom Ward had laughed so
uproariously; for all the affronts seen and unseen given these
people of his own whom he had denied. He had taken a
diploma from their most exclusive college; he had broken
down the barriers of their social world; he had taken the
highest possible position among them; and aping their own
ways, had shown them that he too, could despise this inferior
race they despised. Nay, he had taken for his wife the best

woman among them all, and she had borne him a son. Ha, ha! What a joke on them all!

And he had not forgotten the black and yellow boys either. They had stoned him too, and he had lived to spurn them; to look down upon them, and to crush them at every possible turn from his seat on the bench. Truly, his life had not been wasted.

He had lived forty-nine years now, and the zenith of his power was not yet reached. There was much more to do, much more, and he was going to do it. He owed it to Elise and the boy. For their sake he must go on and on and keep his tongue still, and truckle to Pavageau and suffer alone. Some day, perhaps, he would have a grandson, who would point with pride to "My grandfather, the famous Judge Grabért!" Ah, that in itself, was a reward. To have founded a dynasty; to bequeath to others that which he had never possessed himself, and the lack of which had made his life a misery.

It was a banquet with a political significance; one that meant a virtual triumph for Judge Grabért in the next contest for the District Judge. He smiled around at the eager faces which were turned up to his as he arose to speak. The tumult of applause which had greeted his rising had died away, and an expectant hush fell on the room.

"What a sensation I could make now," he thought. He had but to open his mouth and cry out, "Fools! Fools! I whom you are honoring, I am one of the despised ones. Yes, I'm a nigger—do you hear, a nigger!" What a temptation it was to end the whole miserable farce. If he were alone in the world, if it were not for Elise and the boy; he would, just to see their horror and wonder. How they would shrink from

him! But what could they do? They could take away his office;
but his wealth, and his former successes, and his learning,
they could not touch. Well, he must speak, and he must
remember Elise and the boy.

Every eye was fastened on him in eager expectancy. Judge
Grabért's speech was expected to outline the policy of their
faction in the coming campaign. He turned to the chairman
at the head of the table.

"Mr. Chairman," he began, and paused again. How
peculiar it was that in the place of the chairman there sat
Grandmére Grabért as she had been wont to sit on the steps
of the tumble down cottage in the village. She was looking
at him sternly and bidding him give an account of his life
since she had kissed him good-bye ere he had sailed down
the river to New Orleans. He was surprised, and not a little
annoyed. He had expected to address the chairman; not
Grandmére Grabért. He cleared his throat and frowned.

"Mr. Chairman," he said again. Well, what was the use
of addressing her that way? She would not understand him.
He would call her Grandmére, of course. Were they not
alone again on the cottage steps at twilight with the cries of
the little brutish boys ringing derisively from the distant
village square?

"Grandmére," he said softly, "you don't understand—"
and then he was sitting down in his seat pointing one finger
angrily at her because the other words would not come. They
stuck in his throat, and he choked and beat the air with his
hands. When the men crowded around him with water and
hastily improvised fans, he fought them away wildly and
desperately with furious curses that came from his blackened
lips. For were they not all boys with stones to pelt him
because he wanted to play with them? He would run away to

Grandmére who would soothe him and comfort him. So he arose, and stumbling, shrieking and beating them back from him, ran the length of the hall, and fell across the threshold of the door.

The secret died with him, for Pavageau's lips were ever sealed.

ELLEN FENTON *

After twenty-two busy married years, Ellen Fenton sat down and reviewed her life one morning.

She had been busy for twenty-two years, busy and happy, until somehow, the time had slipped away almost without her knowing how it had gone. It was Eugene's nineteenth birthday to-day, and Eugene was her second son. Heretofore their birthdays had come and gone and made but little ripple on the surface of her life, save that caused by parties or merry-makings or the extra labor involved in the making of birthday cakes. But this birthday of Eugene's somehow seemed to mark an epoch in her life. He was to leave for college soon, too, whither Herbert had preceded him by two years.

"And there isn't anything I want for my birthday so much," said Eugene thoughtfully, "as that tiny etching of Whistler's down at Miller's Art store."

He was a grave boy with an artistic tendency which his father had striven in vain to correct.

"Who is Whistler?" Ellen inquired thoughtlessly.

Eugene looked pained at first, then indifferent and answered carelessly, "Oh, just an artist, mama mio."

* Typescript.

It was not the words so much as the tone that stung her. It seemed to place her at once outside the pale of his life. She had winced a little, then flushed, then said no more. But when breakfast was over she went up into her little study where she was wont to go every morning to cast up household accounts and issue orders. She sat staring at her neat ledger and methodical arrangement of bills with unseeing eyes, and laid bare the past twenty-two years with merciless precision.

She had married at eighteen and she was deemed an exceptionally bright girl in her day. She had reared four sons; tall, strong, manly fellows; the youngest of them was already in the High School, and she felt that she could in sooth, breathe and rest for awhile. She had mothered them as few women do nowadays; loving them without spoiling them, exacting obedience and obtaining love, devotion and a chivalrous regard from all of them. She had kept in touch with her husband's business, and knew every detail almost as well as he himself, so that she could have stood at the helm at any time in his absence. She had ruled and ordered a large household of servants, and overlooked a summer home with a farm attached. She had served on every committee of any account in public matters in her town; had been a loyal and hard working church member; an enthusiastic club woman; a practical charity worker, and an ardent spirit in local politics as far as was compatible with womanly dignity. She had been foremost in every public movement and had never neglected home or husband or children. She was looked up to by every one in the town; was pointed out as the model woman; while those writers, ever ready to point a moral and adorn a tale, constantly held her up as the worthy and progressive twentieth-century woman with a large field, who was unspoiled by semi-public life, and unnarrowed by a large family.

Ellen reviewed her past years thoughtfully. Surely, surely, in all this busy life she must have found the right manner of living; surely, there could be nothing more? Mr. Fenton was wont to declare as he smoked leisurely of evenings in the library that he had a model wife, a model home and model children. What more could a woman want?

Yet, Ellen was conscious this morning for the first time that something had eluded her, and that that something, or rather the lack of it, was responsible for the new feeling of discontent, even unhappiness that assailed her.

"It is like what the French say of us American women," she said, laughing as she unscrewed her fountain pen and turned to her accounts, "We don't know what we want, but we want it very much and we want it right away."

But the accounts were uninteresting, more than that, she found it impossible to arrange them, and after a few futile attempts at adding columns of figures, she threw down her pen and frankly resigned herself to staring at the wallpaper and to thinking it all over again.

"Why mother?" It was Eugene who entered the room and stood staring at the unwonted sight of "the busiest woman in the world" as they called her, sitting idle at the desk, staring hard as if the roses on the wall were actors in a strange drama, and she the sole spectator.

"Why mother, is anything wrong?"

"Nothing, my son. I am merely thinking a little, getting acquainted with myself, as it were. Close the door when you go out and tell the others not to disturb me."

Eugene went out softly, too surprised to broach his errand.

Ellen sat a long while as if reading the wallpaper. That was it, she had not become acquainted with herself.

"And as for my husband, Herbert Fenton," she spoke

aloud, "we are not even on bowing terms with each other."

They had lived together, and loved and been happy to-gether. They had accumulated wealth and acquired honor in the eyes of their townspeople; they had fulfilled their social, charitable, and religious duties punctiliously, oh, so punc-tiliously, and neither of them had felt very strongly about the matter. Their lives had flowed on serenely and carefully, and since the first glorious months of their honeymoon, their souls had scarcely touched. Their ups and downs had been emi-nently respectable ups and downs; no breath of scandal, or fear of disgrace or thought of misery had come near their lives, and they had walked down the years, each clad in an impenetrable armor of invulnerable respectability and com-monplace decency. Ellen thought to-day with a tinge of bitterness, how often she had, Pharisee-like, thanked her gods that her life had flowed so smoothly, "for the sake of the children" as she put it. Yet, she had flattered herself that her prosperity had not made her narrow. She had never withheld a helping hand to the deserving unfortunate. She had never been hard on the sinner, but had given freely of pity, rather than sympathy, and aid and love, such as she understood it. She suddenly realized this morning that even her best and most well-meant efforts must have seemed cold and heartless from the viewpoint of those whose souls are attuned to sympathy by virtue of their own experience of sorrow and misery.

She began to understand why she had sometimes heard herself referred to as a cold woman, whose bright smile awed, rather than reassured those who approached her with petitions. She had always laughed away such suggestions before, and had been wont to assert that with some people mere dignity and reserve were so foreign to their natures that they could not understand it when they met it in others. She confessed now lamely enough, to herself, that in reality her heart had remained untouched and unswayed.

She rose, paced the room restlessly, then strayed aimlessly downstairs, through the drawing room, library and halls. The atmosphere of the house reflected her life and personality. It was massive, conservative, quietly elegant. The pictures were reproductions of the recognized, standard masters. Raphael and Murillo predominated, with stiff family portraits. There was no room in the Fenton household for frisky nymphs or the strange impressionistic vagaries of modern art. Botticelli would have been frowned down. Burne-Jones and Rosetti were not to be mentioned. Turner was but a name, and not a familiar one; while Sargent was un unknown quantity. The coloring of the house was quiet, heavy, old-world. Strange, Oriental combinations and modern upholstering would have seemed as out of place as a bit of Bohemia in a Grand Ducal palace. The library was filled with the old authors, those who had been the recognized standard since the early Victorian era. The Fentons had rather gloried in their library and prided themselves on their literary taste, because it was standard. Somewhere on an upper shelf were volumes of Boccaccio, because he was an old recognized storyteller; but Ellen had shuddered once after reading a rather virile and outspoken novel of a latter day woman and had declared with gentle vehemence at the club meeting that a really moral woman would have found it impossible to have written such a book.

She fingered the music on the piano absently. Beethoven and Mozart, Haydn and Bach for serious moments; Mendelsohn and the Italian school for lighter hours. Ellen played well. In the busy stress of her life, she had not let her music fall into disuse. But she did not care for Wagner, he affected her unpleasantly, she had been wont to declare; Chaminade and all that school were names to her; she had never heard a comic opera, while the lighter, more popular music of the day was a sealed book which she had no desire to open.

Of these shortcomings, she was but vaguely aware as she wandered listlessly from room to room. She could not tell what was the trouble, save that suddenly she felt old and out of the order of things, and she knew not why. In bringing up her sons in an atmosphere quiet, conservative and old-world, she had felt that she was doing the best for them and for herself. Yet, in some intangible, subtle manner this morning she felt that she, the most modern woman, so-called, in the town, was the very epitome of narrowness and old-fashioned ideas.

She was still standing by the piano fingering the music when her husband entered the room breathlessly.

"Why, Ellen," he said, and there was a note of surprise in his tone, "I have been in your office waiting for you for a half hour, and I couldn't imagine where you were."

She had not been conscious of the passage of time since leaving her little study, and it irritated her suddenly to find that so slight a deviation from her usual habits should cause the expression of wonder, almost consternation on her husband's face.

"Why, may I not come in here and look at music in the morning?" she asked sharply; then flushed at her own rudeness, as Herbert Fenton did not reply, but led the way back to her study.

He seated himself thoughtfully and watched her with curious, intent eyes as she fidgeted about the room before she sat down. It was unlike Ellen to be nervous or erratic in her movements. Her gentle, calm self-possession had been a source of pride to her husband and friends and a cause of self-gratulation on her own part.

"Well?" she queried somewhat impatiently, as Fenton said nothing, but continued to watch her with that curious, intent gaze. She faced him as she spoke, and their eyes met for an instant. Was it fancy, she wondered, or did she seem to see reflected in the depths of his quiet gray eyes some of the same discontented awakening that tugged at her soul?

"I have been having a talk with Eugene," he began, and there was a hesitancy and wistfulness in his manner that made her sit down suddenly and gasp.

"Yes?"

"He—he—doesn't want to go to college, Ellen."

She heard him unmoved. Two hours ago such a statement would have seemed impossible, absurd, unheard of. For a Fenton not to wish to go to college was as incomprehensible as it would have been for a Fenton to have become a clown or a mountebank or a street-sweeper. The boys had been reared from their infancy to understand that they were to go through an academic training at college, at least, and after that, to choose their own vocations in life. But here had arisen one unruly member.

Two hours ago Ellen knew that she would have cried out aghast in horror at such a thought. Now she felt that she sympathized with him. She too, felt strong within her the desire to kick over the traces in some way, and she felt nearer to her son than ever before.

Fenton watched her narrowly, as she sat silent after his statement.

"What do you think of it, Ellen?" he asked at length. She stared at the wallpaper before making a reply.

"What alternative does he suggest?" she said slowly.

Fenton looked at her with a sudden elevating of his eyebrows. He had expected a quietly passionate outburst at the absurdity of the idea, and he felt relieved by the gentle manner with which she received the news.

"He proposes to go abroad to study—art." He paused before the last word and pronounced it lamely, looking at his wife to see what effect it might have upon her. She remained unmoved, only a slight flush rose in her cheeks.

"What do you think of it, Herbert?"

"I?" He was helpless at once. "I? Why, you know, Ellen, I always leave such matters entirely to you."

She drummed her fingers on the table and pretended to think it was a harmless subterfuge. Something was whirling within her, an indefinable feeling that she too, wanted to say aloud, as her son had done, "I don't want to do the same thing; I want to do something different." She felt strong within her the desire to go to him, and laying her cheek against his, pour out this new sensation and sympathy, for she felt that he must understand.

Fenton waited patiently. He felt sorry for her for he thought he knew how deep-rooted was her disappointment at this disaffection of Eugene. He would not speak, for he respected the grief which he felt she must be undergoing. Finally, she looked up, and he was slightly shocked to find her eyes bright and hard, and her smile as quick and ready as though it had been a mere matter of deciding an entree for dinner.

"Let the boy go where he wants to go," she said quietly, "He will be the better for it."

Fenton confessed to himself, that after all, he was disappointed. While he had experienced a certain sense of relief at her not bursting into tears, he felt a little hurt to see her take so lightly what he thought should have wrenched her to the core.

"Then it is settled, Ellen?" he asked.

"Yes, settled. Eugene perhaps knows better what he is fitted for than you or I. And after all, Herbert," her lips twitched queerly, "We are happiest doing what we are best fitted for."

He had not heard the last part of the sentence, so absorbed was he in his own thoughts.

"Don't you think it a long way for him to go alone?" he queried doubtfully. He knew that that should have been the woman's thought and he felt a quick little resentment that his had been the first feeling for the boy's safety.

"No," said Ellen decisively, and again her husband felt that bewildered sense of having lost his mental rudder, "No, it will be good for him to get away from the home atmosphere, from all that detracts from his chosen work; from us and our narrowness. Let him go." She had grown suddenly vehement and rising she threw her arms above her head and turned to her husband.

"Yes, let him go. If he stays here he'll get into a rut like the rest of us, and he'll be as narrow as a line and imagine he's as broad as the universe."

Thus it happened that Eugene went abroad, instead of following staidly in the footsteps of his brother and his father and his father's father. There was a certain amount of bustle and hurry and excitement incident to his going away, and Ellen found herself with neither leisure nor inclination to hug her newfound self, but she had the feeling all the while that locked away safe in the innermost recesses of her heart there was a secret joy that she would take out some day and hug it fondly and caress it, even though it would have to be put away again under lock and key.

When Eugene had gone finally, she turned again to her household duties. The other boys, with the exception of the youngest, were off at school, and she should have found plenty of leisure for thought; but there were the clubs, the societies, the church guild, the charities, the board meetings, the visiting committees, the staid magazines to read under a pretense of "keeping up with the times," the accounts, the occasional looking in at the business down town so that she would not lose her grasp of affairs. It began again, all the petty round, with its detail of trivial incident that she had once thought indicated such broad and general culture. Her vision was clearer now, or was her point of view merely changed, or her standards readjusted?

That year, there was an unusually brisk discussion going on in one of her clubs—the Advanced Woman's Club of the town—concerning the election of delegates to the National Convention. Ellen had served them long and faithfully as president, and finally had resigned and held an honored place on its board of managers. She was usually elected every year as delegate, and now the question under discussion was not whether she should be sent as delegate, but how many would be sent with her. She had come to the meeting late that evening—an unprecedented thing for her, and she stood somewhat startled when she heard that she had been elected as principal delegate.

"I can't go, really, I can't," she protested lamely.

"Mrs. Fenton would have us think that she can't leave her household and other duties, when we all know that she has everything under such perfect control that her affairs simply run themselves in her absence," laughed a little member a trifle enviously.

"No, it isn't that," said Ellen. She looked about her timidly. Most of these women were old friends of hers. They thought they understood her thoroughly and perfectly, but how much, after all, did they know about her? How much, in fact, does any one of us know about the other, even our most intimate daily companions? Something within her bade her speak, throw down the gauntlet, as it were. She was not satisfied with her daily life, now then, was the time to proclaim the change she would make; yet she shrank from too open a breach. All the instinctive conservatism in her nature rebelled at the prospect of a scene; yet in all honesty, how dare she accept the conditions of public life any longer and still cherish ideals and long to live up to them?

She rose to her feet with sudden determination.

"Madam President," she began firmly, "I regret to say that I cannot accept the honor which the club has bestowed upon me again, because I do not feel that I can conscientiously do the things required of me."

Intense quiet fell on the room at once. An electric thrill ran over the women. Each one felt that somehow she was going to assist at the disrobing of a skeleton, and there was breathless interest immediately.

Ellen locked and unlocked her fingers nervously. She knew if she spoke conscientiously that her career in the town as a public-spirited woman was at an end, and the long-striven-for, hard-won honors were dear to her after all, even in the light of her recent mental experiences. Like the proverbial flash of life's vision before the eyes of a drowning man, she saw all her career as club-woman, public speaker, trustee, office-holder pass before her. Not lightly was all this to be relinquished, and relinquished for an idea, a quixotic, visionary thought, which after all, might prove untenable. She might place herself in the position to tempt ridicule, and then regret it, and wish to creep back into the fold.

The silence grew unbearable, the dozens of pairs of eyes turned upon her, seemed to burn into her brain. She unclasped her hands once more, and continued abruptly;

"Madam President, certain revelations that have come to me lately, I—do not misunderstand me—I mean not revelations of a nature to touch upon anyone's life but mine, mere psychical revelations—" she was getting deeper and deeper into the sea of abstruse speculation.

"It has occurred to me lately that I have worked so hard in the past fifteen years or more, that I am not quite equal to the nervous strain that club life puts upon a woman who is deeply interested. In the light of that, and for the sake of the members, who, like myself, wish to see our organization represented in the best possible manner, I must decline and beg that you will not press me further."

There was no immediate reply from the chair, and a perceptible quiver of relief swept over the room. After all, they had been spared what promised at first to be a scene. Ellen still stood erect. She had recovered her poise and the easy, unmeaning, polite phrases fell from her lips as of old. But she was dissatisfied. It was not for this that she had arisen. She had been cowardly enough to seek the easier way out of the difficulty, and her message still remained undelivered. She waited an instant, then continued gently,

"It has happened that within the past few weeks I have undergone several mental shocks." The strained look returned to her listeners' faces. She went on, and spoke easily, gently, calmly; her self possession completely restored; her calm faith in her audience's patience unshaken. As nearly as she could describe it, for she was not quite sure of her own position yet, she tried to show that there were things beyond the mere outward living they were all doing; beyond the mere expression of a "good and useful life." She told frankly, for Ellen was no coward, and she felt she owed it to her associates to share her experiences with them; that while she could not tell just what there was lacking in all her past life, she knew the lack was there, and she would find it, and remedy it, if possible. She finished with an earnest appeal to all her listeners to do likewise, to "find themselves, and thus, like Kipling's ship, of whom the last lecturer had spoken so charmingly, to be more worthy, stronger and more capable in every way."

There was a dead silence as she sat down. A few perfunctory expressions of regret were uttered by the president; another delegate was chosen without enthusiasm and the meeting adjourned in a chill gloom that settled on everyone's spirits. Some one or two members came up afterwards and clasped her hand for "expressing so beautifully what they had all felt for so long," but she felt the insincerity of their remarks and hurried away depressed and disgusted. She knew that she was being discussed with unflattering frankness, she knew that she would be misunderstood, and that some would even go so far as to intimate that her mind was unbalanced. She had known that it would be hard, but how hard she had never guessed until that past hour. She was disgusted with herself, too, that she had not found the strength within herself to keep her mental experiences sacred; simply to have announced her retirement, and let the others do the conjecturing. She was conscious in a shamefaced manner that what she had fondly imagined strength of character and a desire to help her friends to her peace of mind, was merely the old desire for public approval and applause.

She found the task at home a harder one. The family, including the servants, was inclined to look askance upon her changed mode of life. No longer did the routine of her busy days flow on undisturbed and serene. She spent long hours gazing out of the windows, when by all the laws of her household, she should have been at her desk. She was given to going out a great deal on long walks, and returning with little to say; she who had once shared every little experience of the day at the dinner table. She could be seen at any hour of the day, reading, poring would be better, and her new taste was as catholic now as it had once been circumscribed. It had been once that she had never found time to read at any hour of the day.

She felt herself changing, developing. Now that she was taking time to grow, she remembered that she had a soul, apart from the religious conception of the idea, and it interested her to see it expand, like the wings of a butterfly creeping from its chrysalis. The one regret she had was that perhaps she was not as interesting to those about her as she was to herself.

She had always been a woman, who in addition to the multiple cares of her household and public philanthropy, to use the cant phrase, "lived her own life." She was discovering now that the term was a misnomer. The average woman, she found, who "lives her own life," in reality, lives others', and has no life of her own. In all the richfulness of the real meaning, did Ellen now enter. She was living her own life indeed, a life in which sordid little bickering, nor foolish ideas of petty preferment had no place.

But Ellen was not a selfish woman, and it was inevitable

that she should regret that she could not share this new experience with her husband. Still, she shrank from any more self revelations. The memory of her club experience was still bitter, and how was she to know if she explained herself to Herbert Fenton that she would not again be playing to the gallery?

She sat at a little table in a cafe overlooking the river with all its broad sweep encircled by green, fir-clad hills. It had been once that she had shuddered at the thought of taking luncheon in a place so Bohemian as this. It was Bohemian, in that its prices were reasonable, its location beautiful, and its clientele not of the millionaires; more than that, it was clean and respectable. Ellen often lunched there now; she could sit by the window and dream, and lose herself, as it were, in the blue mists of the hills, and the clear stream of the river. She was sure not to meet anyone she knew, for her friends would have elevated their noses at such an out of the way place. Sometimes, she brought a book and read as she nibbled at her luncheon. It was poetry to-day, modern, forbidden poetry, and not a phase of regret was in her mind that she was wasting the time that might have been put in reading parliamentary tactics or reports of board meetings.

She dropped her book and gazed out of the window. She was happy in a dreamy, self-sufficient way. She had found herself, and henceforth she knew the world was nothing to her, be it harsh or gentle in its opinion, it could not touch her real self again. She knew that her sons' lives had branched from hers like independent streams from a common lake-source, and that each would go adown its own way, regardless of any interference on her part. Yet, so strong was the woman-love within her, and so forceful of habit that she regretted her husband's inability to be with her in her new inner life.

Self-sufficient as she knew herself to be now, she loved
Herbert Fenton, and she longed for his companionship in
spirit, and longed, too, that he could attain the peace she
knew. They had spent many years together, and though she
knew now, that theirs had been a mere superficial intercourse,
she felt that her happiness would be complete if their lives
could be rounded out together in actual comradeship.

Suddenly, Ellen felt a touch on her arm, and looked up in
surprise to meet her husband's wondering gaze.

"Why—why—Herbert," she said, "is anything wrong at
home?"

"No," he answered slowly, seating himself by her side, "I
was merely surprised to see you here."

"I often come here to lunch."

"So do I, but my lunch-hour is usually later," he made
reply. "I didn't know you knew of this little spot, or," he
paused, and looked hard at her, "or would come if you did
know."

"Well, I have done several things lately that I wouldn't
have done before, you know."

"Yes?"

"Yes. Herbert, I wish you knew and understood." She
reached her hand across the table as she spoke, and he clasped
it warmly. In a little Bohemian cafe one does not mind
clasping another's hand at the table, nor does anyone notice
it. She seemed to notice his whitening hair, his careworn
face, and tired, compressed mouth with more keenness than
before. He had wasted his youth and life and all that life
meant in the mere acquiring of wealth, and had reaped
nothing but material benefits for others, while he would go
to his grave, soon perhaps, without ever knowing what he
had missed.

"Perhaps I do understand, dear," he said quietly, "perhaps Ellen isn't the only member of our household who is 'finding herself.' "

She started and blushed. He continued to smile at her, and stroked her hand gently.

"I have made arrangements to retire from business, Ellen," he went on in the same quiet tone.

"But you—" the wifely business interest was aroused at once.

"Yes, I know I said nothing to you about it, because I saw you were passing through a new experience, and it could not have helped you any to be taken up with mere business details, nor in your state of mind, could you have helped me any."

Ellen flushed again, guiltily this time. Had she neglected her duty, the first thing after all, in her pursuit after herself?

"I am glad, Herbert," she returned heartily, however, "now you will have time to rest—and live."

"I know. We will be comfortable, even wealthy, and the boys' future is assured, and we will rest—and live."

There was a moment's silence, while both looked out of the window at the blue misted hills, and the swift rushing river. Fenton was the first to break the silence.

"There is so much we don't know, Ellen, so much that we don't know we don't now, and so much that we never will know, and won't even know that we don't know. I am conscious that I am talking like a broken phonograph, but it just expresses it, does it not, dear."

Her only reply was a little pressure of his hand, and there was silence again.

"It is not my place to talk," he continued, "men don't usually say out the things that are deepest within them—"

"Nor women either," she retorted quickly.

"Not quite over the women's rights idea?"

She blushed again. She felt strangely embarrassed in the presence of this new Herbert. She knew him only by the new personality within herself that was reaching out for its affinity, and she was not yet so sure of herself as to feel at ease with a companion spirit.

"As I was saying, dear, none of us usually speaks out the deepest sensations of the heart, so that I did not feel hurt at your silence of the past months. I knew through what you were passing by the experience of my own inner consciousness, and but that you saw so little of me you would have recognized that I was going through the same metamorphosis as yourself."

"I wonder why?" she mused.

"We have lived together so long, I suppose," he replied whimsically, "that unknowing, we have become really one, although we have both been lamenting the fact that we were so distant, one real self from the other."

"And now we know and understand," Ellen answered gratefully, "henceforth, we will know each other, and be real companions and comrades such as we never dreamed possible in other days."

"The world forgetting, but the world forgot," he quoted.

"And where we reach our lives out to touch others, how much broader will be our sympathies and understandings."

Ellen was happy, supremely so, for in finding herself, she had also found Herbert, and he had found himself and her. But how many lives were wasted, how many went out into the Great Unknown, all unconscious of themselves or their fellow-men, she mused sorrowfully, as they sat there with clasped hands, while the quick winter twilight settled over the distant blue hills.

THE PEARL IN THE OYSTER *

The commencement was over, and the friends of the graduates
had ceased crowding around them with congratulations and
gifts, and well-meaning, but conventional phrases. The lights
in the church were beginning to lower one by one, and
already the decorations and floral Latin motto began to take
on the leftover, dingy look that yesterday's flowers wear. The
graduates themselves still stood, smiling and happy, conscious
that the world lay before them, an unopened oyster, needing
but their young fingers' tender pressure to open and yield
them its pearl. That had been the phrase of the valedictorian,
and the class had applauded it as not only original and
beautiful but deeply, metaphysically emblematic.

Like the rest of the class, Auguste Picou felt that the phrase
held an especial meaning for him. After the commencement,
he went home and sat himself down while the entire family
gathered around him in awed adulation. He smiled indulgently upon their faces and pictured himself the fond possessor
of the world's pearls, bringing them home for the edification
of his mother.

"Maman," he said softly to the fondest of the group, "I
will make you proud yet."

"Ah, mon fils," she sighed happily, touching the medal on
his breast, "I am ver' proud now. You are mon fils, mon
petit fils. I am ver' proud."

It was the first time in the history of the Picou family that
one of its members had graduated from a school. It was an

* *The Southern Workman*, 1900.

innovation that had at first been resented by the many aunts and uncles who felt that they had a proprietary interest in the only child in the family. Tradition demanded that Auguste should go to one of the many parochial schools in the vicinity of his home, and after a certain course, that is, after the supreme event of the first communion, should consider his education complete and be ready to take up his life work, whatever it might be, presumably cigar-making or bricklaying.

But Auguste had ideas of his own on the subject, and after the event of the first communion was over, he insisted upon keeping on at school, and what was a still worse innovation, he selected a school far uptown, an American "institution for the higher education of Negro youth." That was what its catalogue said. He had learned of it from a friend, a boy around the corner, and when he showed the catalogue with its cabalistic words to his mother, she made protestations loud and long.

"I won't," she declared vehemently, "You shall not go. My son wid what dey call Negre! Non, non!" And she called in the uncles and aunts and wailed that his father had been dead so many years that Auguste could not remember how fine a man he was without having come in contact with "dose American schools."

But Auguste, as has been said before, had a will of his own, and Frank Boyer, the boy around the corner, had inflamed his imagination about the school and the fun to be had thereat. So he overruled uncles and aunts and mother, and went his way rejoicing. Now that he had graduated, had won a medal and was accredited a very bright young man, he smiled down upon their adoring faces and dreamed of the day when he should astonish them even more.

But it seemed that the astonishing process was destined to

be a long one. He set out upon a quest for work, and came home day after day disgusted and disheartened. He might have gone in with one of the uncles, Uncle Pierre, the cigar-maker, but he detested the trade. He might have served as 'prentice hand in a jeweler's on Royal Street, but the pay was too small for so big a boy, and so time slipped away. It was in one of his long quests that he bethought himself of Frank Boyer, and he put his case before him. Frank was meditative.

"Well," he said slowly, "I could get you a job, or rather a fellow I know in our shop could, but it wouldn't be one like you'd want with all your education."

Auguste replied gloomily that he wanted any kind of work with decent pay. Already he had gone idle several years longer than custom in their set allowed.

Frank shook his head, "You won't like it," he said, but nevertheless he introduced Auguste to "the fellow," who in turn introduced him to the proprietor of a billiard hall, a famous resort of politicians, and there Auguste soon found himself at work.

Madame Picou was overjoyed. With her purple calico dress rustling and black sunbonnet waving in the air, she hastened to Tante Norine, who, as Auguste's godmother, had always taken most interest in the boy, and imparted the good news. Tante Norine pressed her thin lips together and looked judicial.

"Mais," she said, "a billiard hall."

"Ah, Norine," said Madame Picou, nodding her head sagely, "you do not understand. Mon fils, he say it is but one stepping stone. He weel do bettare w'en he gets one start."

And all the uncles and aunts, when this was repeated to them, nodded their head sagely, and approved of Auguste's course as was their wont.

In the billiard hall, meanwhile, Auguste was fast forming

curious friendships. The proprietors and customers did not know or care about his home and antecedents. Sufficient it was to them that he was neat and sprightly and obedient. In the intervals of taking cash at the desk and moving about to watch the players, he was imbibing a mixed set of ideas about the political situation of the city and the value of certain kinds of supremacy.

He and Frank were still fast friends after a year's work on St. Charles Street. Frank looked upon Auguste as a sort of protegee of his own, and did him the courtesy never to visit him at his place of business.

The billiard hall in question had been started primarily to draw customers from nearby saloons, and because it was over a clothing store and jewelry shop, it boasted that it discountenanced drinking. This was a boast merely, for it was already the age of electric buttons and discreet, white-coated messengers, and lower St. Charles Street, especially below St. Charles Hotel is sprinkled thickly with glittering signs and glass doors.

One of the most regular customers was Tom Craig. Craig was of the type usually spoken of in ward meetings and rallies as an "old war-horse." He took upon himself the task of initiating Auguste into the mysteries of the political situation, and Auguste proved an apt and ready pupil.

"Tell you, Auguste," said Craig one evening, as he lounged over the desk in the inner hall. "Tell you, man, politics is the only thing. Chuck up your job and go in to work for your ward and all that. I'll pull you in."

Auguste laughed, but his eyes glistened.

That night he and Frank were in the theatre. Frank was applauding the play, and his eyes glowed with enthusiasm, but Auguste found scant interest upon the stage. His mind was intent upon his thoughts. He glanced at Frank's handsome brown face, and felt himself conscious of a momentary thrill of disgust. If it were not for Frank, he would not have to be sitting up here in the side of the gallery reserved for Negroes. He himself could pass muster anywhere. It was only on Frank's account that he was known to be one of those who belonged in the side gallery.

He was distrait and absorbed the rest of the night. When they were about to leave the theatre, he muttered some hasty excuse, and hurried away from the building, glancing furtively about him as he came out and made his way up the half square to Canal Street. He had suddenly become ashamed of being seen on the streets with Frank, and more than that, he was ashamed to be seen coming out of the "back entrance" of the theatre. He promised himself that he would treat himself to an orchestra seat when he next went. And he further promised himself that he would be seen with Frank no more, no matter what the nature of the occasion.

"You see, it's just like this," he explained to Laura the next evening, "Frank's an all right enough fellow, and I like him lots, but you see how it is, a fellow doesn't want to be hurting himself by going about with someone who will give him dead away. Now, I'm not a bit prejudiced against dark people; why, my grandfather was a dark man, but if you're going to get on, you just have to be careful. Why," he added, a sudden thought striking him, "why, suppose Frank should come down to the billiard hall. It would make me lose my place."

And Laura assented. She was fair and beautiful, and she had known Auguste all her life. By a tacit understanding between their families, it was understood that some day they would marry. This was an agreement that suited everyone concerned, and unlike most such affairs, promised to run smoothly to a happy ending.

It was then that Tom Craig resumed his labors as a proselyte.

"I tell you, man," he said over and again, "I tell you, man, you're cut out for a politician."

Auguste laughed, but he listened eagerly while Tom Craig unfolded the mysteries of ward politics and the city machine.

So a year passed, and Auguste and Laura were married. The uncles and the aunts had insisted upon a big wedding, as became a rising young man and a demure, convent-bred girl. Auguste had protested, but he was overruled, and the ordeal over, they settled themselves in the little cottage that was to do duty as home. In the matter of location, Auguste had had his way, in spite of the tearful protestations of both families. He had taken a house "uptown" on Erato and Camp Streets. His excuse was that it was near his work. The fact that he had a deeper one than he saw fit to give was apparent to Laura, but she forbore questioning. It was enough to her that they would be together.

Laura's maiden aunt, who had done duty as a mother since the girl's babyhood, wept much. It was as though her child were being taken into a foreign country. It is heresy almost for a Creole to cross the dividing line of Canal Street and pass into the unknown land of America beyond.

Now-a-days, Auguste walked no more timidly through the billiard hall. He had become a personage in his way, and the management had raised his salary because he attracted customers to the place—men who clapped him jocosely on the shoulders; called him "old fellow" and pressed the electric buttons many times, to the glee of the white-jacketed men who appeared.

Auguste and Tom Craig were fast friends, and Mrs. Craig having called on Laura—they were neighbors—an intimacy had sprung up between them. Then Mrs. Craig brought a friend, and there was a little gathering at the friend's house, and thus Laura was fairly launched into the social swim of that particular neighborhood. She sighed a little, but as Auguste was so beamingly happy, resigned herself to her new friends. She was lonely and unhappy, for after paying one or two perfunctory visits, the several families downtown had ceased to come. It was too far, they said, and though she paid her weekly duty calls, they were never returned. By a tacit agreement, she and Auguste never mentioned their families to the Craigs nor their set.

Into the mysteries of ward-meetings, primaries, local tickets, machine politics and party management, Auguste was now initiated. He was eager, enthusiastic, devoted. He spent much time explaining it to Laura. She listened. She was interested, because he was, but she sighed softly, because it seemed to her that this thing of which he talked so much was building up a wall between her and the old friends downtown.

It happened after many months that Auguste felt that the time was about ripe for him to have that position in the City Hall which Tom Craig had once strenuously urged belonged to him. He pictured himself a high-salaried magnate and Laura in a larger house with a finer and more extended circle of acquaintances. Then he sought out Tom Craig and laid the matter before him.

Craig was inclined to treat the question lightly, even superciliously.

"Why, man," he averred, "you see—well, now what do you want with a job like that? It won't bring you nearly so much power. Why, you don't want to bother your head with such things. What you want to be is a ward leader, that's what you want."

Auguste considered the fact that he and Craig lived in the same ward and that the latter was not inclined to abate one jot or tittle of his power therein, so that there was but little chance of another's prominence. But he bent his energies to the coming municipal election in April. He was everywhere, speaking, declaiming, proselyting. He was earnest for the success of his party, the old ring machine, and his name filtered into the newspapers, and down into the old part of the city where the aunts and the uncles read of him.

Tante Norine shook her head, "Eet is not right," she said, "he is on the wrong side."

The April election came and went. The ring machine triumphed, and after the blare of the trumpets of victory had died down, Auguste went up to claim his reward.

It was not forthcoming, of course. He was put off from day to day with vague promises that gradually dwindled down to studied, bald evasions. He saw other men, men with red necks and thick brogues, come up and snatch away from him the prize he coveted. A vague rumor about him began to float through the streets where he was known, and some of his friends slapped him less heartily on the back. Mrs. Craig's visits to Laura were losing the charming informality which had once characterized them, and were becoming state functions when Mrs. Craig talked grandiloquently about her family connections.

"You see, Laura," said Auguste one evening, as they sat on the stoop, "an American has no chance in these city matters. Every thing goes to the Irish. Well, I'm tired of the billiard hall, and I'm going to quit."

With Auguste, to say was to do, and it was not a great while before he had passed the letter-carriers' examination so creditably that his appointment soon followed.

"One thing about this," he said, "a man doesn't have to pretend he is what he is not in order to keep his job."

It happened that his beat was downtown, the old familiar neighborhood, and his daily rounds filled him with homesick longings. He thought bitterly on the tenderness of the home ties, and the old friends whom he had given up and forced Laura to give up, for what? For the superficial friendship of an inferior class of ward politicians' wives. He began to think of certain fine qualities in the old friends that were missing in the new ones, and he mused bitterly over his own folly in supposing that he could be contented with the life he had been leading.

"Laura," he said one evening, "how would you like to move downtown?"

Laura clasped her hands eagerly and murmured a few caressing words in the forbidden patois they had used as children.

The baby was already four months old, and it had not yet been christened, because her mother-heart could not be reconciled to the garish cheap newness of St. Theresa's church, with the memory of the dim old beauty of the ones downtown. Visions of her old girl friends, and of the joy of having the two families about her adoring the baby, filled her heart, and she laughed aloud joyously.

When they were settled downtown, however, it was not quite so easy to fall back into the old life from which they had been gone for nearly two years. They could not adjust themselves quite as readily as they thought, and the old friends felt and showed a certain resentment at their former defection, and were still more bitter that they had come back into the fold.

Laura shut her teeth bravely, and tried not to notice the changed conditions. When she asked Marie Alexandre, her old chum and bridesmaid, to be godmother for the baby, Marie, with pursed lips and averted face, had invented some excuse, so Laura had fallen back on Tante Norine, who was always kindhearted and forgiving.

Auguste, meanwhile, was up to his ears in a new idea.

"It is true," he said to Laura, "that none of my family ever were slaves, but since I am of the race that was in bondage, I think it but right that I should throw my fortunes politically with the party that freed us."

He was practicing a bombastic, high-flown style of utterance. He felt that he would need it soon. Deep down in his heart, farther down than even Laura could see, he had another reason for his sudden apostasy. He wanted power, political preferment, position, recognition. He was ambitious, he had always been so. He wanted the pearl in the oyster, but thus far it had eluded his grasp. He had found the old ring machine deficient as an oyster-opener, and he had cast it aside to take up national politics and the party then in power at the Custom House. He realized that the municipal party was filled at that time with men who cared little or nothing for brains or eloquence, and if it did, it was large enough to look among its numbers and find them. With the other side, especially in this city, the contingent was so small that any man with a reasonable amount of intellect might shine among them. In the one, he was as but a drop in the bucket. In the other, he might be a noticeable quantity.

"Better to be a king among dogs than a dog among kings," he laughed, and laid his plans accordingly.

But there were conditions which had to be faced, which were awkward, not to say unpleasant. It was awkward, for instance, if he wished to take Laura to the theatre and took seats in the orchestra, to look up at the side gallery and there encounter some of the very men whom he was trying hardest to conciliate. And yet, he could not bring himself to take his wife to the side gallery. It was still more awkward to recognize these political friends in the streets when Laura was with him, and they were about to step into some restaurant. He found that during his stay in the billiard hall, he had dropped into the habit of saying "nigger" when it so pleased him. It was hard to remember that that word was the shibboleth of all that he wished to hide from the party he had now taken up.

Yet, in his zeal to be first, he made a profound impression upon the leaders of the party. He outdid himself. No speaker in the campaign was more earnest than he; no proselyte was more zealous, no haranguer worked harder. He began to feel the thrill which the wielding of power brings. He enjoyed his ability to sway the crowd before him. At times his brain reeled with the stupendous force of his own imaginings. He saw unlimited vistas of power before him. He began to lay plans and to dream dreams that would have surprised Laura, could she have known them.

They had been living downtown a year now, but still the formal stiffness of their old friends had held out. There was no forgiveness in the hearts of these conservative Creoles for those who had deliberately chosen an inferior class of common Irish for their companions, and then had, in a way, sneaked back to the fold. It was like the religion they professed—stern, implacable and unforgiving to the children who deserted it, but calmly conscious that some time they would be glad to come back and sue for mercy.

November was but a month off, and then the national election would be held. Auguste had no doubt but that his party would be successful, and then for his reward. The offices and berths in the Custom House were many and the intelligent and aggressive members of his party were comparatively few. Auguste's eyes were on a comfortable little commission at three thousand a year. He did not yet aspire to big offices like the Collector of the Port. He knew that such berths always went to the old heads of the party. Nor yet did he care to drop to a mere inspectorship at a thousand a year. He would be modest and have a medium office, and in later years, this simplicity of his demands would be remembered.

November came, and with it the momentous Tuesday. The day had not yet died into the grayness of twilight before the grim news was known. The old party had lost, had been swept overwhelmingly to defeat, and with it all hopes of this state's little contingent which had hoped to retrieve the ill fortunes consequent upon its losses eight years before.

Auguste was keenly disappointed, but he reasoned that at the worst nothing could happen to him personally. He held a civil service position, and political influence could not move him. He would devote the four years intervening before the next election to strengthening his position in the party, and by making his services more or less invaluable, be able when the victory came, as come it must, to demand higher recognition.

Then one day he noticed Laura. She was growing thin and pale, and there was a pathetic down-droop to her mouth that smote him. Was he neglecting her? he asked himself, and he began to try to make amends for any slight that she may have fancied. But Laura continued to droop. She was a gentle-natured woman and she loved friends and society, and she was denied both. Auguste's strenuous efforts on behalf of the defeated party had not abated the contempt of the Third Ward men one whit. They scoffed him for a turncoat, and their wives wondered audibly why Laura's uptown friends did not visit her. Sometimes she wished bitterly that she could go back to them, but that was impossible now, for their racial identity was known everywhere. Auguste was a prominent man, after a fashion; but his prominence hurt rather than helped himself and his wife.

It was quite a year after the election before the party in power began to invent excuses to depose the civil service employees in the city. Only a few heads fell under the headsman's knife, and naturally, they were those who had been most zealous in the fight against putting in the present administration. Auguste was handed a little yellow envelope one day. He stood looking at it vaguely, absently, a hot mist of wonder and shame and resentment enveloping him. Then he heard a chuckle and looked up to see two men lounging about laughing at him. One was Dennis, whom he had known in the billiard hall, and whose vote he had once gained for a corrupt alderman. The other was his boyhood friend, Frank, to whom he had scarcely spoken since that night, long ago in the theatre, when he had felt a disgust at his brown face.

He stumbled home somehow and blurted it out to Laura. She sat staring at him with wide wondering eyes and bloodless lips. He began to reproach himself bitterly for what he had brought upon her and the two children, but she arose and went to him where he sat bowed and broken.

"Auguste," she said chokingly, "this isn't home any longer. Let us go away somewhere."

He looked at her vaguely. He knew what suffering she must have undergone to have spoken those words; she, the most home-loving and conservative of women, she who hated change and new things so much. He rose and took her in his arms.

"Yes, petite," he said, "we will go away somewhere where we are not known, and we will start life again, but whether we decide to be white or black, we will stick to it. And politics—well Laura, cherie, we will let them alone."

The next week when they were packing to go away, he came across the old school diploma, and sat reading its Latin inscription bitterly. The words of the valedictorian came to him again, and he could not help but wonder with a quickening of the heart if the pearl within the oyster were destined ever to be his.

ELISABETH *

It so happened that Elisabeth found herself alone in the world with nothing left but the shreds of a long-ended romance; an income large enough to keep her from actual want, and small enough to keep her busy planning how to make it stretch over her needs.

* Typescript.

"I am too old to think about marrying, and too young to go to the poorhouse," she mused. Then she walked to the mirror and stared hard at the face reflected there. "Too ugly to be attractive, and not ugly enough to make a living in a sideshow. Great Heavens! What a failure I am! I don't know enough to do anything with my life, and I know too much to be self-satisfied."

She was bitter, and the consciousness that the bitterness of this mood was becoming her normal condition gave her an added pang. She clasped her hands loosely on her black gown and stared hard out of the window. It was a cheerless view that met her eyes; gray skies over a park that was gray too, with week-old snow, unswept away and grimy with the soot of the city. Gaunt, bare brown trees, with a few huddled miserable birds crouched on their forbidding limbs completed the view. It was in harmony with Elizabeth's mood, and she shivered in sympathy with the birds.

Elisabeth's father, a dreamy, speculative man, totally unfit for his occupation of civil engineer, had died three years after the family had come to New York, leaving Elisabeth and a feeble mother practically alone in the loneliest city in the world. This had been nearly eight months before; and every morning after that Elisabeth had risen hopefully.

"Do you think you are better to-day, mother?" she would inquire. Always the same reply came, however, "Yes dear, but very weak."

And Elisabeth would sigh and go away in tears, for she knew what that meant. Her dream, and her mother's dream, was to go back to their former home.

"It's a little backward country town," Elisabeth would say, with her rare smile, "but it's home."

Daily the mother grew weaker; daily Elisabeth's hopes sank

lower; until one day, the familiar cheerful cry of "Better, dear, but very weak," was not heard at all.

That was the end. Elisabeth was alone with a pittance of an income, and a deep, miserable longing to follow her mother out into the cheerless gray of the winter skies.

"I suppose I may as well go home," she said, but the prospect was not alluring. She had no relatives there but a spinster aunt who was very deaf. Going home meant, of course, living with her, and Elisabeth shuddered at the thought of daily contact with the ear trumpet.

"I must work," she decided, "and there's no work to do there but to teach or to sew, and I can't do either." She knew too, that like most provincial towns, there was no place for one bordering on spinsterhood. It would not be long before she would be discussed at tea-drinkings. She fancied she could hear the minister's wife saying kindly, "Now there's Elisabeth Parrish, poor girl, I don't suppose she'll ever marry," to which the doctor's wife would reply knowingly, "Oh, no, Elisabeth must be, let me see, she was fifteen when Emma was born, I know, and Emma is full sixteen now, you know." And old Mrs. Shelton would shake her head and say, "Oh, well, poor girl, she never did get over Rob Halsey's death. She was to have married him the day he was buried."

No, she shook herself vigorously. She would stay in New York and fight it out if she could. If she could not, well, home would be the last resort. So, like a million others, she went into the maelstrom to be cast up exhausted with the prize of life, or to be sucked under to death as the fates should decide.

It was a lonely struggle, lonely and hard. Had it not been that there was enough of her small pittance left to keep her from want, she would have gone down in the fight and the waters must have closed over her head. She found work after a long wait. That it paid little was nothing; it was to her liking, and it was something to occupy her.

Then Richard Morriston came into her life.

She toiled in a downtown office, up so many flights of stairs that she had never taken the time to count them. Richard Morriston came in and out of the office and talked to her employer. Sometimes after he had known her for a while, he would come to her chair and chat with her a bit. The days that he did this went by swifter than the others; and she would work feverishly, a soft flush on her cheeks, her eyes brightening and flashing with happiness.

Richard Morriston was a staid enough personage, whose sole purpose in life seemed to be the accumulation of more money than he knew what to do with. Elisabeth thought him handsome; perhaps he was. He was big and strong and clean looking; his brown eyes looked at you straightly and honestly; his square jaw and determined mouth might have reminded you of a bulldog, but for a look of tender sympathy that would steal into his eyes at times. All these things Elisabeth had treasured in her heart of hearts. She knew the merest inflection in his voice; the smallest change in expression; the least gesture he would make. He had become so much a part of her life that she could not remember when he had not been in her world.

At first, he would come into the office occasionally—only on business. Then he began running in every day, lingering longer by her chair each time; sometimes even seating himself. Perhaps, it was un-business-like, but Morriston was a personage in the estimation of her employer, who was not to be despised or thwarted in his desires. She knew his footstep outside the office door, and flushed and paled by turns when he entered the room; and all the while she was blooming into new life as a faded rose revives in a vase of cool water.

It was one evening in the late spring when the wistaria hung its purple blooms heavy with fragrance over the paths in the park. Elisabeth bared her head to the soft breeze and strolled happily down the path and across the bridge toward the lake. It was joy just to be alive in the dusk of a spring evening; to watch the glow in the western sky reflecting itself in the calm surface of the lake. She found one of the little arbors on its edge and sank down on the seat humming softly to herself. She was happy, she could not have told why; why she sang nor why she laughed when the black swan, sailing majestically to his nest in the golden glow, spread his wings and whirled disgustedly when an impudent little duck paddled across his path. Then she felt a presence near her and turned with a quick little throbbing at her throat.

"I was walking too," Morriston began apologetically, "and I was rude enough, when I saw you to follow you here. May I sit down?"

She made room silently for him on the little seat, and for a moment neither of them spoke. Elisabeth could not; there was so much happiness tugging at her heart, that she dared not trust her voice lest it betray her.

"Isn't it beautiful?" she ventured at last.

"Restful, peaceful," he made answer, "after all the weary turmoil of the day downtown, to turn to this," he waved his hands comprehensively over the lake with its placid waters enameled by the low foliage, "it seems like another world."

"If we could only live in it always," she murmured.

"Perhaps we wouldn't like it so well," he said smiling down tenderly upon her, "we should probably be yearning after what is called 'life,' bustle and heartache and worry."

She sighed and was silent again. Somehow their hands met and his closed over hers in a tight warm grasp. It struck Elisabeth with a sudden pang that that grasp, tender and strong, was the one thing she had missed in her life, and the missing of it had embittered her whole existence.

For a while, they were silent, watching the glow fade out of the sky, melting insensibly into the silver moonlight. Then, Elisabeth could never have told how it happened, Morriston had put his arms about her, and kissed her once, twice, thrice, full on the lips, holding her close to him.

"Elisabeth, Elisabeth," he murmured.

"Oh, I love you," she murmured, "love you so much. I never dreamed I should have the joy of telling you so."

"Do you love me?" he queried. There was a faint inflection of surprise in his voice; she noticed it, and sat upright.

"Yes I do," she said almost defiantly, "I know you could not possibly care for me as I care for you; your life is full, and you are happy—oh, you could not care for me. You don't know, you don't understand."

He clasped her hands again, "Yes I do," he said gently, 'I do care for you, more than you know," and he drew her closer to him and kissed her once more.

Then Fate intervened in the guise of some young girls, gum-chewing and giggling. They rose and walked silently away, instinctively bending their steps toward the Fifty-ninth Street entrance.

A curious constraint had come over them. When they spoke, it was to utter merest commonplaces. At the park gate he paused.

"May I see you home, Elisabeth?" he asked softly.

"Oh, no, no, please don't, indeed, I'd rather you would not. Good-night, good-bye, thank you," and with a little nervous laugh, she hurried away, and left him standing stupidly in the gate.

"Oh, what have I done?" she wailed when she reached home, nervously wringing her hands and pacing the floor. "What must he think of me, after that? I didn't know what I was saying, I forgot myself."

She threw herself on the bed and writhed in an agony of shame. She remembered every look, every intonation of his voice. The blood swept over her face in a hot wave as she recalled with a sudden rush of memory his look of utter surprise, almost embarrassment when she blurted out her little confession. His after tenderness, she decided, was born of pity, not of love. She writhed again, and hot tears of mortification trickled down her cheeks.

"What must he think of me? How can I face him to-morrow?"

She dragged herself reluctantly down to the office next day. He must come in some time in the afternoon, she knew, and he would come to her desk, and she would have to face him with the awful consciousness of last night's mistake. The morning hours went by all too swiftly. It had been before that the hands of the clock had dragged like laggards for her; to-day they swept round the dial with the resistless force of task-masters urging her to a hateful duty.

Two, three, four o'clock; he had not come. She rose to go home with a choking sense of disappointment. She had dreaded meeting him and yet the feeling that he had purposely stayed away, stung her. He was ashamed of her; he wished to give her a chance to adjust herself; he had not meant that kiss; he was just playing with her; and she—she had bared her soul to him, and perhaps even now, he was laughing pityingly at her. She passed a restless night, and went out next morning, mentally bracing herself for an interview wherein she was to be cold, dignified and distant; he confused, embarrassed and pleading.

There was no such interview, however. He did not come again that day, nor the next, nor the next. A week, ten days passed, and she had no word from him. A dumb, cold despair had settled upon her, mixed with a certain contempt. He was afraid to come near her again. Instead of being brave to tell her that she was wrong, or better still, allowing her to tell him herself, he had played the craven. She told herself a hundred times that she did not love him any more; that her contempt had strangled whatever love she might have had, and each time she knew that she was trying to deceive herself, and failing miserably.

It was after nearly two weeks of this dumb misery that she overheard the clerk, McLaurin say to the assistant book-keeper, "Too bad about Morriston, isn't it?"

She paused with her pen poised in the air, breathless for the reply.

"Isn't he better?" the other asked carelessly.

McLaurin turned three pages of his ledger, erased some figures from his pad, scratched his head and seemed to deliberate an unconscionably long time before he replied. Elisabeth's heart was choking her, and there was surging noises in her head. How could he be so indifferent? How could he help but know that she would hang on his next words as a dying man clings to the last warm touch of life? An age passed and she went through all of purgatory before McLaurin replied, "Um—yes—but he mends slowly. Man can't be as sick as Morriston was and get up in a week, you know."

She stumbled home in a mist of happiness and love and

pity. So he had not shunned her after all; he had been ill somewhere; ill unto death, perhaps, and she had not known it. If she could only have nursed him; have been near him just for a little while. It made her tremble with the measure of her own helpless impotence to think that somewhere in the city another was ministering to him, while she was outside of his life; perhaps even of his thoughts. She thought she would write, or send him flowers; but she feared lest he might think her forward again. There was nothing now to do but to wait and hope and pray, and watch the laggard clock in the office as it dragged out the afternoons while she expected him every day.

Morriston came in at last, pale and languid looking. Her heart throbbed with a great yearning pity at the sight of his weakness; then she smiled into his eyes, and grasped his proffered hand, meanwhile murmuring commonplaces of sympathy.

That was all for that day. He had begun to reproach her with not inquiring after him, but before she could explain, he was called away, and the current of everyday affairs parted them.

A few evenings later they sat again in the little arbor by the lake. The black swan sailed majestically athwart the sunset; the faint sound of the city died in the whispering leaves of the trees.

"I have been wanting to ask you all along," Elisabeth was saying breathlessly, "to forgive me for that rash statement I made to you about a month ago. You must know I did not mean it. I—"

"You did not mean it, Elisabeth?" there was a keen edge of pain in his voice.

"I—it was the water, and the sunset, and—the—the—

evening softness, I suppose, that made me forget myself.
There is nothing else I could say that would excuse such
boldness. I know what you must think of me; you think that
I am like all the rest of the women, trying to ensnare you
because you are—, or well. Don't think that of me; I did not
mean one word."

"You did not mean it?" he reiterated dully.

"No, no," she was biting her lips to keep back the real
words from her heart, "I want to be your friend, Mr.
Morriston, I may, may I not?"

"You were flirting with me, Elisabeth?"

"I flirt?" she laughed bitterly, "Do I look like a woman
who would flirt?"

"But you said you did not mean it?"

"Let us be friends," she waived the question, and put out
her hand.

"Friends? Perhaps." They were walking down the path
and neared the gate. When they reached it, he put out his
hand, "Friends? That is not what I expected from you,
Elisabeth. Goodnight."

He was gone before she could call him back, or could say
the words that were clammering for utterance. She sighed a
little, went home, and woman-like, having stoically lied her
chances for happiness away, cried herself to sleep.

The next day she heard that Morriston had gone abroad
for his health.

Three dreary months passed. Elisabeth ate and drank and
slept. She went to the office every day and went through a
mechanical routine of work there. She walked in the park,
and met friends, and made visits, and when the heat grew
too sultry, she went out of town where she could hear the sea
boom all day, and watch the ships sail across the horizon,

and wonder if he might be on one. Then one day, she got a letter from him.

"I have tried to put you from me, Elisabeth," he wrote, "but it is no use. Your face comes between me and everything on earth and in Heaven. You know you are beautiful, do you not? I can close my eyes and see your soft brown hair, and your tender eyes, and that dear way you have of looking at me with your soul in them. You do love me, Elisabeth. I know you did not mean what you said the last time we met. It hurt me to have you deny that you did, when all the while I was trembling to take you in my arms and kiss the little white lie from your lips. I was hurt and angry, and I went away from you and tried to forget you. I understand how you must feel about it; but you must not think of that, but be my own true, brave Elisabeth, and let me love you and care for you as I wish. When you get this, I shall be near you, for I am writing aboard ship, and shall post it in town."

When she had finished reading, she looked up to meet his eyes upon her, and for once the decorum of the office was upset.

"But it was bold and forward," she protested later. They were back in the park. The fullness of summer had come and gone, and the leaves trembling in the sunset were singing their little death songs in their autumn gowns.

"No," he denied vehemently, "it was sweet and womanly."

"I would not have done it," she said musingly, "but you kissed me first, and in the fullness of my joy I thought that you must love me or you would not have kissed me."

"You were right, I have loved you longer than you will ever know, Elisabeth, and when I kissed you it was my way of telling you so."

And who shall gainsay a man when he shuts off all argument by closing one's lips?

THE LOCKET *

Sister Angela was in a flutter. A message had come for her that morning, a message unexpected and disturbing. True, any message to Sister Angela would be disturbing, used as she had grown to the quiet, uneventful routine of the convent.

"Your mother is dying, come at once."

In the first rush of her grief, she had gone to the Mother Superior and laid the ominous message before her. But the Mother Superior was old, very old, and had outlived most griefs and joys. It was nothing to her that the Sister's mother was dying, or that the Sister herself had wept until her face was drawn and lined and her eyes red and black-ringed. Her voice was calm and steady as she said:

"My child, your grief is unwise. We must all die, and your sainted mother will not rest in Heaven."

"Yes," Sister Angela sobbed in reply.

"You may go to your mother to give her the last comforts of religion."

Sister Angela wiped her eyes and was grateful. It was not usual, but she was only a novice, and the world outside of deeds of mercy was not quite dead to her.

She was to go in the evening. She fluttered about her tasks helplessly and nervously. To her it seemed that the iron gates of the gray building had shut out the life of the world forever. Had it not been so sad an errand, she could have found it in her heart to sin and be glad to escape once more.

When the time came to go, the passionless, even voice of

* *The Home Magazine.*

the Mother Superior reminded her of her duty to the church.

"Remember, my daughter, the world may be fair, but it is sinful, and no fit place for you. Come back untouched by its sin. You will take your full vows in a few months, remember."

In a few months!

"And, my daughter, you know our rules. What is ours belongs to our Most Holy Church. We can have nothing of our own."

Sister Angela bowed her head mutely. Her family was a wealthy one, and they were outside the pale of the Most Holy Church. They would not understand such a statement. It was enough to them that one should give up the world and go out as a Sister of Mercy, to nurse unpleasant people, and to live miserably, comforting others.

Her mother was almost gone when Sister Angela reached her home the next morning. Nothing but the elder woman's indomitable will and determination to see this youngest child had kept her alive. Her face was already set and gray when the novice arrived, but her black eyes were aglow with the last bit of vitality, and embraced her daughter's form with a tenderness that her hand clasp feebly imitated. Sister Angela was a sort of black sheep in the family. Her brothers and sisters looked askance at one who could desert her own people for a "fanatical devotion to an idea," as they phrased it, and her appearance before them now in a strange garb, and an humbly submissive air, only irritated them the more instead of reconciling them.

The mother's hand grew feebler and she made a gesture for Sister Angela to grope under her pillow and bring forth a small object there.

"It was your grandmother's locket," she whispered huskily,

"it has always been cherished in the family. It was her grandmother's and has come down through generations, always going to the youngest child. I have kept it secure for you. It would have made me happy, my child," she was reproachful, even in death, "if you could have handed it down to your children."

Sister Angela was mute as she clasped the heirloom. It was thin and worn with age, curiously carven, and shaped like none that we see now. She remembered it well. When she was a young girl, sometimes as an especial favor it had hung on her neck. Someone, whose name she had tried to forget, had kissed it once when its curious charm had gleamed against her neck.

"Keep it, it was always for you," said the mother, and lapsed into silence and more grayness of face.

The after days were hard ones for the novice. The funeral was a Protestant one, and the people stared when she knelt and told her rosary. They stared curiously at her garb, and there were whispered comments about her. It was a rural community, where Catholicism was associated with emigrants and Irish, cheap labor and Sunday picnics. She was a religious alien among them, and she had not worn her nun's garb long enough to be unhurt by the attitude of her erstwhile friends toward her. She felt too, the strainedness of her family's affection, and she prayed hard not to grow bitter before she left the small town for the convent.

"Is it not enough," she found herself murmuring resentfully between the prayers on her rosary—"Is it not enough that their narrowness drove me to the Holy Church, but that they should despise me now?"

She had loved one not as wealthy as her family deemed right for her to marry, and, being denied each other, he had gone away proudly. When he said he would wed another, whose family, as he expressed it, "was less illustrious, but more human"—she became the novice, Sister Angela. She had closed that chapter of her life tightly and never dared let herself think of it, but it came rushing on her now, tempering her sorrow at her mother's death.

There would be a will-reading, and then they would all be dead to her again. They assembled in the somber library the day after the funeral. The widowed mother had divided the estate equally among her children, and Sister Angela was now a wealthy woman. When it was all over she lingered until she found herself alone with the family lawyer.

"May I—May I—?" she began timidly.

"Yes? Yes?" He was a gruff old man in manner, but really very timid and bashful at heart.

"I want," she said, "you know I—of course, I don't need any property or money."

He looked at her over his spectacles curiously.

"No?" he said, "Why not?"

"I—my—we—that is, we do not hold worldly goods. It is forbidden, you know."

All the while she was guiltily conscious of the weight of the locket pressing against her breast.

"No property, no money?" said the lawyer incredulously.

"Nothing."

"Ah—ah—I see. Your order is strictly communal in its interests?"

"Yes, I suppose so," she was blushing violently now. What if the locket were to be made a communal belonging?

"What do you wish me to do then?" He was an ardent Bellamyite, and here was something that seemed to approach the ideal condition.

"There are some formalities, I suppose," said Sister Angela vaguely, "about turning over my share of the estate to—to—"

"To be divided among your relatives, of course?" he assented, dipping his pen in the ink.

"No!" She startled herself by her vehemence, "No! It is for our order, for my convent." She was bitter again, though she crossed herself and prayed to be delivered from evil thoughts. They, the brothers and sisters, had driven her to renounce her share of the world and they should not be the gainers thereby.

The lawyer wrote a few moments, then he looked up at her keenly.

"You wish to deed everything belonging to you, everything unreservedly, even your share of jewels and such things?" He inquired.

"Everything unreservedly," she repeated, and then blushed again. Her heart beat against the locket, and each beat seemed to strike a little gong on it which sounded, "Lie lie lie; you are keeping me."

The lawyer took her confusion for timidity and the reaction from the strain of the last few days, and so gently led her to her room. She threw herself across the bed, with her hands pressed against the guilty, accusing thing, trying hard to stifle her wicked thoughts and desires.

The Mother Superior met her with her usual calm imperturbability when she returned. The disposition of Sister Angela's worldly goods had been discussed within the gray walls, and the Mother Superior's face, as far as it was able, expressed satisfaction.

"You are a worthy handmaiden of the Church, my daughter," she said benignly.

Sister Angela's heart leaped at the unwonted praise, then sank again as cold as lead, for the locket thumped rebelliously under the folds of her thick gown. She had taken it out on the train once or twice and gazed at it longingly. With each glimpse at its curious, worn, amethyst-studded surface, she became more and more determined to keep it in the face of sin and misery. Why should she give up her mother's most cherished possession?

All that first day it lay hidden, and there was no thought of the danger of it being found. With night came the dormitories and the watchful eyes of the other nuns, eager to see that the novice, so lately gone forth into the world again, was not contaminated by her contact with dross and earth. Her hands trembled as she unloosed her robes, and hid the locket in her discarded garb until she could creep under the friendly covers and clasp it tight again. The morning would bring another problem, she knew, and prayed for courage to face; then chid herself that she prayed for help to sin further.

"Lay not up for yourselves treasures upon earth, where moth and rust doth corrupt, and where thieves break through and steal, but lay up for yourselves treasures in Heaven, where neither moth nor rust doth corrupt, and where thieves do not break through nor steal; for where your treasure is, there will your heart be also."

The priest's voice droned drearily through the gospel. Sister Angela stirred uneasily as she knelt. It was Ash Wednesday, and the last day of her novitiate. Could she take the final vows tomorrow with this heavy sin still upon her? Had she not perjured her soul time and again in her confessions? Had she not purchased each absolution at the expense of her very heart's blood? She hung her head in very shame at the thought, and yet, had she not suffered to keep this last keepsake of her mother's? All the stern Puritanical Protestantism in her nature had risen and joined forces with the later learned tenets of her new faith, and mocked her and put her to shame for the deceit she was practicing.

Had it been a matter between her religion and her love, there would have been no question in her mind what to do. She would not conscientiously have deceived her faith to give herself happiness, no, nor even to have brought happiness to one of those, to whom, according to the world, she owed allegiance. But this was something which involved her mother, and a memory of generations. She believed that she was sinning for the principle. Just how this was, or what was the principle, was not quite clear in her mind, but she thought she was carrying on the work of keeping in its right place the precious heirloom that had been handed down to her from years agone.

For months now she had hidden her treasure in divers places. Some fortunate days she had dared to carry it in the folds of her coarse gown across her bosom. There were other red letter days, when going abroad on some errand of mercy, she had been able to take out the treasure and gaze at it longingly. It was the last link that bound her to the world which grew fairer the further it slipped from her grasp. She hugged it as a jewel rarer than some fabulous undreamed-of stone. Not one regret had she for her lost wealth, gone to swell the coffers of the Church, but she knew that it would be a wrench from which she would not soon recover if the locket were to be taken from her.

The priest's voice droned on through the mass. There was a drowsy stillness in the chapel, which his voice seemed to accentuate, the tinkling host-bell punctuated his murmurings with a mechanical irregularity. Sister Angela sat upright, her hand clutching her bosom frantically.

"Lay not up for yourselves treasures—"

But her locket was not a treasure. Intrinsically, it would hardly have paid for a mass to be said for the poorest sinner who claimed the mercy of the convent. It was an heirloom. Her dying mother had entrusted it to her to preserve from vulgar contact.

Still, to-morrow, she would have no relatives save her Sisters in Mercy; no memories which she might think of; no property save that which all could claim, and it would only be right and fair and true to hand the bauble to the Mother Superior with a full confession of her sinning for the past months.

She paused in the courtyard as they paced from chapel to their duties. It was a mild day with a suspicion of spring in the air, in the already swelling buds on the somber trees that stood in prim regularity around the yard. Some saucy sparrows, little full-chested hoydens, clustered in a gnarled cottonwood and chattered vociferously, gossiping with gusto and joy. Sister Angela looked at them sadly. What mattered it to her if somewhere birds did fly high in the blue ozone and mate and nest and joy in their young? Such things were not for her. She would hide her bauble and go her way to her death. For to-day there was fasting and prayer and stern soul-seeking—always with one thing to hide—and to-morrow the final veil.

It was near dusk of the evening when the Mother Superior came to her where she knelt on the cold floor of the chapel. A storm was raging within her, though she turned a cold white face to the Mother's gaze.

"It is quite unusual to ask a novice about to take the final vows to go out," began the Mother Superior, "but I must suspend the rule in a case of this kind."

Sister Angela dropped her eyes quickly lest the fire in them should be seen and commented upon.

"There is a case of distress which needs immediate attention," continued the Mother slowly, "I can hardly bear to send you, my daughter, but the rules of our order are, you know, to give aid and succor no matter what it cost us. There is not one of the Sisters, save you, unassigned to duty to-night, and you must go. It need not keep you from praying, my child, for strength for to-morrow's holy ordeal."

Sister Angela made no demur; her breath came quickly. To go out once more before the end of liberty, to walk under the stars before her freedom was over. It seemed too good to be possible. She listened mechanically to the Mother Superior's directions, and left the convent her eyes dimmed with anticipation of this one last hour alone in the night and the street before the morrow.

It was past twilight now, and the few lamps that lighted the suburban street punctuated the darkness, rather than relieved it. Mechanically, her hand stole into her bosom and drew forth the forbidden trinket. To-night, she must confess. Tomorrow she must part with it. Too long, already, it had stood between her and absolute faith and repose. Either it must go the way of the rest of her personality—or she must continue to sin and be frightened and anxious, conscious of wrong-doing, and too weak to put it aside.

She stood under a street lamp gazing longingly at the locket.

"Suppose I throw it away here, now," she said breathlessly. It seemed such an easy solution of her problem. In the dusky shadows it would be lost, and her life to-morrow would begin sinless and stainless and unsoiled by worldly goods. Still she put it to her lips and then started guiltily. A footstep sounded near, and she made a nervous effort to put the locket back into her breast. Her hands trembled with fear. It was only a passerby, she assured herself, but what would he think of her, a Sister of Mercy kissing a trinket in the street? She grew more nervous and the locket fell in the dust at her feet.

The man was near her by this time and heard her little cry of distress and saw her stoop and grope helplessly.

"Allow me," he said courteously, and began to look in the dust with her.

"What did you lose?" he asked.

"Oh, nothing, nothing," she wailed, "it is nothing. I don't want it anyway. I was going to throw it away. It's nothing. I must go on."

"Nothing of the kind," he said firmly, as he struck a match. The gleam of the amethysts met his eye at once, and he straightened himself as he picked it up with a little ejaculation of satisfaction.

"Now," he said, holding it out to her. The match still lighted was in his hand, and it threw an upward ray of light on the pallid face hidden in the shadows.

He looked an instant, and crept nearer holding the match close to her face. She tried to turn away, to run, for the lamp had lighted his features from above, but he threw the match to the ground and caught her fiercely.

"Margaret—you?" he cried hoarsely.

Her head hung, but she placed her hand meekly on her bosom.

"Sister Angela, now," she whispered.

"Sister Angela, nonsense! You are my Margaret, and I

have found you," he exulted. "Great God have I wandered from place to place, searching you to find a Sister Angela? Oh, no; you are mine, I tell you, Margaret."

"I belong to the church," she said, and again would have withdrawn her hand.

"You belong to me," he exclaimed joyously, still holding the hand tightly.

"Where is your—the girl you said you were going to marry?" The woman in her hand triumphed over the nun-to-be.

"Nonsense, I never said so. Margaret, when I heard your mother was dead—I—well—I knew the chief obstacle to our marriage was gone, and I hurried to you. They—" he put a world of scornful emphasis on the word. "They told me you were dead to them, and I thought the worst had happened. So I set about to find you anyway, with bitter, murderous thoughts about you, and I find you thus, my little pure-souled angel."

"They did not want me to enter the convent," she said simply.

"But you are going with me, now," he affirmed.

"No," she wrenched her hand away, "you forget. I am going now on an errand of mercy. Let me pass. To-morrow I take the vow."

"You'll take it over my dead body. Margaret, we know we love each other. Come, little one, we can't afford to play with our happiness thus. Come with me now. I can arrange it all so easily, and no one will be the wiser. We need have no fears for the future. You know your heart will be with me should you shut yourself away in that prison, or give your life over to prayers and regrets. You owe something to life, and to me."

The trinket still gleamed in his hand. She thought of her mother's words. After all, it ought to be passed on to another generation. Then she glanced at his face and a great wave of loving pity surged over her as she noticed his drawn lines and graying temples.

"But my errand," she wavered, "perhaps it is some dying man whom I should comfort."

"Someone else will do it for you. Your duties as a Sister of Mercy should begin and end with me. Think of yourself, think of me, of our two wrecked lives if you persist in leaving me; think too, Margaret," his arm had stolen quietly around her clumsy garb, "of a little home, and children and love. Oh, little girl, don't bury yourself alive. Don't doom us both to lives of endless misery."

"No." She straightened herself again. Almost had she yielded to an impulse to sink unresistingly into his embrace. "No, it is a sin you ask me to commit."

"Is it?" he asked quietly. "Would your life there be entirely sinless? Was not this a sin?" He held out the locket, and smiled at the widening of her eyes. "I know, dear. Do you remember once on your birthday, I kissed it on your throat?"

"Yes, but you have been faithless," she whispered.

"I have been driven to seek my fortune in other places save my home," he retorted, "by the pride of your family. If that is faithlessness, then I have been so—Margaret," he cried sharply. "We are wasting our chance for life's happiness. Come, come, you cannot sin in coming with me."

"I have sinned enough," she said taking the locket from him. "This made me."

"It brought us together. Come, we must hurry." She dropped her hand unresistingly in his, then she paused.

"I have no money, nothing in the world but this locket," she said looking up into his face.

"Thank God, that is enough," he said, and hand in hand they stepped out of the circle of yellow light into the dimness of the long street.

CUPID AND THE PHONOGRAPH *

Science had invaded Frenchtown.

Ma'am Giteau spread her purple calico skirts out on the yellow-washed box steps and vigorously denounced the materialistic spirit of the age all the while cooling herself with a palmetto fan.

"Such foolishness, yaas. Now in my time, eh bien. Young mans ain't now, comme ca—" an ample purple shrug completed the thought.

Inside the little frame house, a phonograph blared tinnily and a music-hall, masculine voice adjured some unseen being with a classic name to "come kiss yo' ba-a-by."

"Dat ees not nise, to talk so, —kees, kees—an' my gal lis'en to dat—Uranié, oh, Uranié—" Her own voice rose shrilly and tinnily above the phonograph.

"Oui, oui, ma mère." Uranié stood in the doorway, slim and alert.

"You come out heah, right now. Sich foolishness, keesin' in daih. You Uranié!" for Uranié turned to go inside.

"Mais, ma mère—"

"Sit down heah!"

* Typescript.

A rebellious whir of starched ruffles flounced by the purple wrapper and a pointed chin tipped itself defiantly at the electric light on the corner.

Inside the phonograph whirred itself into silence, and a young man appeared holding the brass horn in one apologetic hand.

"I beg your pardon—" he began, but Ma'am Giteau waved him into silence with the palmetto fan.

"I t'eenk," she announced majestically, "dat we don' wan' no seech foo'ishness 'r-roun heah, an—I t'eenk dat eef you will eggscuse me, I weel say good evenin'."

The light of a great comprehension dawned upon the face of the young man with the brass horn, and he waved it up and down with a chuckle of glee. The little chin pointed itself higher at the electric light.

"Now, if you will just let me play you a few of my selections—" he returned by way of reply.

"I do not weesh mo'." The starchedness of the purple shrug was majestic, the wave of the palmetto fan was the airy dismissal of a sceptre, but the young man had disappeared into the recesses of the frame house, and in a few seconds there was a tintinnabulation of the Holy City from the uncurtained windows.

Also there was a rustling of purple calico; a ponderous creaking of the frail yellow-washed steps. The young man with the tine horn, the oak box and a straw hat with a flamboyant ribbon moved rapidly out of the sacred precincts of Marigny Street. The chin pointed itself at the electric light, after a brief turn in the direction of the disappearing flamboyant hat band, and Ma'am Giteau resumed her starched and doubly ruffled throne. Silence, save for the drone of the mosquitoes circling in a black cloud over the steps.

"Dat impidence," grunted Ma'am Giteau.

"Maman," announced Uranié next morning coming out into the kitchen, where Ma'am Giteau moved ponderously in the concoction of a court-bouillion—it was Friday, you know—"Maman, dere is one young mans in the par-rloh."

"Dat machine man?"

"Oh, no, Maman," there was a roguish twinkle in her eyes, but otherwise her manner was demure as every well-regulated convent-bred maiden's should be.

Ma'am Giteau's morning gown was guinea blue and somber; Ma'am Giteau's morning manner was ponderous and foreboding. The crisp young man in the scrubbed front parlor, surveying the waxen wreath framed in black velvet upon the white wall turned with effusiveness to greet her.

"Madame Giteau?"

"Yaas sir," non-commitally.

"Madame, I am delighted to form your acquaintance. It is a pleasure indeed to come in contact with one who is so evidently up to date in every particular, who in fact, not only enjoys the best music composed by the master minds of the present and the past, but who in the absence of the ability to possess a piano has determined to possess that music in a concrete and handy form. I am a representative of the Palladian Music company. My partner, Mr. Davenant, Davenant, madame, my own name is Jones, madame, Jones. Well, as I was saying, my partner, Mr. Davenant, whom you have met, and who assured me of your courteous treatment and evident desire to own and possess one of the famed Palladian talking and singing machines, in fact, madame, my partner, Mr. Davenant was telling me that you are interested in our machine, and—and—my partner, madame—"

The glare in Ma'am Giteau's eye would have mixed a more

experienced "representative" than Mr. Jones. But Ma'am
Giteau was fascinated as well as angry. It was seldom that she
met anyone who could talk more volubly than herself, and
this crisp young man seemed to be her match.

He paused and mopped his face.

"As I was saying, madame, my partner was telling me—"

"Wall, yo' po'dner-r was tellin you one gret big sto'y, yaas.
He push hees way een wid dat scan'lous teeng. Go way, go
way—" Ma'am Giteau waved a plump hand in the crisp
young man's face, for he threatened to break into speech
again. "Don' you come heah wid no seech foo'ishness!"

He backed suddenly before this onslaught, and might have
come to grief on the marble topped center table had not
Uranié appeared in the door between the parlor and dining-
room.

"Oh, ma mère," she wailed.

Ma'am Giteau waved one blue clad arm to and fro.

"Dose machine," she gasped, "are one deesgrase, an' you—
you—Uranié, go to the back of the yard? Nevair—nevair—"

"Only one dollar down," protested the crisp young Jones,
backing to the open front door, "and fifty cents—"

The crashing of the door cut short his further remarks.
And Ma'am Giteau was alone with the tearfully protesting
Uranié.

"Such a nise young mans too," she sobbed.

"Eh, nise? You weel go back to the convent, see eef you
don'."

Now your self-respecting Frenchtown housekeeper must
needs wash her steps precisely at twelve on Fridays with the
mysterious yellow wash which brings good luck the following
week. Uranié, her bare arms gilded with the contents of the
pail hummed mournfully at her task later that day when a
hand-bill dropped on the face of the box step last wiped.

She paused and read, crouched in a kitten-like attitude on the last step. Her eyes widened; her breast rose and fell; her lips parted with the breath of quick resolution. Then she thrust the bill in the open chemisette of her demure blue frock and hurried indoors.

Now, mind you, she had forgotten to wash the lower step, and that is just where the trouble began.

That night it was sultry and close; mosquitoes circled in ominous clouds about the heads of the occupants of the steps on the banquettes. In the distance on Villèré Street momentary flashes of gold told of the swift passage of "dose 'lectric car" that went briskly up and down before the homes of protesting Frenchtown citizens. For had not "dose car" cut off the leg of poor little Johnnie St. Amant? They were wicked things and to be tabooed. No self-respecting citizen would be found on them. Uranié rested her little pointed chin in her little sunburned hand and contemplated the golden flashes meditatively.

"Eet is hot, Maman," she cooed persuasively.

"Eh, Bien," was the testy reply, "eet is always 'ot een summare."

"Wouldn' you lak a nise ride?" There was more persuasive coo in the voice.

" 'Ow you go'n geet r-ride? You got no 'orse, no buggee; 'ow you can r-ride?"

"Let me show you, Maman."

Would you believe it, that little coo and gurgle actually persuaded Ma'am Giteau to Villèré Street where the brilliant cars gushed up and down in the glare of the narrow hot street. Ma'am Giteau backed away from the rushing of lights and vowed that no persuasion could induce her to ride in one of those death-dealing monsters. Uranié protested almost in tears that there was no danger. Ma'am Giteau knew better.

Had not one of those clangy things cut off the leg of poor little Johnnie St. Amant?

But your demure maiden, convent-educated and only child of a doting widow usually wins her way if there is sufficient incentive behind it, and at the other end of the Villèré Street car was the dream-prophecy of the hand-bill, still crackling in the demure little bosom. Behold then, Ma'am Giteau nervously erect on the seat of the open car, telling imaginary beads with quaking fingers of cold moisture, with plaintive scream at every bump and jolt the car gave as it plunged through the long narrow street uptown, up to the fairy regions, up towards Canal Street, wonder of wonder streets, not to be visited save at Mardi Gras or Christmas time, for there at the end of the route was the heaven of the hand-bill.

A phonograph parlor! That was what it had said. An amusement concern with slot machines, whatever they may be; refined pleasure for ladies and gentlemen. Why not explore these American amusements? reasoned Uranié the demure, with her little savings hoarded in her bead chatelaine. But of the ultimate end of the going Ma'am Giteau should know nothing until the time for disclosure had come. Moreover, amusement parlor, penny-in-the-slot phonographs, graphophone, courteous young man in the flamboyant encircled straw hat—it would be a dull intellect, indeed, that could not follow such an obvious line of reasoning. Who knows what may happen in the enchanted world above Canal Street?

Bang! To the accompaniment of shrieks and prayers the light in the car went out with an all too splendid suddenness; the car lurched and rocked, and Ma'am Giteau throwing up protesting hands to the dimly seen advertisements voiced deep her imprecations on the ungrateful fille who had brought her old age to such a tragic end.

The conductor protested that the oar had merely jumped the track; that in a few moments all would be well, and "if the meanwhile the ladies would alight—"

Ma'am Giteau descended tremblingly into the noisy glare of Villèré and Bienville Streets. She felt first of her bones to be sure that they were sound, then with a sturdy spreading of her skirts turned to the woebegone Uranié.

"We weel walk home, yaas."

"Oh, mais, Maman," was the tearful protest, "eet ees too far. Evair t'eeng soon be a'r-right."

"We walk home," was the sole response. Indeed, Ma'am Giteau had started briskly downtown. Then in a flash of comprehending misery Uranié remembered that lower step that she had not scrubbed. It was fate.

Now if you know the distance from Bienville to Marigny Street you know it is a good mile or more, and this was a hot night when the cottonwood trees hung their leaves limply from motionless stems, and the beetles blackened the arc lights and fell in thick masses on the banquettes. Also, Ma'am Giteau was quite stout, and the purple wrapper trailed behind in heavy flounces. She had known that no good would come of testing fate on one of those devil-cars. Le bon Dieu intended man to go as fast as the feet of a mule would allow, and it was a sin to attempt to go faster. Moreover, had not little Johnnie St. Amant—

Thus grumbling, she stalked along ponderously, making a great show of walking with little progress. Uranié was silent, solemn; there was nothing to be said, in fact.

A red flash of lightning tore across the black sky, and with a roar, the tropical storm burst upon them as they were crossing the Basin bridge. The little schooners rocked up and down and righted themselves to the sudden fury of the wind;

the bridge creaked ominously and showed the raindrops like black polka-dots on a white frock. Ma'am Giteau gathered up her skirts in front, leaving a purple train in the back, and started to run for the friendly shade of the shops on the Orleans street corner.

"Here, Maman," cried Uranié, pulling her across the green stretch beyond the bridge. They leaned breathless against the side of the shoe shop under the shade of the wide shed canopy with which every shop in the district protects its patrons from heat and storm.

But you should have seen Ma'am Giteau's wrath. It was as fine in its way as the tropical storm which blew through the narrow street creating havoc with the open windows and the shutters and the gay awnings. Was she in her old age to be subjected to such indignities and dangers? Did not rheumatism stare her in the face, and a cold that no tisâne brewed by mortal could cure? The sight of a haughty, glittering car flashing by with a ball of blue fire adorning the juncture of the pole and the wire was fuel to the flames of her indignation. To think that she had been inveigled into a thing like that, thick with the flames from the heavens!

"Pliny, come kiss yo' ba—aby!" came a tinny voice almost in their ears.

Ma'am Giteau started as if shot with the blue flame from the car and Uranié clasped ecstatic hands.

The rain thundered on the tin roof, but loud above it Pliny was adjured to do his osculatory duty, and when he had apparently satisfied all concerned, a joyous whirr announced the Holy City—in quartette. The dense rain beat under the shed, and Ma'am Giteau and Uranié flattened themselves against the wall to escape its drenching. Gone was the starch from the purple flounces, drooping was the crispness of

Uranié's muslin ruffles; wrathful was the heart beneath the purple basque; sublime indifference to the storm fluttered beneath the white surpliced front. The last strains of the vision of the world to come died away; there was a little pause, a murmur of good-byes from the shoe shop, and with an "I beg your pardon, Madame," the flamboyant hat band waved in front of two pairs of interested eyes.

"I beg your pardon, but this is indeed an unexpected pleasure."

Ma'am Giteau turned a damp but dignified shoulder upon the intruder with the oaken box and the brassy horn.

Uranié began a softly voluble explanation, which he, who called himself Davenant, waved aside with the horn. Madame and mademoiselle walk home? Never. Did not his surrey stand only at the corner, and would he not be only too happy to drive them home? To walk, that was impossible, even though the rain had stopped, for the gutters were already overflowing and the crossings unnavigable and the thick black mud of a dangerous consistency to thin cloth gaiter shoes and French heeled slippers. Behold then, Ma'am Giteau, silent and almost mollified, disposed on the back seat of the surrey, close to Uranié, while the precious oaken box, and brassy horn, swathed in black flannel reposed on the front seat with the cheerful driver.

But it takes one accustomed to the black New Orleans mud and the treacherous ditches and crossings, the almost tidal waves that rise with the slightest storm to navigate a buggy successfully through Frenchtown. And then, you must remember that Uranié had forgotten to wash that lower step.

It happened when the surrey was bumping across the many tracks of Elysian Fields Street. The wheel slid into a turbulent yellow stream, concealing a track, skidded an instant, and with a snap of springs swayed Ma'am Giteau perilously near the ground. It swayed also the precious oaken box and the horn. It was clearly going to be a sudden and violent disposition of Ma'am Giteau and the hated machine.

There were but two strong arms in the vehicle, and willing though they were, with a protesting horse to guide through swirls of water and mud, they could save but one object, and the most ungallant man in the world, striving to make an ineradicable impression upon a pair of soft brown eyes, and a deliciously pointed chin could choose but one thing to save. Ma'am Giteau was firmly, but gently secured in her seat, the oaken box and the black-swathed horn, tilted, tipped, swayed and went crashing into the swollen gutter, eddied wildly around and disappeared under the little swaying, wooden crossing.

But Ma'am Giteau was safe, and the surrey righted itself and went splashing across the street into Marigny Way.

"Ooo—ooo—" wailed Uranié, leaning over the other side trying to get a glimpse of the vanished magic box, "Ooo—ooo, an' they are so eggspenseeve!"

The gallant driver waved the whip airily, "Only one dollar down and fifty cents—" then recollecting himself, "It is nothing but a sample used for demonstrating." He omitted to state that the sample had cost him twenty-five dollars but what is twenty-five dollars to an invitation to call delivered by a grateful and moist Ma'am Giteau, supplemented by an appealing glance from a pair of brown eyes, luminous above a deliciously pointed chin?

Uranié, smiling in soft dreams of the promised evening call was shocked early next morning at the sight of Ma'am Giteau resplendent in a fresh, stiff afternoon frock of purple, tying on a grim bonnet in evident preparation for a journey.

"Oh, Maman, wha's the mattare?" she cried. Ma'am Giteau seldom went out, save on Sundays to mass, certainly to few places where the bonnet was necessary. That was reserved for funerals.

"I go uptown, to Canal strit, yaas," she announced breathlessly, as one bound to make an unpleasant confession.

"Oh, Maman, take me!" it was the plea of a child, not an eighteen year old maiden.

"You weel stay at 'ome, yaas. I go on de cars."

Uranié's eyes twinkled. "Dose car on Claiborne strit," resumed Ma'am Giteau with awful dignity.

Of course, of course. How good that there were still sensible cars drawn by mules in the manner which was intended by le bon Dieu.

And so, Ma'am Giteau departed in purple portentousness, leaving a very curious Uranié to keep house. There was no way for the maiden to know that the same busy hand that had thrust the hand-bill into her wet grasp the day before had also put one in the window blind for the skeptical perusal of Maman.

The Claiborne Street cars go slowly, and it is indeed a terrible thing to go all alone up to Canal Steet, to find a place only indicated by number on a vague hand-bill, so it was almost noon when Ma'am Giteau puffed back into the safe harbor of Marigny Street. Uranié, watching from behind carefully bowed shutters, opened an eager crevice to admit the rustling of purple flounces—and the very crisp young Jones, who had been so summarily dismissed the day before. Wonder of wonders, he bore in his arms an oaken box and a brass horn peeping from black swathings!

"One dollar down, an' feefty cents a wik," gasped Ma'am Giteau, collapsing into the red velvet refuge of an armchair.

Uranié demurely proferred sangaree impartially to Maman and the crisp young Jones, who departed finally, leaving the treasures on the marble-topped table.

"Eet is foh you," Ma'am Giteau volubly explained to the flamboyant hat-band owner, who called himself Davenant, that night. "Eef yo had not safe me las' night, yaas, I would have fell in de guttare an' per'aps dr-rown. You los' yo' machine to safe me. I buy you one ce jour-la, yaas. Oh, mais, monsieur, you mus' tek eet."

Expostulations were useless in such a flow of French and patois and convent English as poured from Ma'am Giteau and Uranié. Davenant stood helpless.

"But I am not to demonstrate any more," he gasped, "I don't need it. I am in the office now. Well—since you insist, let me call it mine and leave it here. I have no place to put it, you know."

For that was really too good a sale to be lost, after all.

Then what more natural than that he should come every night to give Uranié instructions how to put in and take out the waxen cylinders. For really, it is no easy matter to run a phonograph, and Pliny must be adjured many times a night to kiss his ba-a-by before a satisfactory adjustment can be made of the disks.

Several nights ago Marigny Street was startled by a new and unfamiliar tune sounding from the marble-topped table. All the repertoire of popular melody and sacred song had been gone over many times, now what was this?

And one discerning ear recognized the strains of the Loh-engrin Wedding March feebly and timidly as though rehearsing for a special occasion.

"Dey weddin' pr-resent play dey weddin' ma'ch, yaas," said Ma'am Giteau to the next door box steps, as she waved the palmetto fan above her purple billows.

Science had indeed invaded Frenchtown!

THE ANNALS OF 'STEENTH STREET STORIES *

MISS TILLMAN'S PROTEGE †

"Oh, poor little thing," exclaimed Miss Tillman, "poor dear child, I feel so sorry for her."

And she clasped her hands and shuddered a little in her pity.

Apparently Hattie did not hear. She bent a little closer over her card, and vouchsafed no sign.

"Do you know, Mrs. Morton," went on Miss Tillman, catching her breath now and then in the rapture of her thought, "I'd just like to look after that child, take her under my wing, as it were, may I?"

"That depends entirely upon the little girl's parents. I'm afraid you'll have to consult them about it." Mrs. Morton tried not to speak coldly, but it was an effort.

"Oh, Mrs. Morton, surely, surely, these poor people up here would be awfully glad to be relieved of their cares. I am in love with that child. Such a dear, sweet, patient face. She'd look lovely in a dear white apron with her hair smooth sitting at my feet in my study."

"Well, you know, Miss Tillman, I have nothing to do with the family affairs of our class members. I never touch them." Mrs. Morton had almost said "meddle with them."

Miss Tillman had paid no attention to the latter part of Mrs. Morton's remarks. She turned to Hattie Gurton, "Come

* A manuscript volume that Dunbar-Nelson probably worked on between 1900 and 1910.
† Typescript.

101

here, child," she said in the sweetly imperious manner that had made her a favorite in her particular social circle.

Hattie rose and came to her. She raised a pair of dim eyes and then dropped them and fidgeted as she stood on one foot.

"Wouldn't you like to come and live with me?" demanded Miss Tillman.

"I do' know," replied the child uneasily.

"I have a lovely home and flowers, and a sweet canary bird, and you should have lots of pretty dresses and all the candy you want."

"I don't like candy," returned Hattie.

"Then you shall have cake and a pretty doll."

"Kin Johnny come too?"

Miss Tillman paused. "Sometimes," she said finally.

Hattie regarded her tentatively for a minute and then she edged away, saying in a sudden burst as she reached her seat, "No, I wants to be wid my mama."

Mrs. Morton smiled grimly and Miss Tillman suffered a shade of disappointment to cross her serene features.

"It's a wonder to me how these children can be so ignorant," she said, drawing on her gloves a little impatiently. "I cannot understand it. But of course, they learn better in time. Now that little girl will probably tell with deepest regret when she grows older of her chance to live with a 'fine lady.' It's too bad she can't be persuaded."

"Perhaps there are family ties, and a mother," suggested Mrs. Morton.

"My dear Mrs. Morton, it's absurd. These people are very different from us. I thought you knew that from your long experience with them. Well, good-bye, I must be going."

Miss Tillman had a charitable soul. She was beautiful; she

was fairly wealthy. She sang in the choir of her favorite church; not because of any emolument it might bring, but because she loved to sing and she did not think it right to deprive the world of the pleasure of hearing her voice. She went in for charity as she went in for music. It gratified her artistic spirit to note the supposed contrast between herself, and those "dear people" as she was wont to call them. She was fond of taking her out of town friends "slumming" and if perchance someone to whom she had been kind at one time met her with recognition, she would point out the incident rapturously and expatiate on the gratitude of the lowly. Miss Tillman spent freely and gave money whenever and wherever she was asked, but she did not understand many things. Indeed, it is doubtful if she ever could.

Hattie was deformed. Her eyes were dim and near-sighted, and one of her legs was twisted painfully. But she did not like to be pitied or petted, and she was happiest when it was taken for granted that she was like other children. She had her brother John, who always took prizes at school, and her kitten, and she was happy. They were poor, but she always had enough to eat, and her mother and father, rough generally to all the world, were singularly gentle to her. She went to school when she wanted to, and because of her eyes and her leg, when she chose to stay at home and play with her kitten or sit and look out of the window, there was no one to say her nay. Also, when it suited her fancy, she took Johnny by the hand and trotted over to the kindergarten at the Pure in Heart. It was there that she had attracted Miss Tillman's attention, bending over the card she was sewing.

The idea of adopting Hattie was in Miss Tillman's mind, despite the child's rebuff. She came another day and ventured the topic to Mrs. Morton.

"Where is my little girl?" she inquired in sweet consternation at not seeing her there.

"She's not here to-day," replied Mrs. Morton, "she doesn't always come."

"Poor, dear little thing. I suppose there are times when her mother is cruel to her and won't let her out. Mrs. Morton, you don't know how I am attracted to that child. It seems to me that I must get her out of this awful environment."

"I am afraid—" began Mrs. Morton faintly, but Miss Tillman interrupted her by a request for Hattie's address, and went swiftly out of the rooms on her errand of mercy.

She shuddered as she climbed the stairs which led to the Gurton flat. They met with all her preconceived ideas of the horrors of tenements, for in spite of her charitable proclivities, Miss Tillman had never been at very close range with "her dear people." She felt a delicious thrill of horror because the stairs were dark and the halls ill-smelling, and she found herself unconsciously planning out a letter which she would write to a friend in the country. She knocked at the door which was indicated as belonging to the Gurton's apartment, and when Hattie opened it, she stood peering dubiously within.

"Come in," said Hattie opening wide the door, and Miss Tillman went in, not without a certain little qualm. Who knows what danger might lurk within? And when once the doors are closed, anything might happen.

"Where is your mother, child?" she asked.

"Mama's out."

"Oh, indeed and my little girl is here all by herself as I suppose she must be lots and lots of times. Aren't you dreadfully lonely, dear?"

"No'm," replied Hattie casting a quick look at her corner. Miss Tillman's eyes followed the glance. In one corner of the room a little doll's house had been rigged up, and Miss Tillman could see within doll furniture and dishes and sundry things dear to the hearts of little girls. Also there were various dolls lying about the floor. Hattie's own kindergarten scissors and cutting paper lay on a tiny desk denoting recent occupation. Miss Tillman was conscious of a sudden irritation. She sank into a red plush chair with a yellow silken scarf on the back and murmured so that Hattie could not hear.

"What execrable taste this room is furnished in. It has positively given me a nervous headache. And that piano cover. Ugh!"

The real trouble was not in the furnishing of the room, but that it was furnished at all. But Miss Tillman did not admit this to herself. Then she concluded that this must be a home of vice, and not the home at all for a pure-minded little girl. The idea of the workingman paying for a decent home for his family had as yet not occurred to her.

"Don't you want to come home with me?" she inquired of Hattie.

"No'm."

"You would be very happy there, and everyone would be good and kind to you."

"I wanter stay wid mama."

"Poor little thing," murmured Miss Tillman, "She is ashamed to tell her preference," then aloud she asked, "Do your papa and mama whip you very much?"

Hattie's eyes opened wide in astonishment, "I never did have a beatin'."

Miss Tillman smiled incredulously. She was sure Hattie was afraid to tell.

"Won't you come and take a walk with me?" she begged. Hattie hesitated, "Mama told me to stay inside," she faltered.

"I'll tell mama, and she won't mind," entreated Miss Tillman, and Hattie gave in. She put on her hat and coat, which Miss Tillman noticed with an added sense of irritation, were warm and pretty, and they sallied forth together.

After all, it was a pleasant day for Hattie. They went to some great stores where Miss Tillman bought many things, and they had luncheon in a beautiful restaurant where an orchestra played, and finally, in a noiseless, perfectly appointed limousine, they drove back to 'Steenth Street.

It bore the signs of disturbance, and little knots of women and girls stood about talking eagerly and casting furtive glances at the steps of one of the houses where a policeman was vainly trying to pacify Mrs. Gurton. Mr. Gurton, in his shirt sleeves, stood gloomily looking up and down the street. He had searched, and reported and had telephoned advertisements to every newspaper in the city, and there was nothing else to do.

Then Mrs. Gurton spied Hattie's face in the car, and sprang to her, pushing Miss Tillman roughly aside, and seized the child, covering her with kisses and exclamations. Mr. Gurton, with a man's indifference, was less demonstrative, but he had to clear his throat several times. The crowd gathered around Hattie and made much of her, while on the outer edge of the circle stood Miss Tillman, looking rather foolish.

"I—I— thought I'd bring her back for a bit," she stammered, as soon as she could be heard in the hubbub, "before I took her to my house."

"To your house?" shrieked Mrs. Gurton, while Mr. Gurton stood looking on in open-mouthed amazement.

"Yes,—er—well—I—er—you see, I wanted to take her home with me and keep her for my little playmate."

"There's a mistake here," said Mr. Gurton stepping up, "You've made a mistake, Madam," his tone was quiet, too quiet, Miss Tillman felt.

But Mrs. Gurton shrieked again, "To your house? What on earth does she mean?" appealing to the other women, who only snickered and giggled behind their hands.

"I wanted to adopt her, you know," explained the lady. Her face was growing redder and redder.

"Adopt her? Adopt my child? What do you want with my child? To make a servant or a monkey out of her? She don't want no 'doptin' of yours. She's got a home an' plenty of clothes an' plenty of victuals. She ain't no beggar; she don't need your 'doptin'."

Mr. Gurton tugged at his wife's arm and muttered a command for quiet; but Mrs. Gurton shook him off and continued her shrill denunciations.

"Comin' 'round here takin' people's children, an' a-stealin' inter people's rooms, spyin' an' a-peepin'. I've got the best mind in the world to report her to the station."

Miss Tillman shivered and made an involuntary movement towards the car.

"I—you—" she began, but the policeman had pushed his way to the center of the ever-increasing crowd.

"It would be wisest for you to go home, Madam," he said.

"I didn't mean to harm the child," she returned petulantly.

"Still," assented the policeman, in the same undertone, "it looked bad for you to go in their rooms and get her."

The lady drove away, followed by the laughter of the crowd, and the jeers of "de gang" to all of whom Mrs. Gurton was giving an exhibition of Miss Tillman's fine manner. She was perplexed, nonplussed, chagrined, but ere long before the car had driven up before her own door, she had solved the problem. She lay back in her seat and was proud of the martyrdom she had endured in the cause of charity, and she shuddered at the memory of the thoughtless ingratitude of the poor.

But Miss Tillman did not understand; perhaps she could not.

WITNESS FOR THE DEFENSE*

'Steenth Street had not had such a sensation in years. It really was too good to be true. At last, the disgraced denizen could hold up their heads when any of the 87th Street gang passed through with hoots of derision at them. At last, they could refute the dire charge brought against them that the Mission had "reformed them." 'Steenth Street had won its way back to claiming a right among the dreaded streets of the town, a prestige almost lost within the past year. It was good beyond the comprehension of the mere outsider. One must have been an inmate of 'Steenth Street, and have had all the natural pride of locality to have felt and understood.

Murder had been done; murder, foul, black, unreasoning. It stalked forth in the light of day shamelessly, not seeking the darkness of night to cover its foulness. The sun shone on, bright, searching, pitiless, the river glistened tawnily down at the foot of the hill, unrecking the passing of another human life. A curious crowd gathered and pushed open-mouthed, but not voluble, around the steps of three-thirty.

* Typescript.

The policemen pushed them farther back ever and anon, roughly conscious of their authority, and determined that others should share their consciousness. Now and then, some-one, more venturesome than the rest would jostle his way forward and stand staring stupidly a minute at the steps, only to be pulled back into the crowd by a vigorous, blue-coated arm. Those who were so fortunate as to be on the front row of gaping spectators, gazed long and curiously, with a breath-less, awe-struck manner at a stain on the dirty steps. It was an ominous red dab with splashes and drops about it, also dirty red. It spoke in a sinister language, saying plainer than words that here a life had flickered out into the beyond, choosing the most sordid surroundings for its awful ordeal.

Someone had committed a murder. 'Steenth Street held its breath and compressed its lips. It was not that someone had been murdered; that was not the awful thing. Life was not so valuable in 'Steenth Street, nor so sweet a possession that it should be held in reverence. 'Steenth Street held its breath and compressed its lips in awe-struck joy that someone had actually committed a murder; that within its precincts had been found one unreformed, unregenerate and bold enough to take a human life.

Meanwhile, Belle Williams, crouched in a cell in the nearby station house across Third Avenue and sobbed her heart out, while the gods in blue coats who write things against people in big black-covered books, solemnly recorded that she was charged with the murder of one, Randolph Williams.

"De gang" had lined up in front of three-thirty with solemn precision, Dobson at the head, as one by one the scenes in the clearing away of the tragedy unfolded themselves. Scrappy Franks would have raised a howl when the rigid, bloodstained form was lifted into the ambulance and borne away, but Dobson checked him vigorously,

"Say," he interrogated, "Ain't you got no respect fer de dead?"

Thus admonished Scrappy Franks gulped down his sob and there was silence again. Dobson's own respect was not for the dead as dead, but for the dead when it has given up its life with suddenness and violence, but of that there is no need making too much of a record.

When the officers led Belle out of the house handcuffed, trembling and half-defiant, Gus Schwartz raised a feeble cheer in which "de gang" joined with a vociferation that was a flattering tribute, or should have been, to Belle's popularity. The unsentimental police officers, however, suppressed them with rude words to which "de gang" feeling a certain sense of importance, and a renewed strength of locality, replied with gibes and sneers.

But when Lizzie came out sobbing and miserable, led by Mrs. McMahon, and followed by a policeman who looked as if he would rather have been anywhere else in the world than there, "de gang's" chivalrous instincts were aroused.

"Aw, wot do dey want to take de kid fer?" growled Gus Schwartz, "she ain't done nuttin."

"It's a shame," said Dobson, "dat's a purty child too."

"Let's git her away," suggested Lesie Channing. The spirit of knight errantry was strong within him, and glorious visions of outwitting the whole of the Metropolitan police force for the sake of a forlorn and distressed maiden danced gloriously before his eyes. But it was not to be. Lizzie was pushed into the patrol with her mother, and Mrs. McMahon came back to join the crowd before the steps of three-thirty, wiping her eyes on her apron, and giving voluble expressions and opinions for the benefit of all who might care to hear.

"An' it do be breakin' her heart, poor little thing," she would say now and then, shaking her head mournfully.

All of this was explained by a simple statement made before the gods in blue coats in the station. Belle Williams and her husband had quarrelled in their rooms on the third floor of three-thirty. She had attacked him with a pair of scissors, severed a vital vein; he had run downstairs, and dropping on the front step had died with his head on the sidewalk. That was all, except that the only possible witness to it all had been eight year old Lizzie, Belle's little girl of a former marriage. The gods of the station house were in possession of these bare facts, but there were additional items which 'Steenth Street might have furnished. All the street knew Randolph Williams, swaggering drunkard by profession, bully by necessity, loafer from choice. Not that the possession of these last-named traits would have mattered much, but even in 'Steenth Street, there is a code of honor, and the man who maltreats his fragile stepdaughter as Randolph Williams did Lizzie steps outside the pale, and is henceforth and forever an ostracized being. Thus did Randolph Williams stalk in gloomy and lonely solitude from McEneny's to the dreary halls of three-thirty. He knew why he was shunned, and far from bettering his treatment of Lizzie, he took out upon her body the scorn and contumely of his neighbors.

It was a celebrated case for 'Steenth Street. For so long had woman-kind in this particular section of the world quietly taken its beatings, gone without food or fire or light, while its better half found all three with amusement and jollity thrown it at McEneny's on the corner; for so long had it been that the primitive law of the jungle prevailed, which decrees that the female shall grow uncomely, weighted by the burden of rearing its young unaided, while the male, more youthful and beautiful, bounds away for fresher fields; for so

long had the survival of the strongest been the implacable
law that now when one woman had broken the bonds of
custom and established the right to live and to kill too, there
was great rejoicing. The women stood about in doorways and
halls and discussed the event with avidity. Emancipation was
in the air. The Rights of Woman began to have a concrete
meaning; the cause of Childhood began to have advocates.
Already those who had not believed in the tenets and doctrines
taught at the Pure in Heart retracted their denials and went
boldly over to the enemy.

Lizzie, meanwhile, was in the care of the good women
whose business it is to look after such tiny bits of flotsam as
are cast upon the city's tide. She did not care much where
she was. She remembered Something too vividly to mind
anything that happened afterwards. She was taken every day
to see her mother because Belle wailed and beat her hands
against her breast for her little girl. Lizzie was indifferent,
mechanical; she suffered her mother's caresses, and gave an
occasional perfunctory one in return.

"Oh, my poor little baby," Belle would moan over the
child, "dey ain't treatin' you right. Look at me darlin', you
don't look like my little baby."

Lizzie would look into her face, but before all the kindness
and love in her mother's eyes and tears of joy that were
streaming down her cheeks, the child seemed to see a mask
with distorted features working in convulsive rage and hate
as she had seen it that awful day. She could not understand
why, but she could see no more love in her mother's eyes.

The days after the inquest dragged by drearily enough.
The state was going to make an example of the case. The
section of the city in which 'Steenth Street was located had
been an eyesore to law-lovers for too long. Crime after crime
had been committed and gone unpunished, or nearly so.

Although 'Steenth Street had been nearly on the verge of a reform for several months, still it had had a bad reputation, and must suffer for its former misdemeanors. The District Attorney gathered his facts together and prepared a merciless arraignment against the prisoner. This was a common enough case, but its very commonness made it all the more important that it should be dealt with severely. "The dignity of the law must be upheld."

Meanwhile 'Steenth Street was in a fever. Sympathy ran high on Belle's side and bets were freely taken at McEneny's as to the probable outcome of the trial, which had been fixed at an early date.

To little Lizzie, waiting in the care of the good women, whose duty it is to look after nobody's children, the whole thing was inexpressibly miserable. She had sunken into a lethargy from which it seemed impossible to raise her. The sisters wearied her with their attentions, well-meant, but inadequate. Her heart pined amid the cleanliness and order and regularity of her life among them. The memory of Belle's kitchen, with its combination of the odor of the weekly wash and of savory stews redolent of onions, stirred within her. The memory too, of those fearsome days when Randolph Williams came home ready to belabor her or Belle with a beautiful impartiality, was not without a certain sweetness, for after all was over and Randolph Williams had stalked away, secure in his own dignity and high estimation of himself, she and Belle might creep into one another's arms and sob out certain comforting things to each other; for Lizzie, despite her few years, was mature in the giving of sympathy. But now she thought of Belle with a shudder. The memory of her face, that expression on it before she saw no more, haunted her with dreadful insistence.

However, in due time, as all things will, the day of the

trial came, and great was the excitement in 'Steenth Street. Mrs. McMahon even went so far as to get out the green silk the day before and hang it, airing and uncreasing its many folds on the pulley from her window. On the morning of the eventful day, she arrayed herself, and Solomon, nor the Queen of Sheba were fit subjects of comparison with her. All 'Steenth Street was to be there. It was their trial and it behooved them to attend in large numbers. "De gang" had been heard of trying on new ties and even affecting linen of various degrees of non-whiteness, while Dago Joe's peanut stand had done a rushing business; peanuts in a courtroom being almost as essential as peanuts at a circus, and who shall say that the two do not resemble in some particulars?

However great an occasion 'Steenth Street may have considered this, in the eyes of the lawyers and courtroom habitués, it was a very ordinary affair. Here was a woman, who by her own confession had killed a man, in self-defense, so she said, but she had killed him, no one had ever attempted to deny that, and there was really little to do save to sentence her and go on. It would be a minimum sentence, of course, but it seemed an actual waste of time and of the state's money to prolong the trial for the sake of the interested spectators from 'Steenth Street. Even the yellow journals had failed to take much notice of the case, beyond a few snapshot photographs of the scene of the murder, just as the act was committed, a picture of Lizzie with a description of her innocence and docility. The District Attorney, the various lawyers, and it is to be feared, even the judge yawned as the dreary task of empanelling a jury dragged on. The challenges grew more and more perfunctory; the heavy summer air hung thickly in the stifling room. Lizzie's head fell forward, and the murmuring of the various voices about her blended into a vague pleasant drone from which she was awakened by a gentle hand on her shoulder and a whispered "poor child" from one of the attending sisters.

The hours dragged by. Lizzie found herself wondering why she had been made to come. It was not interesting, and furthermore she could not be of much use anyway. Belle sat and alternately wept or glared fiercely about upon her surroundings. The clerks sucked their pen-handles and stared hard at the flies on the wall. The reporters chatted together pleasantly, or went out in twos or threes, then came back with a great show of hurry and business. Mrs. Morton, of the Pure in Heart, her white face, whiter still in the dingy atmosphere of the courtroom, talked at long intervals with Belle's lawyer, and Lizzie nodded again to dream of Randolph Williams, and to wake with a start of terror as she grasped the hand of the nearest person.

Then there was a recess, followed by a brisker atmosphere in the room. Things seemed to wake up. People came and went before the judge and the questioning fires of the lawyers or the scathing searching of the District Attorney. Everyone seemed so unhappy when they were being questioned and so glad when they were able to take their seats again that Lizzie gazed with wonder at the witness chair. Once she had gone with Belle to the dentist at a hospital, and she had never forgotten the expressions of those who stepped out of the dentist's chair. These people in the courtroom seemed very like those unfortunates in the hospital, she thought. She wondered if it hurt very much to sit down and have those people hurl questions at you, and have these brisk young men write all the while one was talking. She had heard a great deal of talk about "the chair" in the past few weeks, and she thought now that she knew what it was. Of course, all these people had done something wrong and they were being punished by sitting in that chair. Why, yes, it was quite simple. When Mama Belle had killed Randolph Williams, everyone had said she would go to the "chair," and here it was. Only she hoped it wouldn't hurt Mama Belle anymore than it hurt the rest.

Then someone called her name, "Lizzie Williams!"

She answered "Sir," very respectfully as she had been taught and looked about to see who could want her.

"Lizzie Williams!" and the good sister in the black bonnet and white bands about her neck was leading her to the chair. Lizzie clung to her terror-stricken, but tearless. She had long learned that weeping never helped matters any, but she was cold with a grisly fear. Surely she had done nothing wrong? Why should she be punished?

It seemed that there was a curiosity concerning her name and age and various personal matters. They did not ask her to sit in the chair, and at that, the grisly fear faded away and left a gentle bewildering wonderment in her soul. What possible interest could they have in her? The very grave and very earnest white-haired man leaned forward and listened attentively as she talked, and the brisk young men wrote more briskly than ever. Lizzie flung a timid glance at Belle, but she sat with eyes covered with one hand and would not meet her gaze. Suddenly she was a person of importance, but Mama Belle seemed sorry and would not look at her. Was she wrong, and did not mama want to see her punishment?

"Did she know the nature, the sacredness of an oath?"

Why, yes, of course, that had been explained carefully many times at Sunday-school, and in the Sunday afternoon Bible classes at the Pure in Heart. They were very wicked things. Randolph Williams used them always, and the air round McEneny's was usually thick with them.

No. they did not mean that kind. She listened patiently while they explained, then nodded her head with quiet comprehension.

After all, it seemed that they were anxious to have her tell them about mama and Randolph Williams. Her face went pale and a strange fear contracted her heart. It was quiet, so quiet in the room between the questions they asked and her replies, so quiet that the moving of the pencils of the brisk young men smote sharply on the ear. She did not like to talk about that day. The memory of Belle's face was too vivid. The sight of that stark body downstairs on the steps covered with a sheet, the crowd, the blood, Belle's terrified shrieks as they carried her into the station, the clanging patrol wagon, all were too vividly disagreeable. She shuddered, but meeting the grave, but kindly gaze of the black, bonnetted sister, she smiled timidly, choked back the dry sob in her throat, and bent her mind to her questioners.

Oh, how nagging they were! Why could they not let her alone? Why, when she had told them all she knew must they insist that she knew more? Why, when one solemn man got through asking questions must another and still another ask the same questions or more questions, which after all, could be answered in the same way? Of course, she had not seen Belle hit Randolph Williams. She had seen Belle's face convulsed with dreadful anger, and she had run and hid her own in the bed, too glad that the drunken hands were off her small person at last, and when she had lifted her head again, both Randolph and Belle were gone, and there was an outcry in the halls and on the stairs. No, no, no, that was all she knew. No one had told her to say that. She had never lied in her life, not even to Randolph Williams to save herself a beating, why then, should she do so now?

From somewhere a grave voice intervened,

"That will do, gentlemen. The child has been on the stand over an hour."

The rest was confused. First, one of the men who had asked so many questions arose and talked a great deal and sat down amid a stern silence; then the other inquisitive man, the one to whom Mrs. Morton whispered so much, got up and spoke eloquently. At least, someone near her, used the word eloquent, and when he had finished, there was a great deal of hand-clapping and applause. Then the solemn white-haired man said something to the twelve serious men who thereupon rose and went out one by one, for all the world like the men who come out of McEneny's side door on Sunday afternoons.

Then there was silence. It was growing dark, and the lights in the room began to pop up here and there, lighting up strained faces, making Mrs. Morton's and the nervous young lawyer's whiter by the pallor they cast; throwing curious shadows on Belle's worn face and work-knotted fingers, casting sinister lights in the folds of Mrs. McMahon's green silk, making a sort of halo about the judge's white head. Something of the real import of the situation began to dawn upon Lizzie. Suddenly she knew that her mother's life or freedom hung in the balance, and that her words had decided that balance one way or the other. Which way? She looked into all the faces and none seemed to know. What had she done? She wanted to scream the question at the white-haired judge, but he seemed as ignorant as everyone else.

Then the twelve men filed in again. Perhaps they knew.

She rose in her seat; she would go and ask them, but the restraining hand of the sister held her close and from somewhere up there among them one voice rang out sonorously,

"Not Guilty!"

And pandemonium reigned at once in the room. They were cheering and singing and shrieking and women were fainting and she was the center of the pandemonium. Men's voices and women's were crying, "The child saved her!" "The little girl's testimony did it!" "Wasn't she splendid under the cross examination?" "Technicality of the law, you know!" "No witness to the deed!" "If the little girl had faltered all would have been over for Belle!" She was being handed from one to the other and they were kissing her and weeping over her, even "de gang" were thrusting grimy paws at her to be shaken; while Mrs. McMahon swept all the glory of the green silk on the courtroom floor as she knelt at Lizzie's feet and sobbed.

Then someone thought, and took her to her mother, and Belle wept over her too. Lizzie was glad if she had saved her mother as they said she had, but Belle's embrace was not sweet to her; she shrank from it again.

A little later they stood hand in hand on the sidewalk, surrounded by a crowd, but more alone than if they had stood on an unpeopled coral reef. For the mother and child each knew what life held for them. The woman knew that she would walk all her days with the vision of the murdered man stalking by her side; and the child knew that she would never meet her mother's eyes or suffer her caress without a shuddering memory of her face on that awful day.

However, 'Steenth Street knew no such qualms and McEneny and Dago Joe reaped a silver harvest that night.

THE BALL DRESS *

Now it was a well-known fact in the inner circles of 'Steenth Street that Della Mott's father was too poor to keep her properly, so that when she—but that would be beginning at the wrong end of the story.

There was just Dell and her father, and they occupied two rooms on the third floor of three-forty-two. One, which was kitchen, drawing-room and dining-room, had a little cot curtained off in one corner for Mr. Mott. Dell occupied the dark little inner bedroom. Once, in some distant past, there had been a mother, but she was never mentioned. She had walked out one day bearing with her the treasures of the Mott household, and she was not even a memory now.

Mr. Mott was by nature a paternal man. He joyed in children, many of them, and his ideal existence would have been in an orphan asylum. For all of this, Nature was wise in giving him only Dell. Paternal as was his nature, Dell was mother and father and playmate to him. He was a constant source of occupation to her. Still, it was his delight to prate pathetically at McEneny's of his responsibilities.

He tended furnaces and did chores and odd jobs and swept sidewalks, while Dell worked in the box factory when she could, for she had not yet gotten a steady place; and he and Dell eked out some sort of existence. Sometimes he forgot to come home with his earnings. When she was a little girl on

* *Leslie's Weekly*, December 12, 1901.

such occasions Dell would cry herself to sleep supperless and cold. When she grew larger, her modicum of pride had decreased somewhat, and she would go downstairs to Mrs. McMahon's or run credit at the store for supper.

One night Mott came home and found her lying across the bed breathing heavily.

"Where's my pigeon?" he cried.

"I'm sick, pop," she said gently, "awful sick. My head goes roun' an' roun', an oh, I feel awful funny."

Mr. Mott sat him down to think the situation over. He felt confused and awkward in the face of a new situation. Dell had always been a healthy girl. Why, then, was she sick now? He looked about the room, but finding no reply in its cold staring walls, he put on his hat and went out.

"Mrs. McMahon," he said when that lady had answered his knock, "Dell, now Dell, ain't feelin' so good."

Mrs. McMahon was a woman of quick and decisive action, and she started upstairs at once talking all the way.

"God bless the dear brave heart," she cried taking Dell in her arms and feeling the hot head, "An' she's got a fever an' do be makin' herself all worse a-frettin' because her fayther ain't got no supper. She must have a foot-bath and be in bed at once."

The doctor said it was typhoid and the best place for her was in the hospital. Mr. Mott's underjaw tightened and his face took on a look of bulldog determination.

"She shan't go," he said fiercely, almost whispering in his grief.

"My good man," replied the doctor, "Let me assure you, there is no disgrace in going to the hospital. Some of the wealthiest people in the city go."

The doctor knew the tenement horror of hospitals.

"My child in a hospital!" groaned Mr. Mott, while Mrs. McMahon moaned and raised her eyes heavenward.

"She will have care such as you cannot possibly give her, medical attention constantly and the best of nourishment and sanitary care," persisted the doctor.

"Now they want to take her away. They want to put my child in a hospital, and then she'll be gone too. An'—an', — there's just me an' Dell, an' they want to put her in a hospital."

Mr. Mott rambled on weakly and broke into sobs, whereupon Mrs. McMahon burst into fierce invective against the doctor who shrugged his shoulders and went his way.

Dell did not die. She had a hard fight for life however, and she lay for many weeks hovering between death and life. Mrs. McMahon gave up her own household duties to attend her, and there came jellies and things from the cooking class at the Pure in Heart of which she had been a member. Most nights, Mr. Mott slept at the side of the bed, but sometimes, as usual, he forgot to come home, when Mrs. McMahon took his place. But this was not often.

One day Dell sat up, weak and pale with close cut hair, and Mr. Mott sat at her feet and gazed rapturously at her and hugged his knees and even raised a thin cracked voice in song.

"She needs fresh air," said the doctor sniffing at the myriad tenement smells which came up the air shaft. "She ought to have a drive."

Mott said nothing but he worked two days at the livery stable on Madison Avenue and used all his persuasive eloquence to the driver to let him have a carriage to take Dell driving in payment for his services.

It was a great event when that carriage, a rusty one, with

an ancient gray nag and an unliveried driver, drove up to three-forty-two. Word flew from lip to lip and window to window. "Ol' man Mott's takin' Della fer a drive." It was an unprecedented event. Frankie Smith's attempt to jeer at the equipage was sternly repressed by Abe Powers with a grim, "Aw, now, shut up." Mrs. McMahon, who was to go as nurse, had on the gorgeous green silk, a relic of other days and another owner; which she never wore save on state and awful occasions. She fussed and fidgeted about and went in and out of the hall to the carriage a dozen times, finally calling back shrill voiced directions to the small McMahons. Mr. Mott had introduced the driver at McEneny's and the two men had discovered each in the other a secret sympathy and close companionship hitherto undreamed of. Therefore, in the drive, Mr. Mott perched on the box, and they talked joyously, Mr. Mott telling of his awful responsibilities, and they swore a friendship that should never die.

That carriage drive placed the Motts at once on a social plane above Dell's most sanguine expectations. In her short convalescence she had much more attention and offers of help than she had had in her whole illness. Of course, there were some vile cavillers who wondered how "Ol' man Mott had managed it" and others who were Philistine enough to decry the whole matter as something not so extraordinary after all. But there is always envy no matter where one goes and the Philistines could not deny that the Motts were now people of great importance.

So it was thought on account of this acquired status that Dell received an invitation to the great ball of the Firemen's Lodge. She had never been invited anywhere before, and all 'Steenth Street knew how great an occasion was the annual Firemen's Ball. When she and Mrs. McMahon put their heads together over the heavily gilded and decorated invitation they were not long in deciding that the carriage ride had done the whole thing. In reality Mott had wheedled the secretary of the Firemen's Lodge into sending a card to Dell. He had done work for the secretary for a whole week and had taken him to McEneny's before he had proferred the request.

Dell's wardrobe was scanty, and they were still in debt to the doctor. Everyone knows that those who go to the Firemen's Ball are arrayed like unto Solomon, and no makeshift dress will do. After spending a whole day in the dreary contemplation of her two disreputable street dresses and her two muslin shirtwaists, Dell was brought face to face with the crushing realization of the fact which had found voice in Miss Flora McFlimsy's wail.

"Guess you'll be goin' to the ball," said Mr. Mott as he sat down to supper that night.

Dell's eyes were red but her voice was steady, as she said bravely, "Nope."

"No? Why, girl, you're crazy. Why dese girls in 'Steenth Street would give anything to git an invite to de Firemen's."

"I'm not goin'," said Dell, with wavering voice.

Mr. Mott put down his teacup and scowled. "Why?" he asked.

"I've got nuttin' to wear."

"Nuttin' to wear?" he repeated vaguely, "Nuttin' to wear? Why, where—where's—?" He paused, Where was what? Come to think of it, he had never noticed whether Dell had nice dresses or any kind of dresses. It had never struck him that Dell had to have dresses. He sat staring at her with his teacup suspended in air, then he put it down again, and leaning over the table, whispered confidently,

"Pigeon, did you ever know Dad to trow you down?"

"No, pop," said Dell.

"Yer ol' dad's got awful responsibilities, Pigeon, awful ones." He shuddered at the thought of them. "But yer ol' dad'll never trow you down."

He repeated this assurance as he went out, and Dell felt a great contentment as she went to bed that night.

After a protracted stay at McEneny's, where Mr. Mott informed the crowd with solemn gravity that his responsibilities were "some'p'n fierce," he walked away burning with a desire to do something great for Dell. He had a vague idea that she needed something, but he could not remember just what it was. He felt that were he a knight of old of which he had read somewhere, he might accomplish a great feat, but in planning it all out, he became sleepy and went to bed.

Next morning, however, he started out in good earnest to find a dress for Dell.

First, he did a number of chores on Madison Avenue and laid his case before the cook of the household. But she was unsympathetic, and scornfully inquired "Phwat de loikes of dem wanted to go to balls fer?" Then he philandered about the delicatessen storekeeper's wife, but she thought that the account which they owed at her store ought to be paid before Miss Mott attended balls. He went everywhere, did everything, and still was no nearer his goal than ever. This went on for some time, and the day of the ball was coming perilously near. Dell had cried over her wardrobe again and again, and she and Mrs. McMahon had spent long hours in solemn consultation over the matter. They had even tried to see what could be done with the green silk; but it, too, was hopeless. Dell was short and slim; Mrs. McMahon was tall and stout, and it would have been an act of sheer vandalism to have put scissors in its rustling folds.

Then on a dreary day, Mr. Mott fell upon an advertisement in the evening paper,

"Lost, a fox-terrier, with a diamond shaped spot on the neck, no tail, ears unevenly clipped. Answers to name of Dan. Liberal reward, no questions asked if returned to — Park Avenue."

Mr. Mott read this notice several times, and then he arose and went down the streets whistling cheerily to himself as if a great problem had been solved.

When Mrs. Crane, of No. — Park Avenue was called into the dining-room the next day, to see the man who had brought back her beloved Dan, she started back in horror at sight of a strange looking figure. Mr. Mott had decked himself for the occasion in a frock coat, shiny and ancient, which was too tight, and strained piteously at the buttonholes. In one hand, he held a fuzzy top-hat, in the other he was holding out to her a dog, a yellow dog, a dog, unmistakably a product of 'Steenth Street and 'Steenth Street environments.

"Why, that's not my dog," cried the lady indignantly.

"No, mum," replied Mr. Mott humbly.

"Go away from here," shrieked Mrs. Crane, "How dare you?"

"Ah, now, mum, you won't be so cruel. I jest wants an interview wid you. I knew dis wasn't your dog, but I wants to talk wid you."

"I don't want to talk with you," cried the mistress of the house. "Now you must go right away, or I'll call the butler."

"I wish you knew how great my responsibilities are," sighed Mr. Mott, "You wouldn't send me away."

"Poor man," said Mrs. Crane, softening. There were tears in Mr. Mott's voice. "Can I help you?"

"Ah, madam," sighed Mr. Mott again. He was silent for an eloquent moment, then he continued,

"I knew as soon as I saw your advertisement dat you was a good lady, an' I jest picks up dis ol' dawg so's I kin git a talk wid you."

The ingenuousness of the situation appealed to Mrs. Crane's sense of humor, and she smiled sympathetically, "Are you in trouble? Tell me."

Mr. Mott painted his case in glowing colors. Dell's sickness, her motherless condition, her convalescing desire to go to a ball, the first to which she had ever been invited. Mrs. Crane's heart was touched, and she wept, while Mr. Mott sighed over his responsibilities, and the yellow dog whimpered.

* * *

There was no question about it, Dell was the belle of the Firemen's Ball. Her pink silk dress, with its white lace trimmings was undeniably the richest fabric in the room. No one knew, of course save Mrs. McMahon, about the soiled place in front over which a ribbon had been draped, nor of the carefully taken-in seams, and shortened skirt, nor yet of the chalk cleaned slippers. It was a well-known fact, as has been stated before, that Dell's father could not afford her such a dress, so where?—wondered 'Steenth Street, when it saw her go forth to the ball. But Dell danced and was happy, and the yellow dog, restored to its owner, Frank Smith, knew, and Mr. Mott leaned against the wall at the ball, and sighed deeply at his responsibilities.

THE DOWNFALL
OF ABE POWERS*

It being almost Christmas time the attendance at the Pure in Heart bade fair to crowd out the five little rooms. It was the first Christmas that the Pure in Heart had seen and the teachers and leaders were agog with excitement. They meant that the first holidays should be a great event in the annals of 'Steenth Street. Thanksgiving had been only a moderate success, for the poor have so little to be thankful for, that the feast of the Puritans passed by almost unnoticed save for the closing of stores and schools. But Christmas in 'Steenth Street meant more, and even the very lowest ones felt little thrills of expectation whenever they gazed at the green wreaths in the windows, and saw the piny festoons in the warm glow of Mike McEneny's saloon on the corner of Third Avenue. Whether these expectations would be realized or not is a matter of speculation, but the thrills did not hurt, however.

Two weeks before the holiday season began, Mrs. Morton announced at the Sunday afternoon Bible class that there would be a Christmas tree during the holidays. This statement was received with a loud and enthusiastic murmur of applause.

"Of course," Mrs. Morton made haste to say, "we cannot expect to put gifts on our tree for everyone, but we shall try to remember those who have been faithful in attendance and more or less excellent in deportment."

A groan from Lesie Channing broke in at this point. Lesie

* Typescript.

knew that his attendance was perfect, but as for deportment, that to him was as one of the lost arts of the ancients.

"I expect," continued Mrs. Morton bestowing such a radiant smile on Lesie that he braced up and took fresh hold as it were, "that my boys and girls who have been constant since last February, will try to be patient with each other, kind in their manners, and keep ever in mind the real meaning of the season. Then we shall see about the Christmas tree."

No one but Mrs. Morton could have said such a thing. From another source such "softy" would have been jeered, but as you know, that lady's charming personality carried her over many a path so slippery that another, less magnetic, would have fallen down and floundered ignominiously.

The Sunday afternoon class was the most popular one of the week. Not that the subject under discussion appealed most to the habitues of the Pure in Heart, but there were no restrictions as to age or sex so that it was made up of the members of all the week classes; and then Sunday is a dull day in the winter, and the Mission rooms were warm and cheerful. So there was a large number to spread the news, and it was not an hour after Mrs. Morton's announcement that the report was circulated throughout the length and breadth of 'Steenth Street that "De Mission was a-goin' to give a blow-out fer Chrissmus."

Thus it was that Abe Powers, lounging careless ease before Dago Joe's little charcoal brazier, learned the news and pricked up his ears the while he meditatively chewed a peanut culled fresh and hot from the roaster. Dobson it was who spoke to him, standing in abject humiliation before this young aristocrat who could enjoy peanuts and bananas ad libitum undisturbed.

"Wot you t'ink?" he said at last, as Abe Powers made no reply to his announcement.

"It's a guy," said Abe slowly, "she's a givin' you a lot o' con to make you come to de ol' Mission."

"She ain't," cried Dobson, his loyalty to Mrs. Morton overcoming his diffidence in Abe's royal presence. "It's a straight tip."

"When she goin' ter have it?"

"Some time 'teen now an' de Noo year. Say, Abe, you come up agin."

Abe's sole response was a grim growl. In his secret heart, he had resolved to renew his allegiance, which he had allowed to lapse lately, but it would never do to let Dobson think himself possessed of too persuasive powers. He helped himself to another hot peanut, and conversation languishing between them, Dobson departed in quest of a more communicative companion.

On the following Tuesday night, the wood-carving class was crowded, and the dapper little Mr. Barry, opened wide his eyes at the great array of faces, new and old, which greeted him. Abe Powers was there, and with him Gus Schwartz and two or three others who had been dropped from the rolls for non-attendance. Also, were there many new boys, even from the far away precincts of the next street to which the news had spread. It mattered not that they would have to fight their way home that night. In a region of the city where churches were scarce and missions few and far between, the alluring prospect of a Christmas tree was not to be foregone for such a trivial thing as a fight or two.

It was plainly to be seen that Abe was making a great effort at good behavior. He had gone into the contest with determination and he had girded up his loins for the occasion.

This was literal. About the waist of the bulky coat, several sizes too large for him, he had put a school strap and drawn it up to the last notch. This was in evidence of good faith. Scrappy Franks was irreverent enough to make a remark about a sack tied in the middle, but beyond a sniff, and a contemptuous, withering glance, Abe vouchsafed no retort.

When the class was over, Abe was careful to go his way alone. To Dobson's cheerful war cry hurled against the new boys of the next street, he made no answer, and when the battle had begun on the corner of Second Avenue and was waging fiercely up towards the "El" station, he turned and ran home, not daring to trust himself within the sight of temptation.

So a week passed and the Mission continued to overflow. Never had there been such attendance; never such uniform order. Visitors, those whose consciences sent them "slumming" now and then with various results, and those in search of so-called sociological data, were delighted and made copious notes to be incorporated into papers and speeches before great societies. Mrs. Morton's face beamed, and on the following Sunday, she permitted herself to dwell a little succinctly on the glories of the Christmas tree, to the manifest delight of "de gang."

Abe's face alone was expressionless. He dared not hope. Deep within his soul, he longed for a sight of the great tree; for a gift from its branches. He had never seen a real "for true" tree. Those base imitations which are used for advertising purposes in stores he had seen, but the alluring gifts and tinsel ornaments among their branches were never given away, that he knew, therefore, he scorned them. But a tree in a house where the people received things from its branches, that was what he wanted to see, and he had determined to gratify his desire if he had to behave himself indefinitely. Also, but this he dared not hope for, there might be a present hidden away among the greeness and glitter for him.

He was leaning, as was his wont, against Dago Joe's peanut roaster in silent reverie one day, when he was accosted by Gus Schwartz.

"She says," began Gus, pointing a stubby thumb in the direction of three-twenty-two, "dat we kin help."

"Uh-huh," grunted Abe.

"Wanter to go in wid de gang?" Gus felt it necessary to do something heroic in order to keep his past misdemeanors forgotten, if possible. But Abe was a lonely soul, and he objected to having his meditations thus rudely broken into.

"Watcher goin' ter do?" he growled, however.

"Well, she says she ain't got no tree yet, an' us fellers, we kin git her one."

Here Dobson thrust his face into the rapidly growing circle of boys.

"Aw, garn," he said, "He's allus up to some tricks. He wants to swipe one from Macky's. See?"

"Naw, dat won't do," growled Abe. "Youse a great one, you is. T'ink she wants a swiped tree? You git out an' lemme lone." Abe turned away in disgust, and went back to his reveries.

The days went by uneventfully enough, and it was Christmas Eve. The Mission tree was not to be held until three days after Christmas. There was a deep reason for this, for the big missions downtown, who were rich and aristocratic, would have many leftover donations, which they could send to their poor little sister uptown. But of this, of course, 'Steenth Street knew nothing.

There was a holiday frostiness about the air, and Abe shivered a bit as he turned up his coat collar, albeit he whistled cheerily, he scarce knew why. In some mysterious, subtle way, the spirit of the season had gotten into his heart, and he was happy in his little way. He bestowed an affectionate glance on Mary McMahon as he passed her, and leaving her to turn her head away in pretended scorn, he refrained from kicking Willie Smith and strolled adown his way.

And then he saw a sight which made him stand still and give a snort of disgust. There was a fast gathering crowd coming from Third Avenue. It was a hooting crowd, and in it, Abe saw many members of "de gang." He did not need to look at the central figure to know who it was. A queer little sickening thump in his breast told him that, and the snort of disgust was but an outward express of an inner heartache.

Mary McMahon's head was tossed in real scorn now.

"Say, de ol' woman's got 'em again," she snickered.

Abe gave her a wrathful glance and strode determinedly toward his mother, pushing the boys out of his way with no gentle touch. They fell away from his sullen face and blazing eyes, but not without certain terse remarks about the matter.

"Aw, come on," he growled, taking his mother by the arm, "can't you see dese guys ain't got no manners? Git in de house."

At the sound of her son's voice, Mrs. Powers waxed tearful and wept in deep, maternal sorrow that her only child should address her publicly in such a manner. With a firm hand he guided her into the dark hall of three-forty-six, and up a flight of stairs into their one disordered room. There were cries of "Shame!" to follow him up the stairs, and the loud inconsequential laughter from many voices, but in a little while they were safe within their own four walls, and Abe drew a deep breath of relief.

He sat down beside the bed on which his mother had

thrown herself and listened to her drunken snores with fast rising anger. A gloom of hopelessness and misery was settling upon his spirit as the dusk settled over the once bright day. He plunged his hands into his pockets, and gave himself up to bitter wonderings. Just why "de ol' woman" should live nine tenths of her time in a state of liquor was beginning to be a big query with him.

Then Fate, in the shape of the Rev. Mr. Collier, knocked at the door. Abe growled a "Come in," thinking it one of the neighbor women. When the gaunt form of the Rev. Collier appeared on the threshold and his white lawn tie gleamed in the gathering dusk, Abe rose angrily.

"Aw, wot yer want?"

The Rev. Mr. Collier was the pastor of a little long-forgotten church several squares away. His real pastoral duties were light, for the members of his church were few and irregular in attendance. Now and then a vague idea of doing good would stir within him, and he would go to and fro over the territory of the Pure in Heart, and with tactlessness and platitudes, wreak untold havoc which Mrs. Morton would have to spend months repairing. He stood irresolute now at Abe's challenge, but finally entered the room.

"What's the matter with your mother?" he inquired gently.

"Aw, can't you see? She's sick," said Abe.

He spoke glibly enough, but Mr. Collier was not to be put off.

"My good boy," he said, "I fear you are telling me an untruth."

"Wot if I am?" demanded Abe. "Yes, de ol' woman's drunk. Now git!"

"My son," pursued Mr. Collier settling himself into a chair, "You see before you the evil influence of drink. Let it be a lesson to you as long as you live. Never touch a drop of liquor. You see what it has brought your dear mother to. Now promise me—"

"I ain't gointer promise you nuttin'," cried Abe shrilly, "Wot yer takes me fer, eh? Now you git out o' here, I tells yer."

Mr. Collier was surprised into rising. "My child," he began plaintively.

"I ain't no child o' yourn," shrilled Abe again. He paused in the center of the darkening room panting. There was a heartbeat of silence, broken by a sonorous snore from the unnoticed figure on the bed. The sound seemed to rouse Abe to a fury, and with a yell of defiance, he threw himself on the clergyman.

"Now, you git out o' here," he screamed, "you got no right to come here a-preachin'." He was biting, fighting, scratching, kicking, all the while pushing the gaunt man to the door. The Rev. Mr. Collier beat a rather ignominious retreat, carrying away a battered hat and a wondering state of mind. When he was fairly out of the door, Abe slammed and locked it, and throwing himself across the bed beside his mother, sobbed to himself sullenly.

He felt that it was all over for him. He had tried so hard to keep straight for the Christmas tree; he had even refrained from stealing Dago Joe's peanuts, and he had not been in a fight for two whole weeks. He had been looking forward so to the day, and now, the old woman must get drunk, and this man come and preach to him. He felt that Mrs. Morton would hear of it, and throw him out of the pale of the favored ones, and he groaned aloud. There would be no Christmas for him tomorrow, he had not expected any, but there had been hopes for three days after.

"De game's all up now," he said slowly, and so fell asleep.

A ray of sunshine across his face next morning awakened him, and he sat up, stiff and cold and miserable. His mother still slept, and without bestowing a second glance in her direction, he strode out and down into the sunny street. Someone shouted a "Merry Christmas" to him, and kind-hearted Mrs. McMahon, knowing of the night before, asked him in to breakfast. He growled an affirmative to the invitation, although he still felt sore against Mary, but strode first down the street to the sacred doors of three-twenty-two.

That afternoon, Mrs. Morton found a well-thumbed note for her on her desk. It ran,

"Dere Miss Morton, I beat Mr. coller an put him out becos he talked too much an i dont see why we has to be bothered when our mothers is drunk an if you wil plese forgive me an let me come to the tree i will be gode.

signed Abe Powers."

And Mrs. Morton forgave and put a present for him on the tree, although she read a lecture the following Sunday on disrespect for older persons. Abe heard, and was mute, though Scrappy Franks received a punishing from his hands for hinting that the lecture was aimed at one Abe Powers.

THE REVENGE
OF JAMES BROWN *

It was a great day in 'Steenth Street. The tenements and alleys and shops had entered their contents on the sidewalks, on the fire-escapes and in the windows. Something of more than

---

* Published as a young people's story by the Methodist Episcopal Church, 1929.

usual interest was undoubtedly going on. It was not a fight, for there was no excess of jubilation in the chatter of the throng. Banjo Liz was not on a tear again, for there would have been the sound of many voices down in the saloon, with the clattery bang of a banjo pounding on some one's head. There was a sound of horses' hoofs on the cobble-stones, but it was not the familiar rattle of the ambulance, the police or the fire patrol. It was a new sound, the soft rumble of rubber tires and the high-stepping of pampered horses. There was nothing familiar to the denizens of 'Steenth Street. Aristocracy had invaded its sacred precincts and was trying to establish a precedent down near Third Avenue. Aristocracy in silk-lined gowns was walking in and out among the babies and dirty little folks swarming on the curbstones. 'Steenth Street felt itself disgraced and intruded upon. It gave a sniff of contempt and pretended not to be interested, the while its eyes and ears were agog with curiosity and its lips awry with inquiry.

"Hully, gee!" cried Abe Powers, his eyes bulging with excitement, "but ain't she a thoroughbred!"

This was apostrophizing a silk-lined, violet-scented one from the other side of the city, who, alighting from one of the rubber tired vehicles, passed gingerly into the doors of No. Three-twenty-two.

There were more of her kind who went in and some of less thoroughbred qualities who came a-foot. No. Three-twenty-two was the point of interest for the eyes of 'Steenth Street and the stoop and areaway were soon thronged with folks—big ones and little ones—whose necks craned in as the doors opened and whose faces bore mingled expressions.

"An' phwat do they be sittin' up a mission fur?" demanded Mrs. McMahon. "Sure, it's not me, but them wot wurrks out wot needs it." Mrs. McMahon spoke not too loudly, for Mrs. Brown stood near and Mrs. Brown, in addition to being one of the despised class, was—well, she was Jimmy Brown's mother, and if that means nothing to you, why, you'll have to visit 'Steenth Street and there make inquires.

"Now, dey t'inks dey's doin' some'p'n," contemptuously remarked Jimmy Brown, "I wonder who dey s'pose is a going' ter be foolin' roun' here wid dey bible talk?"

"Mebbe dey'll give socials an't'ings," ventured Scrappy Franks.

"Well, dey gotter start mighty soon, er I'll brick-bat 'em onct, an' let 'em see, we ain't stuck on em."

Inside three-twenty-two was a great rejoicing. That is, inside of portion of three-twenty-two on the right. There were five small, stuffy, unventilated, grotesquely furnished rooms, packed to overflowing with humanity in various stages of poverty and wealth. The Pure in Heart mission was being opened with great eclat.

The half dozen earnest women who were responsible for its being felt that they had scored a great point in having present several shining lights of upper-tendom, noted for their charitable proclivities, and the shining lights felt that in lending their presence to the occasion they were scoring two points in their own favor in heaven. So all were satisfied. Below the silk-lined violet-perfumed, and the black-robed and earnest women, was a sprinkling of the substratum for which the mission was designed. Thin, hungry-looking women in strange gowns; stout, overworked women with fretful babies; flashy young women in cheap picture hats, and fidgety children in soiled pinafores.

The leader of the movement was a nervous, energetic woman with a white, sorrow-drawn face, and a voice of caressing monotonous sweetness. She was talking to the assembled crowd about the mission, its inception, its need and its aims. Her talk was lengthy and the children fidgeted worse

than ever. But it was interesting to the older ones to follow
the plan out; how from a mother's meeting here and there,
an informal house to house gathering, the little band of
women had made bold to rent the flat, and begging the
incongruous furniture from various sources, had at last announced themselves ready to begin the task of soul-saving,
child-training and mother-helping.

When the talk was over a little woman sang a hymn,
accompanying herself on the organ; tea was passed around,
the five little rooms peered into, and the Pure in Heart
mission was launched out upon the sea of missionary labor to
take its chances with the tides and shoals which beset all such
craft.

Now, when the last of the visitors had departed, and the
black-robed leaders, too, had left the five rooms in the care
of Mr. William Montmorency Briggs, who was to act as
janitor and lord high keeper of the treasures of the mission,
'Steenth Street settled down to its customary routine, and the
Pure in Heart was, for the nonce, forgotten. There were
other things to do, a fight to be looked after, a cop to be
outwitted, the hucksters to be attended to. 'Steenth Street did
not allow itself long to be disturbed by any one occurrence.
After the first day's wonder, and the few emotions aroused
the first week by the sight of some of its denizens attending
the mission's meetings, 'Steenth Street, as a whole, lapsed
into passive acceptance of the new phase of life opening up
in three-twenty-two. Let as a whole be used advisedly, for
there was a part, a small part, however, which availed itself
of the mission's meetings, and went to them and remained
after to receive what benefits might be distributed. Upon this
part, 'Steenth Street looked, when it thought of the matter at
all, with contempt, mingled with derision and disgust.

But with Jimmy Brown, there were no words too strong

to express his feelings concerning the work of three-twenty-two. He was the leader of the band of whom it was variously said that they were bound either for the island or the chair. 'Steenth Street was noted as the resort of every kind of wickedness, and vice stalked abroad in the light of day unmolested. Jimmy was proud of the reputation of his neighborhood, and for emissaries of the gospel to come into its precincts and establish a "joint" seemed to him an insult too vile to be regarded lightly or impassively. The mission became to him a thing, alive, breathing and alert. He felt keenly the disgrace that had been brought to his neighborhood, and he felt it his duty to slay the giant that had started up and sown the teeth of discord.

You will understand all the more how keenly this responsibility weighed on him when you know that Jimmy was just thirteen years old. But a famous captain was he, and his henchmen came ever to his bidding, never stopped to inquire why or how. Therefore did Jimmy lay dark plans for the undoing of the giant, with the aid of his confederates. It was on one bitter day in March that Scrappy Franks deserted. Abe Powers saw him coming out of three-twenty-two with a woollen comforter about his neck and haled the delinquent before Jimmy, holding court in the cellar of No. three-twenty-two. He fixed Scrappy with a scornful eye and vouchsafed no remark save a scornful "Psst!"

"Ah, youse go on," said Scrappy, "youse kin say, 'psst,' but I gits de woollen comfort, see?"

Jimmy laughed derisively. "I say, fellers, he's one o' de goodies now," he howled. But within him Jimmy's heart ached at the defection of one of his trusted followers to the enemy.

Verbal argument, to Scrappy, was a waste of time, so he

began to defend his case with his hands. There was a mass of legs and arms in the cellar, many howls and a once bright-hued comforter torn into bits and distributed among "de gang" as souvenirs; and Scrappy went forth into the world, comfortless and disgraced, the mark of the deserted on his brow and the lack of warmth about his neck.

It was about this time that Buddy, the youngest of the Brown household, was taken ill with the chickenpox. Jimmy expressed his disgust when Buddy's howls and moans kept him awake in the night, by a muttered, "Kids has allus got some'p'n." Buddy was aged 18 months and between him and Willie, aged 6, there was a sympathy as great as the enmity between them and Jimmy. Therefore when Buddy wailed in the chill darkness of the night because the disease was sore upon him, Willie wailed for sympathy and Jimmy relieved his feelings by punching the curly little head close to his own in the hard bed which they shared. Buddy's chickenpox cast a gloom upon the entire family, or at least, Jimmy ascribed the sorrows which fell upon them to Buddy and his love for that infant waxed less in consequence. He knew that "de ol' man wuz outer wo'k" and drinking heavily, but attached no importance to such an everyday occurrence.

When on one Thursday evening Jimmy came to the one dirty downstairs room that he called home and found Buddy's wailings louder than usual, Willie, tear choked and big-eyed and his mother sitting up in a corner disheveled and miserable, his anger grew large and vented itself in one large expletive. There was no supper, no fire and Jimmy was hungry and cold.

"Aw, where's de ol' man?" he demanded in disgust. When women and children are wailing it is meet that men should take council together and escape the hubbub they raise.

His mother's reply was almost inaudible for sobs, but from the incoherence Jimmy gathered that the paternal one was over at the saloon. The obvious unfairness of this drew from him another terse remark. At the saloon the men could, for five cents, get both food and refreshment, while the women and children were debarred.

"Well, ain't you got nuttin' to eat?" he asked, giving Willie a sly kick under the table. A louder cry from the kicked one and a sullen shake of his mother's head were the only reply. Then, after a minute's silence, Mrs. Brown gathered herself for the fray she knew was coming.

"Jimmy, she began, "you see we ain't got no vittles?" Jimmy grunted assent. "An' Buddy's gettin' wuss; I'm 'fraid he's goin' ter die," and her wailing broke out afresh. Jimmy considerately refrained from saying "Good!" He kicked absently at the leg of a chair. Cold, hunger and disgust had produced apathy.

"There's the mission," said Mrs. Brown, with a gulp.

"Aw, wot you t'ink de mission'll do? Who you t'ink goin' up ter the mission?"

"Well, they helps. Mis' Franks sez they gives you things when you're poor."

"You keep erway f'um de mission, I tell yer. You ain't a-goin' ter git nuthin' dere."

He was telling what he knew was a fib, because his sense of diplomacy told him that it was the only to keep the disgrace from invading his family.

"Well, you git to wu'k and bring in some'p'n."

"Aw, tell dat to de ol' man. He's on a spree. I ain't."

The scarred, feverish child in the corner of the room moaned pitifully, and the sound of its feeble gasps roused Mrs. Brown to a sense of fury. The mother in her arose twofold. She felt the necessity of protecting one child from starvation and of compelling the other to obedience.

"You git right outer here, Jimmy Brown," she cried shrilly, "an' go to the mission an' ask 'em to come down here an' see ef they can do some'p'n."

A hot mist of shame and pride and anger, unspeakable, arose before Jimmy's eyes. "What, go over to the enemy in this way." He set his brow sullenly, and snarled:

"I won't do it, neither!"

"Jimmy Brown, I'm a-talkin' to yer!"

"Aw, rats."

But the maternal will was strong and the maternal arm stronger. Jimmy was spanked, ignominiously, unreservedly, spanked, and Willie chuckled with glee, unholy and unnecessary. Then was the leader of "de gang" thrust forth into the sleet and bidden to obey. He must go down to hateful three-twenty-two and there, because on Thursdays was a mothers' meeting, lay his mother's case before "dem wimmen." A vision of being hauled over by a lot of women folks, of being cross-questioned and forced to tell all about his father's shortcomings, rose and choked him. The pride of family was strong in him and it grieved him sore to have to lay bare to the world, and a world of women who neither knew nor cared, all their pitiful affairs. He raged within himself, and stood stubbornly in the door of the tenement house, resolved not to move, no matter what came of it.

But the street was cold, wet, and deserted. The wind from the East River blew gusty spirals of sleet into the doorways and Jimmy's ragged jacket was painfully inadequate. Over at McEneny's saloon warm lights streamed out and the occasional opening of the door sent forth sounds of cheer and maudlin happiness. The boy thought with disgust of his father over there, drunk and filled with free lunch. The pride he had always felt in the man's capacity for liquor faded into a comprehension of the selfishness of him who left his off-spring to beg. He shivered and strode doggedly down the street. He would go to the mission, for, after all, it was not for himself, and the dread of the maternal arm was still strong, but he would die rather than touch their food. Then he stopped again. How could he ever face the boys? If he explained that he was beaten and made to go, they would cry shame at a boy of thirteen who allowed his mother to spank him. Tears ran down his cheek, tears of shame, anger, hunger, pride. He put up his hand and wiped them angrily away, then looking about to be sure that none of his compan-ions saw him, he ran excitedly into the door of three-twenty-two.

When the ordeal of his interview was over and the good women of the mission had gone with food, fire and comfort to the relief of Mrs. Brown, Jimmy started down Third Avenue, his hands deep in his pockets, his head tucked down to avoid the blasts of wind that rushed up the street. They, the folks, at home, could defile themselves by eating of the food which he begged. Not he. His old hatred of the mission and desire to wreak confusion upon it was dark in his mind. He pondered a plan, but none came. His helplessness smote on him. Then, like a flash, he comprehended a scheme. He would find some means of keeping his mother from accepting its bounty; he would disgust her and through her, others, and the mission would fail ignominiously because it would cease to be called upon for aid. The idea of work, a new one, by the way, entered his mind. He would be revenged upon his mother for her weakness. He would get work to do and eat henceforth without consulting her.

Jimmy did not go home that night, but Mrs. Brown had her hands so full of the baby and the hilarious Mr. Brown, who aroused every one in the house by insisting upon sleeping in the hall, that she did not miss him much. Buddy was better, however, next day and Mr. Brown had departed on a quest for work, when a hubbub down the street near Third Avenue, attracted her from the doorway. Jimmy was fighting his way fiercely, but steadily toward her. His henchmen had turned on him, for when the rumor had come to them that the Brown family were being helped by the mission, they had laid in wait for him and twitted him. But when at his appearance at the corner he was approached, he only said scornfully, "Aw, git out; I'm wu'kin' now." Thereupon they rose to beat him for his twofold defection.

"Where have you been?" demanded Mrs. Brown, fixing him sternly with her eyes, when he had vanquished the last of his assailants.

"I got a job," was the reply, "feller tuk me in las' night and I gotter look after his store."

Mrs. Brown allowed a smile to cross her visage. Jimmy swaggered back in the hall to their room and even poked Buddy with a pudgy forefinger in token of his delight. His revenge was complete. He had shown his mother what her lack of pride had driven him to. Now, she would let the mission alone. She might eat its bread, but he would work first.

As for Mrs. Brown, she was a wise woman and did not enlighten Jimmy as to her opinion on the subject.

OTHER STORIES:
A MISCELLANY

ON THE BAYOU BRIDGE*

The Bayou St. John winds its languid way to the lake. In its dark bosom many secrets lie buried. It is like some beautiful serpent, langurous, sinister. It ripples in the sunshine, sparkles in the moonlight, glooms in the dusk and broods in the dark. But it thinks unceasingly, and below its brightest sparkle you feel its unknown soul. It is silent; not once does it betray the secrets it knows. Looking upon it for the first time, you would shudder because you feel what lies beneath the brown waters.

A man and a woman walked by its silent stream in the gathering dusk of a Sunday evening. Long, red streaks in the water struck the farewell note of a tropical sunset. They walked hand in hand, their eyes fixed on the distant sky.

They had left behind them Esplanade Street with its crowd of gay Sunday idlers, and struck out on the shell-road leading to Spanish Fort. They had passed the retreat of the gray-coated veterans and the houses grew scattered. Reeds, swaying in the wind, showing glistening spots between, told that the marsh land was stretching its hands towards them. They walked on silently, their eyes fixed on the distant sky.

The man spoke first. "Do you think we are wise to go any farther? You will be fatigued, and we can reach no cars to take us home."

She clasped her hands on his arm and implored him piteously. "Ah, ma chere amie, but one leetle w'ile mo'. Eet is fo' the las' time."

*Typescript, written between 1902 and 1909.

147

He shrugged his shoulders, and slowed his pace imperceptibly. Her hand stole around his neck.

"Eet is fo' the las' time? Ah, you do not say non? Tell me?"

Again he shrugged his shoulders.

"Answer me!" her tones challenged. He looked down at
her with indifference.

"It may be. Can I tell?"

They paused; the long red streaks in the water faded and
deepened, like streams of blood on the surface of the water.

"Can you tell? Mais, oui, do you not know? Do you not
know whether you weel walk wit' me or wit' her? You say to
me, eet weel be our las' time, fo' you go to-morrow. Go,
yaas, but w'ere? You have not said, but I know, I know. You
are false to me."

He plunged his hands into his pockets, withdrawing them
as he did so, rather roughly from her grasp:

"Listen to reason, Thalié."

"Non, non, thare ees no raison. You love me an' I love
you. You are mine, mine, do you not know? Thare ees no
mo' to say. Mais, you weesh fo' to go, to anothare wooman,
fo' w'y? Because you are afraid."

He shook his shoulders as one who is hearing an old
argument which he feels it futile to answer. They had turned
and were slowly stepping back into the cold gray of the east.

There was silence, then he spoke slowly.

"I am not afraid, Thalié, to stay with you. It is not fear
that makes me go, it is duty, that's all."

"Duty!" she sneered, "Eh, moi, w'en duty comes in,
pouf—with love. You are cold, cold to talk of duty w'en yo'
heart says love. Eet weel brake my heart—oh, Edouard,
Edouard—" she threw her arms about him passionately and
strained close to him with maddening caresses. "Eet weel keel
me, I mus' love you an' have yo' love."

He stroked her hair with gentle coldness, and put her arms away from his neeck. His quiet self-control awakened a fury in her.

"What right have you to leave me, now? Am I not yo's? Are you not mine? Are you not bound to me by ties which you mus' not break? Ah, Edouard, no one weel understan' you lak me. No one can, pas possible. Mais, with me—I weel be all that she can be an' mo', oh, so much mo'. You weel laugh, w'en you think you almos' los' me. You weel love me so—" The fury died into the tender little coo of the French woman, and she nestled close to him.

He put his arm about her shoulder and stroked it gently. But he quickened his steps into the eastern gray.

"C'est impossible," he breathed softly.

Her lithe figure drooped for an instant; then it stiffened into a rigidity that meant purpose or despair. He was relieved.

They had reached the bridge at the end of Esplanade Street. The lamps were not yet lighted, and darkness hovered in the east, threatening the Bayou.

"Shall we wait here for a car?" he asked, and she assented briefly.

He leaned against the open railing of the bridge and gazed into the brooding waters below. On the distant banks a hoarse cry like a waiting death croaked from the reedy home of an alligator.

She began to speak, slowly at first, then choking with rapid utterance.

"Lis'en to me. You come heah two, t'ree month ago; I fo'git, no mattah. You come to me, seeck and pitiful, an' I care fo' you. Mon Dieu, I love you as soon as I see you. I have no one to love but my seester, my leetle seester so far away, an' I wo'k, wo'k wo'k to help her, because she study an' I mus' help her. Then you come, an' you smile at me;

ah, bon, Dieu, eet ees lak wine. I mos' fo'git ma petite soeur, she I love better than God almos'. She I would geeve my heart's las drop fo', but I mos' fo'git her w'en you come. Then one night, you put yo' arms aroun' me, an' kees me, an' I know heaven. Seence then I pray to you instid of le bon Dieu, seence then, I follow you night an' day, since then I have no life but what I geet f'om you. Ah, Edouard—"

She pressed close to him, clinging, appealing. He pushed his form back close to the open railing, breathing heavily.

"An' now, you weel go to her, to someone else an' fo'git me, but no one weel evah love you lak me. You are mine, do you understan'?"

An open car dashed past them on the bridge; a furious whirl of brilliant lights, fluffy, gay dresses; a rushing mingle of chatter and song and clanging gong. They had forgotten to signal it, and he was disagreeably conscious that there would be no other for a half hour.

"Edouard, Edouard, say you love me."

She shook him gently, both hands on his shoulders.

"No, I do not love you."

He spoke slowly through set teeth as if with a grim purpose.

"Ah—" a wild animal feeling pain for the first time cries as she did.

"I have never loved you."

She covered her face with her hands, and he could feel her tremble in the gloom.

"You were good to me when I was ill and weak, and I respected you for it and admired you and am grateful to you, but I have never loved you."

"But you keesed me—you tol' me that night—"

"No, Thalié, my dear, you are mistaken." He took her

hands, cold, trembling, piteous into his own. "That night in the moonlight I leaned toward you accidentally and you threw your arms about my neck and kissed me, telling your love for me."

"Ah—" she struggled from his clasp and choked in rage, "Do—you—tell me—"

"Thalié, think, think, remember. I have not said once, 'Thalié, I love you, Thalié, be mine.' I have been true to her who shall be nameless between us."

"You made me believe—"

"I have flirted with you, perhaps, I am sorry, but I have not lied to you."

"Eet ees as bad," she flamed, "eet ees worse. You ruin my life, yet you save your honeur too." She laughed shortly.

"I shall go back to her to-morrow. I have not betrayed her nor you. You have led yourself into a delusion, Thalié."

"You shall never go back to her!"

He started, then laughed quietly.

"Let us not be melodramatic, Thalié," he said lightly.

For answer, she flung her lithe body at him with the concentrated force and passion of a springing wild-cat. Her long fingers wound themselves around his neck like steel cords. He gasped and was silent.

In the struggle, the thin crust of civilization was torn off with a wrench of the hand. Life became elemental, primordial. Man fought for life, and life alone; woman fought that which she claimed in a passion of maternity might be no other's if not hers. When he saw that the struggle tended towards his death, he would have forced her into the stream, but he was too weak from the long steel fingers clasped around his throat.

There was a rushing darkness of form flying through the

open railing; a gurgle, a sullen splash. The waters of the
Bayou parted an instant, then flowed languidly on to the lake.

She looked down upon them. "Ah," she said triumphantly.
Then she fled blindly up the somber deserted street. Her
long black hair, loosed in the struggle, streamed behind her.
When a lock touched her forehead, she shuddered as at an
arresting hand.

A square ahead she saw a lighted corner where stood a
chatttering Sunday crowd. The sight restored her to her
senses and she paused in the darkness to bind up her hair and
smooth her dress.

"He is mine," she said triumphantly, "Let her wait fo'
heem."

Then she walked swiftly, proudly, out into the circle of
light. The car was coming; it had crossed the bridge and
whizzed toward her. It was the one they would have taken
together.

She stepped into a group of friends who welcomed her
with shouts of delight, "Thalié, Thalié, Thalié!" they cried,
but she was silent.

One brilliant eyed girl leaned forward and said loudly.
"You friend, Edouard, he left yesterday, n'est-ce-pas?"

She nodded assent, still silent.

The crowd chattered with glee, "She does not know, she
does not know. We do, we do. We have found out!"

She grew cold with a grisly fear, and strained to listen to
the brilliant eyed girl.

"Did he ever tell you the name of his fiancée?" She shook
her head.

"It is not the same as yours, for she is only your stepsister."

"Ma petite soeur?" Her voice was hoarse like the cry of
the alligator with death in its tones.

And the crowd chattered, "Yes, yes, yes, he did not know and you did not know, but we have just found out from his friend who has come."

The Bayou St. John winds its languid way to the lake. In its dark bosom many secrets lie buried.

NATALIE*

Natalie swung herself down from the breakwater to the white sands below, and walked along on the edge of the sea, her feet leaving prints that filled with water, and were quickly effaced. She swung her brown arms in the fading sunset light, and sniffed the whiffs of salt air with keenly appreciative nostril, swinging as she trotted along with long, clean-limbed step. Natalie was happy in her little sunset world down here by the water's edge.

Suddenly she paused and her big black eyes widened angrily. Someone had invaded her territory and was coming towards her.

Down here on the sands at this edge of the beach was Natalie's own kingdom, and woe unto the trespasser who dared within its boundaries. At Mandeville, you know, there are places where the fickle Lake Ponchartrain encroaches too frequently and too violently upon the homes of men, therefore, it has to be kept back by stoutly built breakwaters, as its no less turbulent cousin, the Mississippi river is kept from swamping New Orleans across the way by levees. Then, too, there are spots here and there where the lake kisses the shores in regulation beach-like manner, or mingles with swamp and

* Typescript, written before 1898.

bayou over morass and tangled moss thicket. When the tide was low, one might walk on the sands below until the beachy places were found. Down here at the West End of the town, the natives called Natalie's kingdom because of the absolute sway she exercised over those sands and marshes and little beauty spots of scenery and waves.

Walking towards her now on the sunset lighted sands, evidently taking great delight in wetting her delicate slippers, came a fair-haired, rose-tinted creature, in an ethereal film of fluffy lawn and flower-covered hat. Natalie surveyed her curiously. She knew the type well; the delicate summer boarder who came to idle time away, was afraid of everything under the sun, and generally treated Natalie either with supercilious indifference or with contemptuous patronage. She knew them and hated them accordingly. But this one must be of a different kind, else how did she get down that perilous climb, and why was she unaccompanied by maid or mother? The newcomer was also surveying Natalie with admiration plainly depicted in her eyes.

Contrary to her usual custom, the queen approached the trespasser and said, "Who are you and what are you doing here?" She spoke in French, and the blonde shook her head and said sadly,

"You'll have to speak English."

Natalie's self-importance rose in a corresponding degree as the girl's eyes surveyed her healthful frame with wonderment, and she repeated the question in a mixture of bad English and gestures.

Olivia replied that her family had moved into the house at the corner for the summer. The big house hidden in red roses and magnolia trees.

"The Torrés house?" asked Natalie.

Olivia nodded her head wisely, and discussing the beauties of the place, they walked along the sunset sands. They had just reached the stage when confidences were in progress, when a sharp voice above their heads caused them to look up. They were passing beneath the fishing wharf of the house, and a fretful looking, over-dressed lady with a white lace parasol was leaning over the railing.

"Olivia!" she screamed sharply, "What are you doing down there? Come up here this minute."

Olivia started nervously; it was evident that she was afraid of her mother.

"How can I get up?" she inquired.

"You'll have to climb, yes," said Natalie, "cause the nearest slope is a leetle more than a half mile down."

So boosted up by Natalie's strong, bared arms, and clinging to the scrubby bushes that grew through the cracks of the breakwater, Olivia gained the beach smiling, flushed, triumphant, only to be met with a scowl on the face of the over-dressed lady.

"What do you mean," she said sharply, "by acting like a regular tomboy, and running about with such a person already?"

Olivia hung her head, but said nothing, only walked into the house, and sat on her father's knee.

"Papa," she spoke slowly, and with tears in her eyes, "I climbed down the breakwater just now, and met such a nice girl on the sands. She's what they call a 'Cajan' here; awfully pretty, and nice, and so smart, papa! She speaks such good French, I didn't dare answer her in anything but English. Her name is Natalie Leblanc, and she lives down where the bayou meets the lake. She told me that she never liked summer boarders because they were always so stuck-up, but she liked me, because I seemed to have some sense. And she's so healthy, papa, and strong, why she almost lifted me over the breakwater. And, papa, please sir, mayn't I go with her? She says she'll show me all the beauty places, and teach me how to swim and row and fish and all that."

"Whew!" replied Mr. Spiers, "you two must have flown into each other's arms to have learned all that."

"She's a nice girl, papa; her grandmother is her only relative, and she's a neat girl to be so poor."

"And did you find out how old this prodigy was?"

"Just my age, papa, fourteen years, only you'd never think so. She's so much taller and stouter than I am."

At the supper table that night, Mr. Spiers said to his wife, "Carrie, I want you to let Olivia take off those fancy clothes and get some blood in her face; she looks like a wax doll. Let her run and jump and climb and get sunburned. It'll do her good."

"Gracious me, John," exclaimed Mrs. Spiers, "you'll have the child a regular hoyden; when will she learn dignity?"

"Six years from now is time enough. I hate these little old women that are coming up now. Let her go with the natives, they'll teach her more healthy topics of conversation than that fashionable city set."

Olivia said nothing, but her pale little face lighted with pleasure, and she flashed a grateful look at her father across the table. Next morning, Mr. Spiers went back to the city, and the family settled in their beautiful, rose-embowered, rambling old home for the summer.

Natalie was swinging dreamily on her front gallery in a hammock made of barrel staves and sacking. A peaceful noonday silence hung over all save for the persistent trilling of a mockingbird in the moss-laden old oak tree, and an occasional hoarse grunt from an alligator in the black waters of the bayou. The persimmon tree shook a shower of snowy fragrant blossoms at its foot, as the breezes that came from Nott's Point swept its branches. It was a quaint little, one-sided house, shingle-roofed, and moss-covered, its gray sides guiltless of paint. But the wide gallery that went all around the house was scrubbed white, and sprinkled after the good old fashion, with white sand, while the walk that led from the battered gate was sanded carefully, swept clean, and bordered with precise rows of poppies and larkspurs. Natalie's eyes closed as she dreamily answered the mockingbird's trills with snatches of a Creole melody.

A timid knock roused her to a standing position, and there half opening the gate, stood Olivia.

"Entrez, entrez!" cried Natalie impulsively, "Oh, mais, ma foi, you look nice, you seem sensible now," with an approving glance at Olivia's gingham dress, white sunbonnet and sand shoes. "Stay with me all the day, yes, and we shall have such fun, such a nice time, yes, we will."

So Olivia stayed, and was introduced to the grandmother Mme. Leblanc, very old and dignified and gentle. She was escorted proudly around the big yard with its duck pond and plum orchard; initiated into the mysteries of the artesian well. In Mandeville, you know, slow little town as it is, everyone uses the artesian well in preference to anything else, so that every one has most clear, cold, and sparkling water at all times. This one of Natalie's fell into a big stone basin, overgrown with scarlet creepers, and waterlillies on the clear pool. Upon the stone beneath the trickling stream there was a glass, and Natalie explained how glasses could be colored by simply letting them stay under the action of the water for a day, then the sulphur and iron would turn the white into a

clear amber with iridescent lights throughout. Within the
old-fashioned kitchen there were many glasses which Natalie
had colored, and nothing more daintily clear could be imagined.

This was only the beginning of a close intimacy between
the girls. There were long rambles down the bayou shores
into the piney woods, delicious swings on the branches of the
old oak, that stood sentinel-like over the water's edge, intimacies with the quaint Indians in the St. Tammany settlement;
rowings around the lake's edges and up the bayou in a dory,
singing French songs that Natalie could make sound so
prettily; swims in the brown lake water; a healthy brownness
in Olivia's face, and a pleased sparkle about Natalie in the
newfound affection that was so strange to her.

But she could not be induced to visit Olivia's home at the
Torrés place. "Madame, your maman, cares not for me," she
would say in response to Olivia's entreaties to come to the
house, "and I think it better to stay away. You come to me,
we will be happy, yes."

When Mr. Spiers came over on the steamer Saturday
evening to stay until Monday morning, nothing pleased him
better than to see his "little country girl" so healthy, though
the stylish mother grieved to see the unfashionable tan on the
girl's cheeks.

One day, however, Natalie wanted Olivia for a piney
woods ramble to gather pine cones which would be made into
picture frames. So with bonnet and basket, she swallowed her
pride, and trudged up the beach to the Torrés place. Mrs.
Spiers leaned over the picket fence with a bored expression
and a frown. It was dull in this unfashionable town with
nothing of interest save the daily watch for the arrival of the
New Camelia, which came puffing across the lake's bosom

every evening, the engine's arms working up and down with monotonous precision. One regatta of very miniature pro- portions, with a very tame hop at Colomés' hotel, a daily drive to the post office, with an occasional visitor constituted the round of pleasures for the season. Mrs. Spiers wanted to go home, but Olivia wanted to stay, and Olivia generally had her way with her father. Natalie's voice aroused Mrs. Spiers from an unpleasant reverie.

"Is Oleevia at home?"

She looked up crossly. "Olivia?" she said.

"Yes, madame," and Natalie gave her one of her most polite French bows, while Mrs. Spiers drew herself up haughtily.

"I think you are making a mistake," she said icily, "you probably mean *Miss* Olivia."

"Yes, madame, I mean Ma'amselle Oleevia Spiers."

At this moment, the subject of discussion tripped down the flower-lined walk of the old-fashioned garden.

"Oh, Natalie," she cried joyously, and would have kissed her friend, but the mother held her back.

"Do you mean to tell me, Olivia, that this—this—person calls you by your first name as if she were your equal? Do you permit that?"

Both girls' faces crimsoned; the one with a fair flush of mortification, the other with a darker tint of injured pride and anger.

"Mama—" began Olivia pleadingly, but Mrs. Spiers was thoroughly angry now.

"In the future, girl," she continued addressing Natalie, "I want you to call my daughter *Miss* Olivia. I require that of all inferiors."

Natalie's dark-tressed head rose proudly, "I am not an

inferior, madame," she replied, "in age and in education, I am Oleevia's equal, yes, and in birth, and breeding, I am superior to madame herself," and walked away proudly, swinging her gay-colored Indian basket with erect head, while Olivia burst into shamed tears, and was promptly hustled inside.

Natalie did not go to the woods to get the pine cones, but walked swiftly home and threw herself moodily into the homemade hammock.

"They are all alike," she mused, "these city people with their airs, and I was foolish to try and be friendly. Serves me right, yes. Mais, much as I like," clenching her fists, "I'd pop before I'd call her mademoiselle, ah, non, non!"

Thus ended the pleasant intimacy between the girls, and Natalie went on in her old way, rowing her dory into the bayou, and fishing for the beautiful trout in its black waters; queening it over the children in the village, and dreaming the hot hours of the day away in the hammock or under the big oak. On Sundays, she would meet Olivia at the quaint little old church on the back road, and smile pleasantly as she knelt to tell her beads, or bowed at the tinkling of the hoarse, little host-bell.

The summer passed away, and merged into the autumn months; the poppies blazed red in the gardens, and the goldenrod gleamed in the woods and hedges. From all sides sounded the crack of the hunter's rifle, and the crackling of dropping nuts on the brown leaves in the crisp, clear air. It was pecan threshing time, and all the small town was busy in the work of threshing the pecan trees and packing the long brown nuts into barrels for shipping. Natalie's time was so taken with helping to thresh trees, gathering in the autumn-tinted persimmons and paddling in the swampy lagoons to

shoot the small birds that flocked on the water's edge that
Olivia was almost forgotten.

It was on a Sunday evening that a strong southeast wind
came with a rush and roar over the angry waters of the lake
from Nott's Point, and sent the heavy swell booming high
against the breakwater. Natalie's little kingdom down on the
sands was completely submerged in about eight feet of water,
and the angry waves tossed up onto the shore, dashing clouds
of spray into the very houses.

All the population of Mandeville was out on the beach,
they dared not go on any pier, for every one of them, even
to the steamer landing seemed in imminent danger of being
swept away at any moment. Everyone was watching the brave
little New Camelia as she battled against the wind and waves
coming from Covington and the Tchefuncta river past
Mandeville on the way to New Orleans. Again and again,
shrilly tooting her displeasure did she skim around the landing, endeavoring to find a stopping place, but in vain, and
after a final shrill squeal, she started towards New Orleans,
now bounding high on the crest of a wave, now delving deep
into a trough, the engine arms frantically waving up and
down. Natalie, with heavy black hair, wind-blown and tangled stood in the midst of a crowd of her friends talking
loudly with the rest so as to be heard above the wind and
water, and at the same time furtively watching the evident
distress of Mrs. Spiers and Olivia, who stood apart and
wrung their hands with fright.

Everyone remembers until yet, that awful Sunday night.
How in the pitchy darkness the fearful southeast wind blowing
in the waters from the Gulf of Mexico through the Rigolets,
upturned immense centurion oaks, and crushed solid old
houses as though they were so many eggshells; how the cattle

bellowed as they were swept away into the writhing, tossing waters, and how on the Monday morning, when the slow daylight dawned over the frightened, praying town, it revealed a complete submergment of four feet, with natives perched in every possible place, and the angry lake still tossing its heavy swells over the crushed breakwater, and dashing logs, and wood, remnants of piers and bathhouses into one's very bedroom.

Natalie's house had escaped, and the water yet lacked three inches of being in the rooms; so cheerfully making the nervous grandmother comfortable, she took her dory from its place on the back gallery, and paddled out into the desolate, frightened Louisiana Venice to give her helping smile to the distressed natives, with offers of her home to those whom falling trees or wild waves had made homeless. Picking up struggling chickens from stray bushes, where bedraggled and wild-eyed they had sought refuge, and a mewing, clawing kitten, and piling them all in the stern, too frightened to fight with each other, she rowed up the canal that had once been the main street until she came to Olivia's house. A sudden impulse caused her to ship her oars, and look up into the windows where she saw Olivia's white, frightened face.

"Natalie," called the girl, and ran out on the gallery, while the dory paddled into the ruined yard, "Oh Natalie, mama is so frightened! She is wild to go home on the Camelia, see, it is coming over now, and Mr. Colomés and Mr. Mathias have all been here, telling her she can't possibly get to the boat, and she's having hysterics, and oh, Natalie, I'm *so* frightened!" and she clung to the dory wildly.

At that moment, Mrs. Spiers came out on the gallery followed by M'sieu Colomés, the hotel man, who with shrugs and gesticulations was saying,

"Madame, is ver' unwise, ver' unwise; mais, non, madame will surely drown if she attempts to catch the bateau."

But madame was determined, so with a final shrug at the perversity of "dose Americain," M'sieu Colomés jumped into his pirogue and paddled away in disgust, determining to wash his hands of the whole affair. Madame turned to Natalie with a despairing gesture.

"You can row, Natalie," she pleaded, "take us to the landing."

"Ah," thought Natalie, 'I am not 'that person' now." But she said nothing, only turned and looked out upon the waste of waters. As far as the eye could reach the lake rolled in long, heavy, groundswells that sobbed in sullen anger under a gray sky at the mischief they had done. About a hundred feet from the gallery stood a row of slender storm-swept saplings outlining the edge of the former breakwater. Just at this line, the swells broke sharply throwing lines of foam into the inundated streets. The brave little Camelia was puffing and working in another attempt to reach the landing, but this time from New Orleans. The landing a half mile away showed out into the angry waters a broken pile of lumber, the pier reaching to the shore, reduced to stumps.

Natalie shaded her eyes, and took in the details of the scene at a single glance.

"Eet might be posseeble," she said musingly, "to row down the strit, yes, to the landing pier, then try the waves, but it would be dangerous, yes. Madame, the danger is over, stay in Mandeville until the water goes down."

But Madame was hysterically angry at the idea. Her husband was uneasy, she knew, and there was no possible way of letting him know that she and Olivia were safe. Then just look at those waves, and that was enough! Who knew but in the night they might rise and sweep the entire town away. Even now, the house rocked on its foundations. The servants who had gone out the night before, had not been able to return and the two were alone.

Natalie looked at her earnestly as she talked. Madame had tried all that money and persuasion could do, no one dared brave those waves to meet the boat. Moreover, all the skiffs in Mandeville, save five, had gone to pieces in the storm. Olivia was crying silently, dreading the angry waters.

"For Oleevia, I'll take you," said Natalie at length, "For your 'Mees Oleevia,' " she couldn't help growing sarcastic under the circumstances.

The few people who gazed out of windows and from galleries of the houses remaining on the beach marvelled to see Natalie's brown arms pulling the now heavily laden dory up the street. Mrs. Spiers and the valise were stored in the boat among the wet chickens and the trembling kitten, while Olivia steered. It was easy enough rowing up the street in the comparatively calm water, but the superhuman effort came when it was time to get into the lake towards the boat which had now reached the landing, puffing and blowing, and tugging at the cable which bound her to the broken anchor-post.

It was only a hundred yards out, but it needed a man's herculean strength to pull against the fearful force of the heavy, incoming waves. A foot would be gained, only to be lost and beaten back for three feet or more. Mrs. Spiers, too frightened to speak looked desperately about her, while Olivia prayed silently as she steered. From the deck of the steamer, the Captain and crew watched the dory with a field glass. "If only we could help her!" they cried, but every boat had been swept from the steamer in that awful twenty mile battle from New Orleans.

Pull, strain, tug every nerve did Natalie, and a little headway was made. Now her strength seemed gone, and it looked as if she must succumb and let the boat drift and be dashed into pieces on the shore. But onward she forged, her strong back bending as she plunged the boat through a stubborn swell.

"Oh, Marie, mere de Dieu," prayed Natalie, "dans cette heure de travail, pitie-moi; donnez-moi ton secours."

For a weary hour she fought with blistered hands and failing heart against the surging swells and driving wind until near the sides of the steamer, when a lasso-like rope came whizzing to the dory. Mrs. Spiers, white and trembling made it fast to the seats, and in another instant, they were all on deck, surrounded by the wondering crew, safe, but exhausted, and sobbing, every one of them.

"And after mama being so mean to her too," cried Olivia in the first flush of excitement.

Mrs. Spiers and Olivia went to New Orleans, while the captain sent one of his strongest men to row Natalie home. That night, the Torrés house crumbled to the ground, its old foundation undermined by the water.

But was Natalie ever forgotten? Go to Mandeville to-day and you'll find her there yet, though this happened eight years ago. But see the comforts around Mme. Leblanc—the books and music and pleasant little luxuries. And when Natalie goes to New Orleans for the Carnival week, Mr. Spiers introduces her to everyone as the "plucky little girl who rowed my wife and daughter out of a death-trap, by Jove!"

SUMMER SESSION *

"You were flirting with him!"

"I was not. I don't know how to flirt."

"So you say, but you can put up a pretty good imitation."

"You're mistaken."

"I am not. And a man you never saw before in your life. And a common taxi driver."

"He's not a common taxi driver."

"How do you know?"

"I just know."

"Strange exchange of intimacies for the first meeting."

"I tell you—"

"Shut up!"

"I won't shut up, and don't you dare tell me that again!"

There was a warning note in her usually gentle voice; an ominous tightening of her soft lips; a steely glint in her violet eyes. Logan heeded the warning and sat in grim silence, while Elise ground gears and otherwise mishandled her little car through the snarled traffic of Amsterdam Avenue.

"You told me 114th street, and I waited for you there for a half hour, and I got jammed in the traffic and things went wrong, and this young man got out of his taxi, and straightened me out. And while I waited for you he just stayed and talked."

"To your delight."

* Typescript by "Alicea Nelson," probably ca. 1928–1932.

"What was I to do? Push him away from the running board? I was standing still, and I couldn't drive away since I was waiting for you."

"I told you 115th street, and there I stood on the corner in the broiling sun for a half hour, while you were carrying on a flirtation with a taxi driver, until I walked back, thinking you might have had an accident."

"Don't you say flirtation to me again. You said 114th street. You never speak plain over the telephone anyhow."

"Anything else wrong with me since you've met your new friend—The Taxi Adonis?"

Elise brought the car to a grinding, screeching pause in front of the movie house which was their objective. They sat through the two hours of feature and news and cartoons and comedy and prevues in stony silence. They ate a grim meal together in the usual cafeteria, and she set him down at the men's dormitory of the university in the same polite and frigid silence. Logan glanced at her now and then just a trifle apprehensively. He had never seen just this trace of hardness in her, like the glint of unexpected steel beneath soft chiffon. But his manly dignity would not permit him to unbend. He answered her cold good-night with one as cold, and for the first time in that summer session, during which they had grown to know and like one another, they parted without making a future date.

He waited for her next day at luncheon hour, as she came from her class with a half dozen other chattering summer-school teacher-students. His manner was graciously condescending.

"Shall we have luncheon together?" Lordly and superior as usual.

She flashed her usual violet-eyed smile of delight, but he felt, rather than saw, that the smile did not quite reach the eyes; that the violets were touched as by premature frost.

"What I can't quite understand," he pursued, after he had brought her tray, deftly removed the salad, tea and crackers, and placed the tray behind the next chair, "is, if you are skillful enough to drive from Portland, Maine, to New York alone and without disaster, how you can get mixed up in a mere traffic jam on Amsterdam Avenue, and have to have a taxi driver get you out."

Elise's brows went up at the awkward English, so at variance with his usual meticulous and precise phrasing, and a haunting query clouded her eyes. Logan quenched an embarrassed "Hem" in iced tea.

"I did not drive from Portland," was her final response. "I came from my own town, twenty-seven miles beyond Portland."

There was no particular reason for Elise's driving down Amsterdam Avenue after classes that afternoon, but she did and a friendly red light brought her to a halt at 114th street. Adonis—Logan's sneering cognomen stuck in her mind, and she realized with a guilty start how ruggedly applicable it was—stuck his face in her car window. Poppies suffused her cheeks and dewey violets swam in a sea of flame.

"All right?" he queried.

"Quite, thank you." The light was happily yellow, and she meshed her gears.

"What's the hurry?" He put a protesting hand on the wheel.

"I have an engagement!" She sped away frantically. Adonis whistled at the wabbling career of her little coupé down the street.

She saw him just ahead of her in the cafeteria line next evening at dinner time. She reached for her tray with hands that insisted upon trembling, though she shook them angrily. He smiled daringly back at her. He was even handsomer out of his taxi uniform than in it, and the absence of the cap revealed crisp auburn curls of undoubted pugnaciousness.

"You get a seat, I'll bring your dinner."

"But I—"

"Go on—"

There was a difference between Adonis' ordering of her movements and that of Logan's. A sureness of merry audacity against prim didacticism. She sat at a window table and meekly arranged silver and napkins.

"But I could never eat all that," she protested at the tray, "Beef and potatoes and—and—all that food."

"I knew that's what's the trouble—diet of salads and iced tea and crackers, mentally, spiritually, physically."

Elise ate roast beef and corn on the cob and pie á la mode and laughed at Adonis' jokes, and his whimsical descriptions of man and his appetites. Over their cigarettes she chuckled at his deft characterizations of their fellow diners.

"Eat hay and think hay," he was saying, "thin diets and thin souls. You need a red-blooded chap like me to make you eat food, put flesh on your bones and reconstruct your thinking from New England inhibitions to New York acceptance and enjoyment of life."

Elise's world rocked. School principals used muddled English. Taxi drivers talked like college professors.

Adonis paused and regarded something on his shoulder as if it were a tarantula. Logan's hand quivered in rage, and veins stood up on its pallor "like long blue whips," Elise found herself thinking.

"Aren't you taking a lot of liberties with a young lady to whom you've not been introduced?" snarled the owner of pallor and veins.

Adonis brushed off the hand and the remark with a careless gesture. He arose and bowed elaborately. "Miss Stone and I have been introduced, thank you, by ourselves—and you?"

Elise looked perilously near tears, "Oh, er—Logan—Mr. Long—this is—er—Mr. McShane."

Logan looked stonily through Adonis, "I don't accept introductions to taxi drivers, even if you do eat with them, Elise."

"Oh, please—" she began.

"That's all right," Adonis gathered up the checks. "Just let me settle this with the cashier, and then if you don't mind, we'll go outside, and settle the physical difference between a taxi driver and—" He did not finish the sentence, but the sinister drawl and contemptuous pause made Elise's scalp prickle with shame for Logan.

"You would suggest a common brawl; quite true to type. I hope, Elise, you have seen enough of such ruffianly conduct to be satisfied."

"Quite the contrary," she answered cooly, "I am going out with Mr. McShane in his taxi." It was pure spite, and she had a sinking feeling that she might not be wanted.

"Terry to you," he retorted, "and let's be going. We've got a busy evening before us."

Logan was beside them on the sidewalk, blocking the way to the taxi parked at the curb.

"Elise, don't be a fool." He grasped her arm and wrenched it, so that she gave an involuntary cry of pain. Terence McShane's next three moves were so violently consecutive as to seem simultaneous. His right hand caught Logan neatly on the point of the chin, so that he went down with amazing swiftness; his left encircled Elise's waist and lifted her into the taxi, and both hands swung the machine with a roar and sputter in the general direction of the Washington bridge.

"But you're losing fares," Elise protested.

"Nonsense. If you can stand this bumpety-bump, what's the dif?"

"Its entrancing," she murmured at the river, the sky, the stars, the electric signs on the Jersey shore, at Terry's hatless curls.

"Police call," the radio protested, "calling all police cars. Look out for taxi license Y327D. Driver abducted summer school student. Watch for taxi. Arrest driver. Kidnapping charge."

From their leafy shelter, where somehow the taxi had parked itself—neither could have told when or how it stopped under those particularly umbrageous trees, they stared at the radio's accusing dial.

"Well, I'll be—" Terry swore softly, "What do you think of that worm putting in such a charge at headquarters?"

"Oh, Terry, you'll be arrested and put in jail!"

"Will you go to jail with me?"

'You know I will—oh, what am I saying?"

"Words of wisdom, me darlin'. Let's go. Anyhow I'm glad we didn't cross the bridge and get into Jersey."

Through circuitous ways and dark streets, avoiding police, taxis, inquisitive small boys and reporters on the loose, they drew up in front of police headquarters.

Elise sat demurely on a bench, and began to repair damages to her hair, complexion and neck frills. The little pocket mirror wavered ever so slightly as Logan stood accusingly in front of her, but her eyes did not leave the scrutiny of their mirrored counterpart.

"A pretty mess you've made of your life and reputation,"

he thundered. "Your chances for any position in my school are gone."

Elise put back a refractory curl behind her ear, then tried it out on her cheek again, surveying it critically in the mirror.

"Won't you recommend me for a job, Mr. Principal, after I've studied so hard all summer?"

Terry's gales of unrestrained mirth at the desk made them both look up in amazement. Laughter rocked the walls of the station house, rolled out into the summer street. Captain and Sergeant and Lieutenant and just plain officers roared lustily, all save one quiet plainclothes man, who laid an iron grip on Logan's arm.

"Terence McShane, you were always the best detective in the city," roared the Captain. "And you made him bring himself right into our outstretched arms."

The iron grip on Logan's arm terminated into steel bracelets.

"Okeh, Longjim Webb, alias Prof. Logan Long, the school principal, looking the summer students over for teaching material in his consolidated upstate school, we'll give you a chance in the Big House to meditate on the law against white slavery."

"Your zeal to corral this particular choice bit of femininity made you throw caution to the winds," suggested Detective Terence McShane.

Incredulity, disgust, anger swept the violet eyes. Elise flared into Terry's face.

"You—you—pretending to be a taxi driver. You just used me for a decoy," she raged.

Terry held her protesting hands tight as he whispered below the hubbub of Logan's protestations,

"Never a bit of it, my dear. I loved you the first day you

stalled your car in the thick of things on 125th street, before you even saw me, and I got in the habit of following you around while I was impersonating a taxi driver, to get a chance to know you. Then when I found this—" a wave towards the still-voluble Logan—"had marked you for another one of his prey—well you don't mind if I combined a bit of business with my pleasure?"

Elise's faint "No" was visible, rather than audible.

"It's all right then? Shall it be beefsteak for two?"

"Yes."

"And you won't take back what you promised up there on the Drive?"

"How can I," she laughed, "when my middle name is McBride?"

HIS GREAT CAREER *

The travel-scarred motorcar came to pause in the driveway of the great mountain mansion. "The Squire" as he was lovingly called for miles around, greeted the owner of the car as he rather stiffly set foot on the ground.

"It's good of you to come up here to see us in our mountain fastness," he said warmly.

"Didn't know you lived here until we broke down somewhere in your peaks and crags, and Martin inquired of the nearest civilized house."

The Squire talked cheerfully as he carried the bags of the great criminal lawyer up the broad walk.

"We're having a big house party here," he explained the

* Typescript, written after 1916—probably between 1928 and 1932.

group of guests on the veranda. "My wife's birthday, and when we give a party up here, it means a weekend stay, for we have to go so far for our festivities, it would be a pity to go right home."

The great lawyer was introduced to the fluttering and flattered group of maidens and wives, and to the hearty men who hovered on the edges. He bent his great grizzled frame over small eager hands, while his host stood by, enjoying his embarrassment in the pause before he went to his room.

"And so you're married?" asked the lawyer, as they went up the broad stairs.

"Fifteen years. You remember when my health broke eighteen years ago? I found *her* here in a sanitarium, wrecked too, and 'sick of that disease called life.' Between us, we mended our lives, and then she didn't care for the east and all that it means any more than I did—so we stayed, and here we are."

The great lawyer revelled in the scene, a marvelous panorama spreading out from the window.

"Prominent citizen, leader of the community, and the rest?" he asked smilingly.

The Squire was modest. "Well, we've helped build the community, and all that sort of thing. You can't live in a place without being part of it. And you, old Hard-head, you've become one of the most famous lawyers in the country!"

The lawyer waved a deprecating hand. "I'm motoring in out of the way places now to forget it awhile."

The veranda was not in a mood to allow him to forget. Famous celebrities did not drop into their lives often enough for them to be blasé. The lawyer put down the excellent cocktail that his host brought him in lieu of tea, and inquired for the mistress of the house. She had ridden to town for a last bit of foolery for tonight's costume party, explained the Squire.

The almond-eyed widow was subtly intent on opening up a flood of reminiscences. She fluttered slender hands and widened black eyes suggestively. Even the great lawyer's habitual taciturnity relaxed under the enveloping warmth of her delicate advances. The Squire looked on grimly. He was remembering the night she had sworn to be avenged on the slim, pale woman, who had taken him, her legitimate prey. A wife and a widow since, but the almond eyes still avid for vengeance.

"You must have had some interesting experiences, have you not? Oh, do tell us about some of your early struggles."

The great lawyer expanded under the enveloping perfume of her incense.

"Well," he began, his great voice booming softly in the mountain sunlight, "I shall never forget my first case. I was a briefless barrister, and hungry, or I would not have taken it. Everyone concerned in the affair is dead now, so I can smile at it. My first client was a murderer, a woman. She confessed the truth to me, and expected me to clear her."

"And did you?" chorused an octave of soprano voices.

"Yes. It was the beginning of my career."

A soft intake of breath from the widow, and a flattering flutter from the rest of the veranda left the great lawyer to turn to his host.

But the Squire was oblivious, for coming up the walk was the mistress of the mansion. His soul was in his eyes as he watched her. Her eyes glowed, and her face was wind-whipped from riding; she had taken off her hat and her packages dandled from her arm. The lawyer stood in intent stillness. The same lithe form. The same aureole of auburn hair, as yet untinged by gray. The same still, quiet little face with deep pools of eyes. The same questioning droop of head. She came quickly up the walk and on the veranda with incredible lightness.

"My dear," said the Squire, his voice a protecting caress, "this is—"

But she extended her hand smilingly to the great lawyer, grasping his with welcoming warmth.

"I did not die, you see," she said in her deep, vibrant voice, "The west gave me health and happiness," and still holding his hand with proprietary grasp, she turned to the group on the veranda.

"Mr. Booth is an old friend of mine, too. You see, I was his very first client, and I flatter myself that I started him on his great career."

BY PATHS IN
THE QUAKER CITY *

High noon in a robot restaurant. Your nickels are your waiters and bring your sandwich or coffee to your hand. Far east on a side street off Market, where there are workingmen in caps and grimy coats, the derelict aged, and undersized girls from little shops or factories, pitiful in makeshift finery and thin shoes. Endless streaming in and out of a restless, hurried throng. Tables seat four and sometimes six; oftimes strange

---

*Typescript, by "Al Dane"—probably 1928–1932. Perhaps intended as creative journalism.

luncheon companions. Men stand at counters, feet resting on the rails, and churlishly wolf their sandwiches and coffee.

Here at this white topped table are four; two women, a man and myself. The two women are old, but there is at least twenty years difference between them. Some secret fear of the pitiful aged makes them avert their eyes from each other. The one not so old gulps her tea hastily, and fingers something in her lap. It is a brown paper bag, from which she draws forth tiny scraps of bread, which she eats with shame-faced haste, looking around fearfully. When her tea is gone, she thrusts some hard ends of bread back into the paper sack, rolls it into a small parcel under her arm, and rising swiftly, departs without a backward glance. Her black dress eddies about her shabby ankles; her straw hat nods defiance at the chill wind.

The man laughs. He is blue-chinned, red-nosed. His collar is open and innocent of a tie. He has had trouble navigating the cup of black coffee to his mouth without disaster.

The other one is an ancient crone, toothless, seamed, wrinkled, wispy-haired. She sips coffee, and eats hunks of raisin bread, which she boldly breaks from a loaf in her lap. She confides in me that she bought a fine loaf of raisin bread for six cents, and " 'T'will last me three meals with me coffee. Good nourishing bread." She nods her head, and the loosely tied bow of black ribbon on her nondescript hat waves a joyous affirmation.

The thin little girl who brings a plate of beans to the table draws away scornfully from the aged dame. She smiles toothlessly, unabashed by snubs, and waves her hunk of raisin bread. But the aroma of the beans draws down the corners of her mouth and she pauses. Her hand trembles, her eyes glisten, her head poises as if to swoop upon the plate over which the thin girl picks daintily. Then the old soul draws back, wipes her moist mouth with the back of her hand, and gives the whole table a benevolent smile. "Nothing like good raisin bread and coffee for a square meal," she announces triumphantly.

HOPE DEFERRED *

The direct rays of the August sun smote on the pavements of the city and made the soda-water signs in front of the drug stores alluringly suggestive of relief. Women in scant garments, displaying a maximum of form and a minimum of taste, crept along the pavements, their mussy light frocks suggesting a futile disposition on the part of the wearers to keep cool. Traditional looking fat men mopped their faces, and dived frantically into screened doors to emerge redder and more perspiring. The presence of small boys, scantily clad and of dusky hue and languid steps marked the city, if not distinctively southern, at least one on the borderland between the North and the South.

Edwards joined the perspiring mob on the hot streets and mopped his face with the rest. His shoes were dusty, his collar wilted. As he caught a glimpse of himself in a mirror of a shop window, he smiled grimly. "Hardly a man to present himself before one of the Lords of Creation to ask a favor," he muttered to himself.

Edwards was young; so young that he had not outgrown his ideals. Rather than allow that to happen, he had chosen

*The Crisis 8, 1914, pp. 238–42.

one to share them with him, and the man who can find a woman willing to face poverty for her husband's ideals has a treasure far above rubies, and more precious than one with a thorough understanding of domestic science. But ideals do not always supply the immediate wants of the body, and it was the need of the wholly material that drove Edwards wilted, warm and discouraged into the August sunshine.

The man in the office to which the elevator boy directed him looked up impatiently from his desk. The windows of the room were open on a courtyard where green tree tops waved in a humid breeze; an electric fan whirred, and sent forth flashes of coolness; cool looking leather chairs invited the dusty traveler to sink into their depths.

Edwards was not invited to rest, however. Cold gray eyes in an impassive pallid face fixed him with a sneering stare, and a thin icy voice cut in on his half spoken words with a curt dismissal in its tone.

"Sorry, Mr.—Er—, but I shan't be able to grant your request."

His "Good Morning" in response to Edwards' reply as he turned out of the room was of the curtest, and left the impression of decided relief at an unpleasant duty discharged.

"Now where?" He had exhausted every avenue, and this last closed the door of hope with a finality that left no doubt in his mind. He dragged himself down the little side street, which led home, instinctively, as a child draws near to its mother in its trouble.

Margaret met him at the door, and their faces lighted up with the glow that always irradiated them in each other's presence. She drew him into the green shade of the little room, and her eyes asked, though her lips did not frame the question.

"No hope," he made reply to her unspoken words.

She sat down suddenly as one grown weak.

"If I could only just stick it out, little girl," he said, "but we need food, clothes, and only money buys them, you know."

"Perhaps it would have been better if we hadn't married—" she suggested timidly. That thought had been uppermost in her mind for some days lately.

"Because you are tired of poverty?" he queried, the smile on his lips belying his words.

She rose and put her arms about his neck. "You know better than that; but because if you did not have me, you could live on less, and thus have a better chance to hold out until they see your worth."

"I'm afraid they never will." He tried to keep his tones even, but in spite of himself a tremor shook his words. "The man I saw to-day is my last hope; he is the chief clerk, and what he says controls the opinions of others. If I could have gotten past his decision, I might have influenced the senior member of the firm, but he is a man who leaves details to subordinates, and Mr. Hanan was suspicious of me from the first. He isn't sure," he continued with a little laugh, which he tried to make sound spontaneous, "whether I am a stupendous fraud, or an escaped lunatic."

"We can wait; your chance will come," she soothed him with a rare smile.

"But in the meanwhile—" he finished for her and paused himself.

A sheaf of unpaid bills in the afternoon mail, with the curt and wholly unnecessary "Please Remit" in boldly impertinent characters across the bottom of every one drove Edwards out into the wilting sun. He knew the main street from end to end; he could tell how many trolley poles were on its corners;

he felt that he almost knew the stones in the buildings, and that the pavements were worn with the constant passing of his feet, so often in the past four months had he walked, at first buoyantly, then hopefully, at last wearily up and down its length.

The usual idle crowd jostled around the baseball bulletins. Edwards joined them mechanically. "I can be a sidewalk fan, even if I am impecunious." He smiled to himself as he said the words, and then listened idly to a voice at his side. "We are getting metropolitan, see that!"

The "that" was an item above the baseball score. Edwards looked and the letters burned themselves like white fire into his consciousness.

STRIKE SPREADS TO OUR CITY.
WAITERS AT ADAMS' WALK OUT
AFTER BREAKFAST THIS MORNING.

"Good!" he said aloud. The man at his side smiled appreciatively at him; the home team had scored another run, but unheeding that Edwards walked down the street with a lighter step than he had known for days.

The proprietor of Adams' restaurant belied both his name and his vocation. He should have been rubicund, corpulent, American; instead he was wiry, lank, foreign in appearance. His teeth projected over a full lower lip, his eyes set far back in his head and were concealed by wrinkles that seemed to have been acquired by years of squinting into men's motives.

"Of course I want waiters," he replied to Edwards' question, "any fool knows that." He paused, drew in his lower lip within the safe confines of his long teeth, squinted his eyes intently on Edwards. "But do I want colored waiters? Now, do I?"

"It seems to me there's no choice for you in the matter," said Edwards good-humoredly.

The reply seemed to amuse the restaurant keeper immensely; he slapped the younger man on the back with a familiarity that made him wince both physically and spiritually.

"I guess I'll take you for head waiter." He was inclined to be jocular, even in the face of the disaster which the morning's strike had brought him. "Peel off and go to work. Say, stop!" as Edwards looked around to take his bearings, "What's your name?"

"Louis Edwards."

"Uh huh, had any experience?"

"Yes, some years ago, when I was in school."

"Uh huh, then waiting ain't your general work."

"No."

"Uh huh, what do you do for a living?"

"I'm a civil engineer."

One eyebrow of the saturnine Adams shot up, and he withdrew his lower lip entirely under his teeth.

"Well, say man, if you're an engineer, what you want to be strike-breaking here in a waiter's coat for, eh?"

Edwards' face darkened, and he shrugged his shoulders. "They don't need me, I guess," he replied briefly. It was an effort, and the restaurant keeper saw it, but his wonder overcame his sympathy.

"Don't need you with all that going on at the Monarch works? Why, man, I'd a thought every engineer this side o' hell would be needed out there."

"So did I; that's why I came here, but—"

"Say, kid, I'm sorry for you, I surely am; you go on to work."

"And so," narrated Edwards to Margaret, after midnight, when he had gotten in from his first day's work, "I became at once head waiter, first assistant, all the other waiters, chief boss, steward, and high-muck-a-muck, with all the emoluments and perquisites thereof."

Margaret was silent; with her ready sympathy she knew that no words of hers were needed then, they would only add to the burdens he had to bear. Nothing could be more bitter than this apparent blasting of his lifelong hopes, this seeming lowering of his standard. She said nothing, but the pressure of her slim brown hand in his meant more than words to them both.

"It's hard to keep the vision true," he groaned.

If it was hard that night, it grew doubly so within the next few weeks. Not lightly were the deposed waiters to take their own self-dismissal and supplanting. Daily they menaced the restaurant with their surly attentions, ugly and ominous. Adams shot out his lower lip from the confines of his long teeth and swore in a various language that he'd run his own place if he had to get every nigger in Africa to help him. The three or four men whom he was able to induce to stay with him in the face of missiles of every nature, threatened every day to give up the battle. Edwards was the force that held them together. He used every argument from the purely material one of holding on to the job now that they had it, through the negative one of loyalty to the man in his hour of need, to the altruistic one of keeping the place open for colored men for all time. There were none of them of such value as his own personality, and the fact that he stuck through all the turmoil. He wiped the mud from his face, picked up the putrid vegetables that often strewed the floor, barricaded the doors at night, replaced orders that were destroyed by well-aimed stones, and stood by Adams' side when the fight threatened to grow serious.

Adams was appreciative. "Say, kid, I don't know what I'd a done without you, now that's honest. Take it from me, when you need a friend anywhere on earth, and you can send me a wireless, I'm right there with the goods in answer to your S. O. S."

This was on the afternoon when the patrol, lined up in front of the restaurant, gathered in a few of the most disturbing ones, none of whom, by the way, had ever been employed in the place. "Sympathy" had pervaded the town.

The humid August days melted into the sultry ones of September. The self-dismissed waiters had quieted down, and save for an occasional missile, annoyed Adams and his corps of dark-skinned helpers no longer. Edwards had resigned himself to his temporary discomforts. He felt, with the optimism of the idealist, that it was only for a little while; the fact that he had sought work at his profession for nearly a year had not yet discouraged him. He would explain carefully to Margaret when the day's work was over, that it was only for a little while; he would earn enough at this to enable them to get away, and then in some other place he would be able to stand up with the proud consciousness that all his training had not been in vain.

He was revolving all these plans in his mind one Saturday night. It was at the hour when business was dull, and he leaned against the window and sought entertainment from the crowd on the street. Saturday night, with all the blare and glare and garishness dear to the heart of the middle-class provincial of the smaller cities, was holding court on the city streets. The hot September sun had left humidity and closeness in its wake, and the evening mists had scarce had time to cast coolness over the town. Shop windows glared wares through colored lights, and phonographs shrilled popular tunes from open store doors to attract unwary passersby. Half-grown boys and girls, happy in the license of Saturday night on the crowded streets, jostled one another and pushed in long lines, shouted familiar epithets at other pedestrians with all the abandon of the ill-breeding common to the class. One crowd, in particular, attracted Edwards' attention. The girls were brave in semi-decollete waists, scant short skirts and exaggerated heads, built up in fanciful designs; the boys with flamboyant red neckties, striking hat-bands, and white trousers. They made a snake line, boys and girls, hands on each others' shoulders, and rushed shouting through the press of shoppers, scattering the inattentive right and left. Edwards' lip curled, "Now, if those were colored boys and girls—"

His reflections were never finished, for a patron moved towards his table, and the critic of human life became once more the deferential waiter.

He did not move a muscle of his face as he placed the glass of water on the table, handed the menu card, and stood at attention waiting for the order, although he had recognized at first glance the half-sneering face of his old hope—Hanan, of the great concern which had no need of him. To Hanan, the man who brought his order was but one of the horde of menials who satisfied his daily wants and soothed his vanity when the cares of the day had ceased pressing on his shoulders. He had not even looked at the man's face, and for this Edwards was grateful.

A new note had crept into the noise on the streets; there was in it now, not so much mirth and ribaldry as menace and anger. Edwards looked outside in slight alarm; he had grown used to that note in the clamor of the streets, particularly on Saturday nights; it meant that the whole restaurant must be prepared to quell a disturbance. The snake line had changed; there were only flamboyant hat-bands in it now, the decollete shirt waists and scant skirts had taken refuge on another corner. Something in the shouting attracted Hanan's attention, and he looked up wonderingly.

"What are they saying?" he inquired. Edwards did not answer; he was so familiar with the old cry that he thought it unnecessary.

"Yah! Yah! Old Adams hires niggers! Hires niggers!"

"Why, that is so," Hanan looked up at Edwards' dark face for the first time. "This is quite an innovation for Adams' place. How did it happen?"

"We are strikebreakers," replied the waiter quietly, then he grew hot, for a gleam of recognition came into Hanan's eyes.

"Oh, yes, I see. Aren't you the young man who asked me for employment as an engineer at the Monarch works?"

Edwards bowed, he could not answer; hurt pride surged up within him and made his eyes hot and his hands clammy.

"Well, er—I'm glad you've found a place to work; very sensible of you, I'm sure. I should think, too, that it is work for which you would be more fitted than engineering."

Edwards started to reply, but the hot words were checked on his lips. The shouting had reached a shrillness which boded immediate results, and with the precision of a missile from a warship's gun, a stone hurtled through the glass of the long window. It struck Edwards' hand, glanced through the dishes on the tray which he was in the act of setting on the table, and tipped half its contents over Hanan's knee. He sprang to his feet angrily, striving to brush the dèbris of his dinner from his immaculate clothing, and turned angrily upon Edwards.

"That is criminally careless of you!" he flared his eyes blazing in his pallid face. "You could have prevented that; you're not even a good waiter, much less an engineer."

And then something snapped in the darker man's head. The long strain of the fruitless summer; the struggle of keeping together the men who worked under him in the restaurant; the heat, and the task of enduring what was to him the humiliation of serving, and this last injustice, all culminated in a blinding flash in his brain. Reason, intelligence, all was obscured, save a man hatred, and a desire to wreak his wrongs on the man, who, for the time being, represented the author of them. He sprang at the white man's throat and bore him to the floor. They wrestled and fought together, struggling, biting, snarling, like brutes in the dèbris of food and the clutter of overturned chairs and tables.

The telephone rang insistently. Adams wiped his hands on a towel, and carefully moved a paint brush out of the way, as he picked up the receiver.

"Hello!" he called. "Yes, this is Adams, the restaurant keeper. Who? Uh huh. Wants to know if I'll go his bail? Say, that nigger's got softening of the brain. Course not, let him serve his time, making all that row in my place; never had no row here before. No, I don't never want to see him again."

He hung up the receiver with a bang, and went back to his painting. He had almost finished his sign, and he smiled as he ended it with a flourish:

WAITERS WANTED. NONE BUT
WHITE MEN NEED APPLY

Out in the county workhouse, Edwards sat on his cot, his head buried in his hands. He wondered what Margaret was going all this long hot Sunday, if the tears were blinding her sight as they did his; then he started to his feet, as the warden called his name. Margaret stood before him, her arms outstretched, her mouth quivering with tenderness and sympathy, her whole form yearning towards him with a passion of maternal love.

"Margaret! You here, in this place?"

"Aren't you here?" she smiled bravely, and drew his head towards the refuge of her bosom. "Did you think I wouldn't come to see you?"

"To think I should have brought you to this," he moaned.

She stilled his reproaches and heard the story from his lips. Then she murmured with bloodless mouth, "How long will it be?"

"A long time, dearest—and you?"

"I can go home, and work," she answered briefly, "and wait for you, be it ten months or ten years—and then—?"

"And then—" they stared into each other's eyes like frightened children. Suddenly his form straightened up, and the vision of his ideal irradiated his face with hope and happiness.

"And then, Beloved," he cried, "then we will start all over again. Somewhere, I am needed; somewhere in this world there are wanted darkskinned men like me to dig and blast and build bridges and make straight the roads of the world, and I am going to find that place—with you."

She smiled back trustfully at him. "Only keep true to your ideal, dearest," she whispered, "and you will find the place. Your window faces the south, Louis. Look up and out of it all the while you are here, for it is there, in our own southland, that you will find the realization of your dream."

MRS. NEWLY-WED
AND HER SERVANTS*

Little Mrs. Newly-wed sighed and looked ruefully at her hands. Her New York friend had just exclaimed, "Dear me, where are your diamonds?"

"Oh, I don't wear them all the time, I only put them on occasionally."

"But why," persisted the New York girl, who was on a holiday visit to Washington.

"Well, the truth is, I have had so much of my own work to do that it ruins the rings, so I have to keep them put away."

"How plebian!"

Little Mrs. Newly-wed drew her chair closer, and laid her reddened hand on her friend's arm.

"I know it sounds plebian, and all that, but I lost one of the diamonds out of my engagement ring, while scrubbing out the bathtub and it taught me a lesson."

"Scrubbing out the bathtub! You don't mean to say that you—!"

Mrs. Newly-wed nodded her head plaintively. "It's a long story," she began, "but it's a queer one—in the abstract. When I came here in April, after the honeymoon, I found a maid in charge of the little house. She rejoiced in the name of Carrie. At first, she surveyed me loftily, but finally seemed to make a compromise with her feelings by addressing me as 'Miss Bessie.' They all do that, you know, down here, I mean

---

*Typescript, written between 1898 and 1902.

that they all call folks by their first names. Well, I was trying all I knew to get used to housekeeping, when in a week or so, Carrie informed me that she couldn't do all the work, it was too heavy."

"For two people?" queried Miss Manhattan.

"Yes, and I didn't know any better than to tell her to get someone to help her. She brought in a woman who worked one third of the time, and talked the other two thirds. Never saw a woman talk so much in my life! Well, Dave said he couldn't stand the expense, that one servant was enough for our wee house, so I discharged Carrie."

"How did you do it?"

"Oh, I didn't do it, I couldn't. Dave gave me the money to pay her, then I slipped it back to him, and he sent it up to my room, where I had retreated until I begged him with tears in my eyes to pay Carrie off. So he did."

"And then?"

"Then came Fannie. She was from the country, and didn't know beans. She would let the fires go out just when it was time for dinner, and she kept things in an awful mess. I used to wonder why she took so long to clean the parlor and dining-room, until I caught her one day leaning out the window kissing her hand to a great rusty looking ash-cart man. One Sunday morning at breakfast-time one of the women from the camp—"

"What on earth is the camp?"

"That's that disreputable part of the town just below the Sixth Street hill where a lot of colored folks have congregated. Its called the camp."

"All right, go on."

"Well, this woman came down to the house, and demanded to see me. I was afraid of her, and I suppose I looked it.

" 'Air you de madam?' she inquired.

"I answered in the affirmative. 'Well I wants to know does you low yo' gals to flirt wid othah gals' fellers?'

" 'I have nothing to do with their private affairs' I said with all the dignity I could command.

" 'Well, I jes' wants to tell you 'bout dat Fannie. I took dat gal in outen de street, yes'm I did, when she didn' have 'ary rag to her back. I's been a frien' to Fannie, yes'm I has, Gawd knows, an' she done deceive me!' Just then Fannie came in the dining-room, and the woman turned, and ana-themized her. 'Oh, you needn' hang yo' haid, you little runt, you know you went to de circus las' night wid my Jim!'

" 'I didn't!' said Fannie.

"The woman got so mad at this that I thought she would have slapped Fannie, only Dave sent them both home—and there I was with Sunday dinner on my hands, and no cook."

Miss Manhattan threw back her head and laughed inor-dinately. "Poor Dave!" she said.

"—So I rushed out to Carrie's house," continued Mrs. Newly-wed as though there had been no interruption, and begged her to come back. She said she wasn't well, and she never could work in warm weather anyhow. But she came, and before the week was out, fainted in the kitchen, and had to be sent home in state, with all the neighbors looking out their front windows."

"You poor child," said Miss Manhattan sympathetically.

"Well, Carrie sent her sister Lulu to take her place. Lulu was pretty fair, only she had a young baby about four months old, and she used to disappear at the oddest and most incon-venient times, and turn up an hour or so later, and if I would remonstrate with her she would say in the most pitiful tones,

" 'Sholy, Miss Bessie, you wouldn' hab my baby sta've!'

though I am perfectly sure it was not always the baby that took her out.

"Finally, she left, and Mary came to take her place," Mrs. Newly-wed paused and sighed. "Mary was the queen of them all," she wailed.

"What did she do?" queried Miss Manhattan.

"What didn't she do? Mary was one of the most original young women I have ever met. Soon after she came the things in the pantry began to disappear in the most mysterious manner. If it was tea or sugar or coffee, Mary swore by the seven stars that she knew nothing about it, but sometimes a half of a roast or a broiled chicken would be gone, and if I made inquiries, she would exclaim, 'La, honey, I knowed dat col' vittles wa'nt no good to you, so I jes' natchelly ca'ied it down to a little sick chile.' That sick child certainly had a voracious appetite, for everything and anything went to fill its capacious maw.

"Well after a bit little happenings in the house began to leak out and go the rounds of the neighborhood, greatly exaggerated. I knew Mary was very intimate with the girl next door, so I suggested that she wouldn't gossip our affairs with her friends. I wish you could have seen the aggrieved look she gave me.

" 'Honey,' she said, with tears in her eyes, 'honey, does you fink I'd tell lies 'bouten you? Look hyeah, I's a-goin' home, I ain' nevah had no body 'cuse me o' gossipin'. Don't you know dat Lizzie jes' lives outen de back window to see what she kin hyeah so's she kin add on an' tell her missus?'

"Well, we stood Mary her dirt, and gossiping, and pilfering bravely. She even got sick, and I doctored her, and bought medicine and put mustard plasters on her. But when she patted Dave on the head one day when he went into the kitchen to inquire after dinner, I felt in duty bound to send her back to the camp."

Little Mrs. Newly-wed looked so doleful that Miss Manhattan considerately repressed her mirth, and murmured something sympathetic, though her eyes twinkled.

"Then came Lulu No. 2," continued the little matron, "she was a gem. She is a young girl, and still in school, but it being vacation she was looking for work. Dearie me, what a comfort that girl was. She had her little peccadilloes, but they didn't amount to a row of pins, and I felt perfectly safe in going away, and leaving her in change of Dave and the house.

"But when I came back from visiting mama in Massachusetts, school had opened, and Lulu No. 2 was awaiting my return with impatience. Now there I was with the whole house topsy-turvy, cleaning to be done, carpets and curtains to be placed, and a million and one things to do. Lulu No. 2 said she'd find some one to take her place, and then appeared Eliza upon the scene.

"She walked in one morning while we were at breakfast, and announced that 'she'd try me.' There was a 'magerful' gleam in her eye that was simply appalling, and a cold hard twist to her mouth that was discouraging, to say the least. I didn't want her, but was afraid to say so, and Dave wouldn't help me in the least. So she came, and was enthroned among the pots and kettles.

"We got along famously, for all her magerful qualities. She was a good, earnest worker, and took a fancy to me, but Dave had only to show his face, when she'd stiffen and become sphinx-like at once. I asked her one day if she didn't like him. You should have heard her snort. 'Don' like no man,' she said indignantly, 'don' see whut Gawd put 'em

hyeah fur nohow. My husban's been daid twelve yeahs—an'
I's been a happy 'ooman jes' dem same twelve yeahs.'

" 'Did he treat you so badly?' I asked.

" 'Didn' treat me no wuss'n othah men treat dey wives,'
she growled, 'he beat me, an' tuk all de money I eahned f'um
washin' an' ca'ied on wid othah women right in my face. But
dey's all alike, d'ain't no diffunce in 'em.'

"Eliza was just like an old cart-horse, steady and safe, and
I was genuinely sorry when she told me that she was getting
the rheumatism so badly that she would have to leave."

"Dear me," said Miss Manhattan, "how could you remember all their names?"

"I don't know," groaned the little matron, "Dave proposed
that we make a list of the names, and frame them. He is
always prepared to see a new face waiting the table, and he
says he lives in a continuous state of wonderment as to who
and what next.

"Word got down in the camp that Eliza was going to
leave, and two candidates presented themselves. The first took
me in hand in a patronizing off-hand manner. I asked her
name, and with an air of easy assurance, she said joyfully,

" 'My name? Yes'm, my name's Mis' Cantlett, Mis' Edmonia Cantlett, but laws, honey, you kin jes' call me Edmonia
ef you likes, I don't mind.'

"I didn't take Mis' Cantlett, but chose the other applicant,
Mamie, whose 'mama' according to her version, was a rather
particular person, and laid down some cast-iron rules as to
what Mamie could and could not do while she was here. I
was a little chary of her, but Dave pleaded, 'She has such a
soft sweet dialect,' he said, 'it will be so interesting.' "

Miss Manhattan did not restrain her mirth this time. Mrs.
Newly-wed sighed and went on.

"Her dialect might have been soft, but the yarns she told in that dialect were not. She had to go to church every night in the week, and must go and see her mama at all hours in the day. We breakfast at eight, you know, and one o'clock would find Mamie cheerily singing over her dishes in that same soft dialect, while I had done all the sweeping and dusting upstairs. I paid her off in a few days, and she went back to the camp and reported that I had slapped her face because she couldn't work like a steam-engine."

"What did you do then?" said Miss Manhattan indignantly.

"Nothing," replied the little matron meekly, "there wasn't anything to do. I found Maizie next. She came charily enough, for I was beginning to have a bad reputation in the camp. Her career lasted two weeks, and was fair enough in its way if she did eat the choicest bits of celery, and made the nuts and raisins fly before they came to the table. One morning she arose in a cantankerous mood, and 'sassed' everything in sight, flatly refused to do anything and finally wept, and said she was ill. It was her payday, and after she got her money, she disappeared, never to return. I learned that she had been sneaking out her clothes in small bundles all the week. The last I saw of her, she was selling Christmas greens and holly outside Center market."

"Next!" cried Miss Manhattan.

"The next was Emma, a half-witted girl, whose career was brief and meteoric. She wore me out one whole day trotting behind her, and doing her work over. When evening came, she began to get her hat and coat. I suggested that she remain longer, or at least until I should need her no more. She turned on me like a fury,

" 'No, I ain't goin' to stay. Ain't I done tole you dis mawnin' dat I had to go? Now ain't I? No, I got to go home an' sew, I is. You can't keep me hyeah, dat's all.' So vanished Emma."

Mrs. Newly-wed paused for breath, and absently twirled her wedding ring.

"And now?" queried Miss Manhattan.

"Now? Well, I've sworn off on the camp, and I'm haunting employment bureaus, and meanwhile my gem of a Lulu No. 2 comes in and gives me a hand before and after school and on holidays, and we manage somehow."

"My dear," said Miss Manhattan, after a pause, "how long have you been married?"

"Ten months," moaned the little matron.

"And ten maids!" cried Miss Manhattan," Well, I'll stay single."

"Or stay in New York, where you can patronize the emigrant station," laughed the matron, ruefully regarding her hands again.

THE DECISION*

When Marion Forman married Burt Courtland, the world of make-believe literati of which she had formed a temporary center applauded. It was so Browningesque, quite romantic, and—er—not at all in the conventional, sordid, matter-of-fact fashion of lesser souls. It was, in fact, an elopement, for Marion's mother, through long years of widowhood, had acquired a keenness of vision which penetrated the artistic veneer of Courtland's soul. She had first warned Marion against him, then discountenanced his presence, then threat-

*Typescript, written between 1902 and 1909.

ened maternal authority against suspected clandestine meetings. Marion had disregarded, disobeyed, pouted, then finally eloped. Mrs. Forman sighingly resigned herself to the match, and vowed that no matter what came of it she would never play a part in the Greek chorus of "I-told-you-sos" which she saw in an inevitable future.

The make-believe circle of Bohemia went into soul-raptures for a month, then forgot the incident. For a glorious period Marion basked in the violet light of semi-social approval until another furor came. Then she awakened to the realities of existence and found it sordid.

On one day she had a fit of the blues. This is a disease in which men and unmarried women may revel to their soul's last delight; but to married women, it is essentially forbidden. For might they not wish to indulge even when their lords and masters are also thus inclined? Marion had not learned this lesson, Mrs. Forman having wisely deemed further advice to her daughter superfluous. So when Courtland came home in the full fever of a fit of artistic temperament, he was disconcerted to find his wife unresponsive to his mood.

He sat down by her side and attempted to take her hand, but it lay inert in his palm.

"Are you ill?" he asked with a feint of concern in his voice.

She gave a dispirited negative, and murmured unwisely something about being homesick.

"Homesick!" The word awakened a latent demon in his soul. What right had she to be homesick? Was not her home here, with him? Were not her duties here? He reproved her sternly, then coarsely, then vilely. Marion shrank under the whip sting of his commonness. For several weeks she had suspected the streak of vulgarity in him and it was this that had turned her thoughts regretfully to the gentle refinement of her own home life. She stared at him in surprise to discover a trace of an alcoholic demon in his words and manner. His jaw was set prognathous, his eyes red-streaked across their blue, his mouth loose-cornered. Disgust, shame, terror, horror, seized her, and half-insane from self pity, she hurled the book in her hand at his swaying form and rushed from the room.

For four years she led a life that was a fitful dream of torment, disgust, terror, love, longing for release. He was pitifully ill, and she nursed him back to life with a loving care that astonished even Mrs. Forman, still quietly watching her daughter's Hades of a life. He was successful beyond his most sanguine expectations, and Marion joyed with him, the while she hated herself that she could be happy over his successes. She alternately loved and hated, feared and trusted, caressed and spurned him; and he alternately loved her with the wildest, most insane devotion and lashed her with the most scathing scorn that his ready tongue was capable of. They clung together sadly like two thieves in a world of honest men. She felt the fineness go out of her soul like the gold-dust out of the heart of a flower. When he struck her, she scarcely even wondered. She grew skeptical of all married women and wondered how they could conceal their sorrows so successfully, for hers were suspected by all her friends.

But she loved him, and no matter where he was, or how far into the depths he went in his search after the bizarre in life, she went after him, brought him home, and freshly whited the sepulchre of his being so that no one might know for a certainty.

Then the crash came.

It was not so much a crash as a sudden parting of a chain already strained to the pulling out of the last link. There was a deed that even Marion could not bear, and she left his house and wandered abjectly home to lie sick and wounded in body and spirit for a weary flight of months.

Mrs. Forman watched her curiously; the world of her friends watched her with curiosity. None of them believed that Marion would do more than recover her health before she would rejoin Courtland in the great, dreary new mansion he had but just built for her. Marion stayed on with her mother, inscrutably silent and cold at first, still more inscrutably cheerful, gay and society-loving, when the Lenten season of her illness had passed.

After the first year, Courtland's friends began to lay bets as to how long the separation would last. Courtland had been indifferent when the break came; later he stormed, threatened, and demanded his wife of her mother. Then he pled and wrote her letters that she might read one every day, wherein he begged forgiveness and promised reform. He fell ill and lay at death's door, while physicians telegraphed Marion frantically, assuring her that Courtland's only chances for recovery lay in her presence at his bedside.

Marion read all the letters, signing for the registered ones with a smile of contempt. She refused the money he had placed in the bank to her account; she answered with silence his almost threatening demands for his letters and keepsakes. She treated the physicians' appeal with the same disdain.

"He is not going to die," she told her mother, "If he were as ill as they say, I would feel it here."

Mrs. Forman forbore to remind Marion that she had passionately avowed more than once that all love in her was blotted out, leaving a dull ash of regret and a hollow longing for frivolities.

After the second year, Marion's men friends began to

wonder why she was so long in getting a divorce. When the boldest of them ventured a question, she elevated her brows in disgust.

"Divorce? Why? What for? I'm strong enough to keep Courtland at a distance without the intervention of the law."

"But—er—suppose there should arise a question of marriage again?" he stammered with a longing, caressing look at her beauty grown radiant and youthful again.

"If he wishes to marry, let him get a divorce; I shall not interfere. I'd like to see some other woman go through my experience."

She let herself speak bitterly; she had known the man for a long while.

"But yourself?" His voice was as insinuating as convention would allow.

Marion's eyes grew savage.

"I wouldn't trust the kingliest man that ever trod the world," she breathed through tense teeth.

When in the third year, still evincing a cheerful indifference toward all phases of life that surprised even Marion's most nearly Bohemian friends, the news of Courtland's utter failure in health and finances left her apparently unmoved and uninterested, those who were watching her with the deepest interest and curiosity gave her up in despair as an enigma worthy only of Edipus.

"If Mr. Courtland is lying on his death bed and you *know* he has but a short while to live and you feel that I can soothe him and help him die in peace, send for me. But don't cheat me with a lie in order to effect a patched up reconciliation."

This she wrote to the physician when the rumors came.

"It is only my duty, mother," she explained as she showed the letter before sealing it.

Mrs. Forman quietly acquiesced. She had long since ceased

troubling her brain with finding the fine distinction of the
boundary between hate, love, indifference, and duty. But at
the end of the year, Courtland was out again, though with
broken health and a sadly impaired fortune.

At this juncture an uncle died. He was a misty, vague,
relative, who having made his fortune in the far west preferred to stay there and enjoy life in true democratic fashion,
rather than drifting into the east and fashion and hollowness
and much spending of money. Therefore, Marion and her
mother, being his only living relatives found themselves
suddenly possessed of a fortune of millions; a regular Oriental, Aladdin sort of fortune, three-fourths of which was
Marion's in her own right.

Thus life put on an entirely new aspect for Marion. It
meant independence, affluence, the world treasures of life
opened to her, no matter what it was, she might command it
with an almost imperial dignity. From a life of comparative
poverty, she was suddenly lifted to an almost bewildering
power. If in the dreariest moments of her workday life she
had looked back on the luxuries—dearly bought—that Courtland had surrounded her with, she had compensation now in
the calm contemplation of a cloudless future. If in her most
womanly moments, she had thought of Courtland in poverty
and ill-health, she could show her Samaritan spirit now by
putting him at ease and beyond any future of want.

"And it's the only right thing to do mother," she said
confidingly. "I was poor when Burt married me, and at his
worst he never begrudged me a whim, be it ever so costly.
Now I can settle a sum on him that will put him beyond want
for the rest of his life. Don't you think it a good idea?"

Mrs. Forman applauded the suggestion. Years had taught
her the futility of doing more than acceding to a suggestion
when her advice was asked.

But when Marion's lawyer called to see Courtland about the proposed settlement of fifty thousand a year, he found him politely, but firmly insistent upon refusing any such bounty.

"I don't want her money," he muttered, pacing the floor wildly. "I want HER. She knows. I wanted her when I was rich and she was poor. Now that the situation is reversed I don't want her to throw me a crust and bid me be gone like a beggar. If she wants to help me—let—her come—to me."

That night, Marion lay with burning eyes searching in the darkness for the answer to her problem. The love in her heart, she had said was dead, and ashes lay in its place—but he needed help. She weighed in the balance the two lives that she might lead—a carefree queen with a roseate world before her, or a heartsick, unloving wife, bound to a querulous invalid. Behind her lay the memories of her wild life; a life of blows and caresses; of intoxicating days of perfect love, and depths of degradation and vileness. How could she know that his promises of good conduct would be kept? How could she know but that at the slightest provocation he would not break into his awful passions again? He might live until he died of old age, long after her eyes had closed in sheer misery. She knew that he would be content with no half measure. To go back to him would mean that she must be his wife; through all the heights and depths that she had once trod.

Before her lay the two paths; pleasure and happiness on the one; an unknown formless misery on the other. Which should be the way of her life?

* * *

All night Marion tossed feverishly in the darkness. By morning, her decision must be made, and once made would be unalterable.

In the gray twilight of the dawn she arose, and smiling quietly as at a great burden lifted from her soul, went to her mother's room.

"Mother, I have come to tell you what I have decided to do," she said softly.

NO SACRIFICE*

Stories usually end with the marriage, the chime of the wedding bells, and the "and so they lived happily ever after." Mine begins with the wedding, or rather the engagement. I had met Gerald in a rather romantic fashion. He saw my picture in an amateur magazine, which published some of my verses, and a brief biographical sketch. He wrote me in my southern home, and I was thrilled to the very center of my being when the letter came. For Gerald Kennedy was the leading novelist of the moment. He had sprung into prominence from the middle west, and like Byron, he literally "awoke one morning and found himself famous." That he would condescend to notice the amateurish out-pourings of a little small-town southern school-girl seemed incredible. I answered his letter, and a correspondence grew up, more or less clandestine. My mother had old-fashioned ideas about correspondence with strange men, and I did not take her entirely into my confidence as to the number and length of our letters. Nor of the ardent verses which he sent me—and afterwards sold to magazines, for Gerald was a poet as well as a novelist.

*Typescript, by "Alice D. Nelson," ca. 1928–1931. Written for possible *True Story* publication.

The autumn following the beginning of our romance, I was sent to a small New England girls' college. The glories of the New England autumn will always be associated in my mind with the ripening of my love for Gerald. His letters came almost daily now, and I experienced a thrilling popularity among the girls in school. To be receiving letters from Gerald Kennedy, daily letters, and adorable poems, and passionate outpourings made me the queen of the school. The girls used to crowd around me when my letters came, and I would tantalize them by reading bits here and there, just enough to whet their appetites for more. It was a delightfully happy time. Gerald was begging me to elope with him; he wanted me for his own, unhampered by others, and he did not want the conventional fuss and feathers of a big wedding. He begged me to come to New York, just so he could see his "Dream Girl." Sometimes I felt as if I would just slip away from school, and run over to New York to see him, but something held me back. Maybe it was the thought that down in our Virginia home was a mother who trusted me, and whose heart would break if I should betray that trust.

February came, and Gerald wrote that he was going abroad for a year. He had a lecture contract, and would sail on the fifteenth. He was pathetic about having to delay seeing his "Dream Girl" for another year. I was torn between love and uncertainty. What if I should never see him? What if he should forget me in Europe? I knew that I adored him madly. Torn between doubt and desire, I was shaken to my inmost heart when a telegram was handed me in the gray twilight of the winter day.

"Am giving a farewell party for Gerald Kennedy. Come over and spend a weekend with me. You will be perfectly chaperoned. Barbara Sydnor."

I could scarcely believe my eyes. Mrs. Sydnor was an old

friend of my mother's, and had once visited our home in the south. How she had remembered me and obtained my address I could not conceive, though I suspect Gerald could have told. She was an undoubted factor in literary circles in New York, and to be a guest in her home carried with it much prestige.

The girls shrilled their excitement. "Oh, Aline, you *can't* get away from that now!" they cried, "You *must* go." "Think what it will mean!" "A guest of Mrs. Sydnor's and to a farewell party for Gerald Kennedy!" They adored and envied me in one breath and flew around making additions to my simple wardrobe.

The matron of the school was as impressed as the girls, and that night found me boarding the midnight train for Mrs. Sydnor's and the unknown glories of New York.

The next day and night were like a dream of paradise. Gerald was even handsomer than I had visualized. His pictures—and I had many of them—did not do him justice. They could not show the merry sparkle in his dark brown eyes, the sheen on his chestnut hair, the warm coloring in his face, the subtle play of emotions on his mobile features. That this Greek god could prefer me to the other women who swarmed about him, clamoring for his attention, literally making doormats of themselves, as I thought, seemed incredible. But prefer me he did, and was most frank in the expression of his preference.

We drove together in the park in the afternoon, after a luncheon of literary celebrities. Gerald slipped me away in a manner so adroit that I never knew how it happened. Almost before I knew it he had me in his arms in the luxurious limousine he had commandeered, and was pleading me to marry him before he sailed.

"Marry me, and I will know that you are mine. Then stay

here in New York and wait for me. I'll break my contract, if you say so, and hurry back in a month. But you must be mine, you *must*."

I was swept off my feet. I loved him, and reason was swept to the winds.

The farewell party was scheduled to begin at nine o'clock. Gerald's ship sailed at midnight. It was half-past ten when we entered Mrs. Sydnor's drawing-rooms, filled with excited, chattering people wondering where was the guest of honor. Gerald drew me to the center of the room, under the brilliance of the lights, and throwing his arms about my shrinking form, clad only in my afternoon frock, proclaimed proudly,

"I want to present my bride, Mrs. Gerald Kennedy!"

In the chorus of wonder and congratulations and excitement, I heard a low piteous moan. Marie Weatherford, the tall, handsome brunette from Texas, had fainted dead away.

There was no need to go back to school now. I stayed on in New York, and through Mrs. Sydnor's aid, secured a position as a secretary to the wealthy old Mrs. Hayes, who "wanted something young and cheerful around the house, to read to me and put up with my foolishness." It was a confining position, but my duties were not difficult, and the luxury of the home compensated me for the tedious hours I had to spend within its walls. Gerald's letters were a constant joy. I lived and re-lived that glorious afternoon of our honeymoon. Mother had come to New York immediately after receiving Mrs. Sydnor's message concerning the marriage, and would have taken me back home with her, but Gerald had told me to await his return in New York, and I had vowed to obey him. I was happy, and seeing me so, Mother was content.

The months rolled by swiftly. Gerald was coming home. He had a splendid position in the diplomatic service in

Washington. We would set up our home there, and in the brilliant life of the capital achieve his ambition—to give his "Dream Girl" the setting he thought she merited. So his letters said. I prayed at night that I would not awake and find it all a roseate dream, a thing of fluff and golden light and rainbow thoughts. But when he enfolded me in his arms on the pier as his ship docked, I knew that life for me was the most beautiful and wonderful thing in the world.

That night we went to a homecoming party planned by Marie Weatherford, the flashing-eyed Texas beauty. She was a musician, and in her luxurious studio was staged many a merry Bohemian party. I had gone to one or two during the winter, but in the main, I was lost in the brilliant company. Their caustic wit and brilliant repartee left me lagging far behind with the slower processes of my simpler mind. I did not enjoy Marie's parties, her guests, her food, her drinks, nor her own brilliant, patronizing self. But to-night, since Gerald was the guest of honor, I could do no more than be gracious about going.

I did not know why a pang of jealousy swept through me as Gerald bent low over Marie's hand, and held it rather long to his lips. I felt somehow out of things, as she took possession of him and surrounded him with her personality, to my complete exclusion. I noticed the sly smiles of the guests, the covert remarks, the winks and nods, and the side glances at me, where I sat in a corner on a divan, repulsing the attentions of first one and then another of the sons of Bohemia, who seemed bent on "consoling me."

The party grew wild and wilder. The punchbowl was refilled again and again, and cocktail shakers were kept in a constant ferment. My stomach had never learned to assimilate alcohol, so for the sake of keeping decency in any party to which I might be bidden, I always refused everything. I did not know that I was dubbed a "flat tire" and a "wet blanket." I only knew that I did not like to get sick, so eschewed the things that were physically repugnant to me.

Gerald was in fine fettle. His glass was never empty, and Marie kept close to his side, constantly plying him with more and more liquor, cocktails, punch, champagne. I heard expressions all around me that set me into a dismal train of thought. "Gerald's running true to form, isn't he?" "The old boy hasn't lost any of his thirst." "Guess he drank Paris dry and is back to finish up New York." "Just like old Jerry; he'll be going the rounds again soon."

I grew cold with terror. After all, what did I know of Gerald, the man I had married? I had seen him only one afternoon and evening, and that was our meeting, our courtship, our wedding and our honeymoon. I had been reared with an old-fashioned horror of the drunkard. Had I married one? Vague rumours that had filtered through the air concerning Gerald crystallized into my thoughts. I had not noted them before, so absorbed had I been in our love and my happiness. But now I remembered dimly that the terms "Rounder," "Man about town," "Good fellow" always seemed on people's lips when they spoke of Gerald.

Someone proposed a cabaret as a fitting finish to the party. We piled into cars and taxis and poured into a nightclub, into the blare of the music, the unlovely nudity of the performers, the heat and stale air, the covertly smuggled flasks of gin, and the close-clasped dancing. I was sickened at the breaths of the men who asked me to dance. Gerald seemed to have forgotten me. My heart ached at the farce of this, his first night at home after an absence of a year. He and Marie seemed to have so much more in common than we had. She was ever leaning over his shoulder, lying in his close embrace as they danced on the crowded floor, holding her lips to his, fondling him as I would never have dared to do.

From one to another cabaret we went, and another and another, until I lost count of the weary route. We stumbled up to daylight from the last place. The party had dwindled to one car, in which there were only Marie, Gerald, some sleek-haired, mumbling youth, whose name I had forgotten, if I ever knew it. Gerald had "passed out," as Marie called it. In other words, he was beastly—no, I will not call it beastly, beasts do not so defile themselves—he was ghastly drunk—unconscious.

"Best come to my apartment and let him sleep it off," suggested Marie, with a sneer.

Something awoke in me, and I turned on her defiantly, "I will not take him to your place," I said, "he is my husband, and I can care for him."

She laughed, a slow sneering laugh that maddened me. In anticipation of our happiness together, I had engaged rooms at a hotel, and we went there together, leaving Marie and her friend to find their way home.

Gerald was all penitence the next day, and I found it easy to forgive him. I was very young, and very much in love, and he could exercise a most disarming charm. We were very happy for a few days, and then another party, and another lapse. I saw Gerald for what he was, wild, undisciplined, spoiled, a prey to the baser emotions roused in him by women like Marie. I ran all the gamut of emotions that the traditional wife of a drunkard runs. There were days when I felt that I must separate from him and go my way alone. Then the prospect of a life without Gerald stretched a dreary, blank, gray path, leading nowhere, barren of hope or joy or love, and I had not the courage to go through with my resolution.

Marie loomed like a ghastly Nemesis. There was no use in trying to deceive myself as to the relations between her and Gerald in the past. I believed him innocent of her now, but she took delight in taunting me with her previous intimacy with my husband, of the closeness of their friendship, of their community of interests and friends. She took a fiendish delight in making me the outsider in my husband's life. Gerald pretended that I was oversensitive, that Marie was, in reality, a good friend of mine, trying to teach me the way to be a social success.

"You must not be a little fool," he said to me once angrily. That hurt. To think that the man I adored could speak to me in such a manner, and because of another woman was almost more than I could stand.

Fortunately the call from Washington came and we hurried south. I was all excited eagerness at the thought of being alone with Gerald, of the new and strange life of which would be a part, of the home I would make for Gerald, of the part I would play in his interesting life. I would begin to write again, and he would be proud of me once more. We would be together, and we would make a home, which would be a center for the brilliant people in the city. I could not help but discuss my plans with Gerald, and he seemed as brightly eager to help me as he had once been in the earlier days of our love.

But alas, the brilliant, sober-minded, serious and thoughtful circle which I had hoped to grace eluded me. Gerald had a fatal gift of attracting to him the butterflies of life. I found myself swept into a swift set of false ideals, false standards, false lives. Gerald was busy in the office all day. He had engagements in the evening with those who could "advance" him, so he said, and his nights were taken up with a round of social engagements, winding up too often in nightclubs, road houses, dawn dances, early hour house parties. Weekends were a nightmare to me—a joy to Gerald. He had definitely relegated me to the position of a little, inconspicuous hausfrau. Neither my health nor my inclination permitted me to keep up in the mad whirl in which he lived and moved and had his joyous being. Gerald liked another women, plenty of them, and he did not seem to care how I fared. If I went places with other escorts, he was satisfied provided I did not interfere with his butterfly of the moment. That his house was well-managed, his servants efficient, his wife ready to act as hostess for whatever party he brought home or chose to "pull," that the machinery of the household was well-oiled, and that there was always plenty to eat and drink when he wanted it, were his major concerns. The fact that we were running a hotel and not a home did not annoy him in the least. I drifted into a dull acceptance of the situation. I was too numbed in my soul to know whether my heart was broken with disappointment or not. I seemed like a somnambulist, walking along the road, without knowing or caring whither I went.

It was at the height of a particularly brilliant season in our second winter in Washington that Gerald came to me in a diffident manner, quite foreign to his usual air of masculine self-assertion.

"Er—Aline—" he began slowly, "—er—Marie Weatherford is coming to-morrow for a visit—"

"That woman in my house," I interrupted breathlessly, "Why Gerald, what are you thinking of?"

"There's absolutely nothing the matter with Marie, but

your own nasty-minded suspicions!" he flared up, crimson with rage. "I've promised her a season in Washington, and she wants to come now."

"There are plenty of places where you can put her up without insulting me by bringing her here," I retorted.

"What do you mean by insult? How dare you imply that I am insulting you by bringing one of my friends to the home?" His anger was so out of proportion to the cause of it that I knew him guilty of my suspicions.

"Gerald," I answered slowly, "I know perfectly well that you and Marie have been meeting in New York ever since you returned from Europe. I know about the weekends you have spent with her at various house parties on Long Island; I know you love her more than you love me. My only wonder is that you continue to live with such a drab little nobody— but don't rub it in, don't bring her here—" I could not help the choking sobs that finished my sentence.

Gerald seemed ashamed. He patted my back, and wiped my tears with his own handkerchief.

"You're all wrong, little girl," he said gently. "I know I'm pretty wild, and I've been neglecting you a bit of late, but it doesn't mean a thing. You're always the first with me, you know it. But there's just something in my blood—you can't understand it, you little white rose, but there's no other woman in my life, however black it may seem."

And thus, with fair words and tender caresses and kisses he lulled my fears and suspicions, and made some of the old riotous happiness of our earlier days come bounding back to my soul. Marie came as our house guest two days later.

I will draw a veil over the weeks that followed. It is such an old story—the guest of the home, who betrays the wife. An old story, a universal one, differing only in its sordid details. And it was one of those sordid details that brought about a crisis in our lives.

The Citoyens' Ball was easily the most brilliant affair of the season, and Marie was busy planning her costume, turning the house upside down with her preparations to be the QUEEN of the assemblage. I dreaded going. I knew Gerald would have no eyes for me, and I had no heart to plan a gown. But some instinct of self-preservation made me go through with the ordeal. Because Gerald had always called me his "White Rose," I chose white satin and white roses and pearls and a white ermine evening wrap. Marie was as radiant as the red rose which her gown simulated. We went together, first to a gorgeous dinner, Marie escorted by a somber-eyed young Parisian, at that moment the darling of the younger set.

Gerald showed uneasiness. Marie was tauntingly beautiful, and she seemed bent, either on making him wildly jealous, or it may have been, she wished to show her power over M. Meriam to the younger women, who adored him and envied her. After his one duty dance with me, Gerald resigned himself to watching Marie, to torturing himself with jealous furies at the evident absorption in her handsome partner.

I was dancing by them once, he and Marie, and I overheard him threaten her with dire misfortune if she did not cease torturing him. I heard his low, pain-fraught tones, her taunting, sneering laugh—and I felt sorry for Gerald.

The climax came when he saw her leaving the hall nearly a full hour before closing time with M. Meriam. I saw Gerald rush to the door and intercepting them, apparently expostulate violently. I saw Marie's light shrug of the shoulder, her sparkling backward glance, and the attitude of blank despair with which Gerald watched them as they swept away, leaving him standing alone. A short time later, he followed wildly. He had forgotten me. I was left alone, without an escort at a formal ball.

It would have been humiliating beyond words had it not been for Laurence Owens. He had been a patient and un-obtrusive admirer of mine all winter. I had smiled to myself at his gentle devotion, his subtle attentions, the delicate way he had of letting me know that he considered me a wife neglected, and that he would be my consoler if I would allow him. I was so in love with Gerald that all men seemed as trees walking, even in the face of his most flagrant infidelities, so the subtle attentions of Dr. Owens merely amused, without tempting me.

But this night I was grateful for the quiet way that he came to my side at once. He had seen the whole wretched panto-mime, and without saying a word, he let me know what he had seen, understood and sympathized. He danced with me, and took me down to supper. When I pled a headache, and expressed a desire to go home, without a word, he escorted me to his car, and we drove away. I was so crushed, so humiliated that in the safe darkness of the car, I let the quiet tears flow. I did not even notice that he had taken me in his arms, and was gently kissing away the tears, that he was murmuring words of love to me and telling me of his desire always to protect me. I fled to his warm comfort as a child flees to its mother's breast; I was conscious of no other feeling than that of a tired child who lays its burdens on the breast of a mother or father.

But Dr. Owens felt otherwise. I cannot describe the subtle way in which he insinuated himself into my life. Gerald had left the house when we got home. I found a note from him saying that he had been sent to Cuba, and had gone to New York by an early morning train, and would sail from there. Marie shrugged her shoulders when I announced this at luncheon, and that evening, she too, left for New York. I was alone again, with my wretched thoughts and the insidious attentions of Dr. Owens.

Shall I tell it all? I loved Gerald madly, but his absence, the cold little notes I had from him from Cuba, the knowledge brought me by someone that he had spent a week in New York, and was seen constantly with Marie, who had apparently repented of her escapade with M. Meriam—all these left a great, cruel wound in my heart, and it was easy for the tender consolations of a sympathetic and understanding person to find grateful acceptance. Dr. Owens was so unobtrusive, so gentle, so subtle in his attentions that I drifted into an affair with him almost imperceptibly. I was astounded after a bit to find that people were beginning to place us together at dinners; that we were supposed to accompany each other to parties, that, in other words, we were acknowledged as having an "affair," and that it seemed the proper and accepted thing to do.

"Faciliis descensus avernus." I had ceased to think in the terms that had been mine when my mother talked to me of the fundamentals of life, and stressed the beauty of wifely fidelity and the loyalty of married couples. I picked up a newspaper one Sunday morning. In the rotagravure section I saw a picture of the fashionable set in Havana. There stood Gerald in his flannels, and laughing and leaning on his arm, with what seemed to me a malicious smile lurking in the corner of her mouth, was Marie, in the latest and most daring sport outfit. When Dr. Owens came to me that evening with his honeyed whispers, I let down the bars of my resistance. What was life without Gerald's love? Why not snatch a bit of happiness for myself?

Many a woman has lulled her uneasy conscience to rest by telling herself that she is a wronged and wounded wife; that her husband does not care what she does; that it is the accepted situation in her set; that the seventh commandment is as outmoded as the hoopskirt and the bustle, and that if she is hurting no one by her actions, there is no harm done; that life is such an uncertain thing, she had best snatch what happiness she can whenever and wherever she can. I say many a woman has lulled, or tried to lull her conscience to sleep. I tried. I failed. I could not be happy in the devotion with which Dr. Owens surrounded me, in spite of his most earnest efforts, nor the easy drifting on of our lives together, either unnoticed by the swift set in which we moved, or covertly winked at.

Gerald returned from Cuba a wreck. For three years he had gone a pace that would have killed a Samson. He worked hard, and he never spared himself in the doing of his duty. He played hard, and he played every spare moment that he could get. He wrote much, and there were contracts for stories, and for a novel, that drove him to write at whatever cost. He loved hard, and he loved many, but he reserved his passion for Marie. He had scores of friends, or shall I say hangers-on? who battened upon him and sapped his vitality, what was left, and constantly urged him to more and greater excesses. He came home in the late spring, a shadow of his former self, with a racking cough that made specialists shake their heads and look grave and talk to him learnedly and seriously.

He tried to go back to work, but he was soon down with

pneumonia. Nurses. Doctors. Consultations. Hospital. Oxygen treatments. I threw off the well-meaning sympathy of Dr. Owens. I forgot everything save that Gerald was the love of my life. I became nothing but a praying machine. I felt that God was punishing me for my sins, and I wallowed abjectly in a slough of despond, from which I emerged only when the doctors informed me that the crisis was over and that with care, Gerald would soon be well again. But he recovered only to face shattered health, the threat of tuberculosis, and an order to go to the west, Arizona or Colorado.

I loved the Rocky Mountains. Here I had Gerald to myself, for awhile, at least. He had a year's leave of absence. Our wants were few in our little ranch house, on the edge of the plains, with a view of a curving sweep of the snow-capped Rockies, from Pike's Peak to Long's Peak, a hundred and fifty miles of grandeur. Gerald slowly won his way back to health. We rode horseback together. He hunted jack rabbits and climbed the foothills. At nights we read and talked together, and some of the camaraderie of which I had dreamed came to our lives. It was glorious, early in the mornings to scamper across the plains on our sturdy ponies, followed by the big sheep dogs, which were a part of the outfit of the tiny ranch. We learned how to build campfires, and laughed at our efforts to toss flap jacks in the frying pan in accepted cowboy fashion. True there was a veil between us—a veil whose thickness was tangible and real. It was formed of the memory of Gerald's past, and the thought of my own. I could not hold him guilty when I remembered that I had sought consolation. I knew too, that he must have heard rumors of my flirtation with Dr. Owens, there are always busybodies in every city to help bring about divorces. I often wondered why he had not reproached me. Thus, though there was comradeship, and almost happiness between us, there was also a sense of suspense, of waiting for a crisis.

It came. We returned one lovely crisp day from a long ride up the trail of the foothills. A ride that was long to stay in my memory as the last of our lovely experiences together. It had been a day of almost unbelievable happiness. Almost the veil had been withdrawn. Several times I felt that Gerald was on the point of confessing his sorrow at having tortured me with Marie. And if he had, I should have told him all the truth about Laurence Owens, and we would have thrown aside the old bitternesses, and started life anew with no cloud between us, no barrier to our perfect understanding and love. But somehow, whenever he began to speak, and I knew in my heart that the moment had come, he would hesitate, clear his throat, and I knew that the golden opportunity was gone.

We were riding home slowly when he leaned over to me. "Aline darling, there is something I must tell you, something I want you to tell me, so that we can begin a new life in truth."

My heart beat so fast I thought it would choke me, but I nodded my head for I could not speak.

"When Marie and I—" he continued, and then we heard a shout, a honking of the horns of many automobiles, and looking across the plains toward our little ranch house, we saw it literally surrounded by cars, out of which people poured, shouting across the mesquite and sage brush, and waving joyous and excited signals.

We spurred our horses to a gallop. When we were near our house, Marie ran out to meet us radiant in her knickers and boots, sombrero and kerchief. She nodded to me, but laid her hands on Gerald's bridle, and laughed into his eyes as he wonderingly demounted.

"You folks needn't think you're the only ones in this neck of the woods," drawled Dr. Owens, as he took possession of my hand. "We've got a house-party of thirty up at the Que-Bar Ranch, just seventy miles away, and as soon as we got you honeymooners located, we drove down all of us, in flivvers and what not to pay a sociable call."

And here it was all over again, Marie, Laurence Owens, the whole silly, gushing, guzzling, dancing, drinking, gambling, gossiping, scandalous set from back home, here in the clean pure air of the mountains, defiling it with their breaths and vapid words, forgetting sunset and sunrise, seeing in the wonderful moonlit and starlight nights, only opportunity for unwholesome flirtation and scandalous romance, oblivious of the purity of snow-capped peaks, grateful only to the clean-washed ozone, if it gave them fresh appetite for drink.

Two weeks of this. Of the visits of the house-party to our ranch, of our return visits, or weekend stays, of the parties, the all-night carousals. I saw Gerald slip back, back, away from me, back to Marie, away from the joys of hard riding, clean living, simple pleasures. Dr. Owens sought to drag me down too, back to a place with the others, where he might give me "consolation," but my soul revolted. Even Gerald's obvious neglect of me, and the succumbing to the lure of Marie, could not tempt me to wreck my soul further.

One night ten or twelve of the crowd came to our ranch for dinner, cards, an all-night party. I sickened of them long ere midnight and would have gone to bed and left them to their own devices, but someone had pre-empted my bedroom to sleep off a too potent dinner. I went outside, and climbed up in the crotch of a crooked catalpa tree, where I was wont to sit on sunny days, and look at the magnificent panorama of plain and mountains. Hidden in the long leaves of the

trees I could hear all and see all, and not be visible. I saw
Dr. Owens prowling around the lot looking for me, I knew,
and chuckled in unholy mirth at his evident discomfiture. I
saw Marie and Gerald come out arm in arm, their heads
close together, and vanish in the moonlight toward the old
barn. I watched couples sentimentalizing in the moonlight,
and wondered vaguely why that kind of thing had ceased to
allure me. I must have fallen asleep in my comfortable crotch,
for when I was conscious of my surroundings, I noted the
faint glimmer of dawn in the east, and saw Gerald and Marie
coming from the direction of the barn toward the house.

They passed directly beneath my tree. Marie's voice was
soft, filled with tenderness that I did not know possible.
Gerald's tones had that gentle wooing note that always set my
pulses athrill. And they were making plans for their future.
Marie was the aggressor. I did not mean to listen, but I
could not help it without disclosing my presence. They
stopped where I looked directly down upon them, and Marie
seemed to have gained her point, for Gerald took her in his
arms finally, and they pledged themselves to a life together
beneath some skies, far away from the interference of the
world.

When they had gone into the house, and I knew by the
bustle and stir that the party was disbanding, I slid down
from the tree, up to my room, packed a case with the barest
necessities, hastened into the barn, saddled my horse, and
while the crowd was shouting good-byes to Gerald, slipped
out the back road, and putting spurs to my pony, sped away
across the plains to Silverdale, twenty miles away, the railroad
station in the opposite direction from the one we usually used.
I gave the horse to the station master to be returned to the
ranch and boarded a fast express for the east. I had tied a

note to the saddle of the pony to be given Gerald. It was brief.

"Gerald: I overheard you and Marie planning your life together. I will not stand in the way of your love and happiness. You can get a divorce if you want it. I will not contest. Aline."

You might have thought that I would flee to mother for love and sympathy but I did not want any. Something hard filled my heart and soul, and sympathy seemed mawkish and unnecessary. I heard that Gerald had resigned his post in the service, and had gone to Switzerland for his "health." Marie seemed to have dropped from the public eye at the same time, but whether people connected the disappearance of the two I did not know. I refuse to see any visitors in Washington, as I dismantled the house, and disposed of the furnishings by sale or storage. Dr. Owens haunted me with his attentions, but I persisted in my determination not to see him or to resume any friendship with him. I blamed him and rightly so, for engineering the whole house party to the Que-Bar Ranch and wrecking my little paradise on the plains.

When the house was completely dismantled and disposed of, I fled to New York, and in a comparatively short while had a job in an office. A job so foreign to the life I had lived for the past five years, although it was in a publishing firm, so taxing, so confining, so challenging to my every capability, that I found no time for repining, for worry, for anything but keeping myself efficient and fit. It was a gruelling task, but it was my salvation.

Now and then vague echoes of Gerald seeped through to me. He had returned from Switzerland, I heard, and tried to get back his old post. But younger, stronger, steadier and more efficient men had taken their places in the service, and

Gerald was outmoded from his year or two of idleness. Now and then I ran across stories from his pen in the magazines. But they were very poor, and I fancied were accepted only because of the lustre of his name. A scathing series of reviews of his new novel foredoomed it to failure.

I often wondered in my leisure moments where he was and what he was doing. Now and then I saw his name in the papers, a habitue of the New York nightclubs. My own path would never cross his. I was a woman in the business world, whose straight and narrow road went monotonously from office to the woman's club house where I lived. There was an occasional bypath to a theatre matinee, a concert, an art exhibit, a game of bridge with some of the other women in the club. I went sedately gowned and soberly marcelled. Men had no place in my life, save as employers or business associates. I could neither hate nor love Gerald. When I thought of him seriously, I wondered why I had not been served with a notice of our divorce.

Riding down in the subway one day my eyes fell on a glaring headline in the morning paper:

GERALD KENNEDY ONCE FAMOUS NOVELIST DRUGGED AND LEFT TO DIE

I read, with a strange fear clutching at my heart, the lurid story which followed. Gerald had been found apparently lifeless in the area-way of a house of none too savory reputation, his pocketbook, stickpin, watch, cufflinks, overcoat, all gone. Apparently he had been drugged, robbed and thrown into the street, the victim of the gangsters with whom he had evidently felt safe in one of his excursions into gang-land. They had probably thought him dead, else his life would not have been spared.

For days I made inquiries at the hospital to which he was sent, without giving my name. When I heard he had recovered enough to be dismissed, I ceased my interest. Again I lost sight of him, but not for long.

From now on Gerald's name figured in the papers constantly. He was the center of escapade after escapade of the most unsavory nature. There was hardly a raid, a disgraceful story, a disreputable brawl unless Gerald was the storm center around which the turmoil revolved. It seemed to me as I read of his drunken life that he must be trying to drown some unhappy memory. When I saw an account of the marriage of Marie to a Hungarian count, I knew what it was. The papers were filled with stories and pictures of the magnificent international marriage—for Marie's father was immensely wealthy in Texas oil lands, and she was well able to purchase a European throne, if she wished it.

So poor Gerald had been thrown into the discard? I could not help a throb of pity for him as I looked at the pictures of the wedding in the rotogravure papers. "Poor boy," I said to the pictured wedding procession, "She might at least have had you for one of the ushers."

Shortly after the wedding I received a summons to come to the office of a lawyer, one of the biggest in New York. I went with a strange choking sensation. At last Gerald had filed suit for divorce. Although I had been expecting it for four years, I could not help the weird emptiness in the pit of my stomach at the thought.

The lawyer was kindly-eyed and gentle. He smiled as I entered the room.

"Sit down, Mrs. Kennedy," he smiled at me, "I have a shock for you. You might faint, and I don't want you to fall too far."

"I never faint," I assured him, "I can stand anything."

"Are you sure?" he asked, still smiling.

"Absolutely," but I took the chair he placed for me.

"Well, I have the pleasure of announcing to you that you are the sole heiress of ten million dollars."

"Ten million dollars!" Things did go black before me for a moment, and then I caught on to myself and held the world down before it went off into a sky rocket. "But who would leave me ten million dollars? You must be joking."

"Did you ever hear of Jackson Weatherford?"

"Mother's only brother," I answered promptly, "but he died when I was a little girl."

"Not died, disappeared. Changed his name. Went west. Bought a worthless ranch, and lived to see it one of the greatest oil fields in the section. He never bothered to write you folks, because he was in a pet about some family disagreement. But he always kept in touch with your lives, and intended if ever you were in need to come to your assistance. He was particularly interested in your career after you separated from your husband, and before he died, just six months ago, in fact, he was so impressed with your pluck and grit that he made a will leaving you everything he possessed, except for a few minor bequests to followers and servants."

"His wife, children," I manage to whisper.

"Never married. It is all yours."

And now, here I was sole heiress to millions in stocks, bonds, valuable city property, oil wells, a dazzling Cinderella dream, the sort of thing that you think of as impossible, preposterous. I was dazed, and it took me literally weeks to get a grip on myself. I dreaded giving up my job for fear the drama was only a figment of the imagination, and I should awake jobless and penniless.

Eventually after many weeks, months, rather, of tiresome adjustments, conferences with lawyers, visits to my "estate" scattered in various parts of the country, eventually, here we were, mother and I settled in a lovely mansion on the Hudson River, a dream home, with everything that the heart and soul could desire. Friends, of course, flocking to me from everywhere, and the treasures of the world mine for the asking.

But again the fatal newspaper. I was having my breakfast in bed one morning. My room was a dream of loveliness. Outside of the long windows I could see the river sparkling in the sunshine, within the room a bower of roses, fragrant, beautiful. The tray sparkled with glass and silver, and the most fragile china. The dainty breakfast might have been prepared to tempt the appetite of a capricious queen. I lay back among the silken coverlets and lacy pillows, and idly picked up the morning paper.

GERALD KENNEDY, ONCE FAMOUS WRITER
PUT OUT OF SANITARIUM
FOR NON PAYMENT OF BOARD

Poor Gerald, fled in his extremity to the cheapest and most unsavory of refuges against the ravages of disease, and thrown into the discard because he had not money to pay his board.

I went to Mr. Brewster that morning with plans for Gerald. I was the queen, now, he the beggar lad. I could afford to reach down to him in the gutter of his extremity and give him largess. Knowing Gerald as well as I did, I knew that my benefactions would have to be anonymous. He would die rather than take a cent from the women he had wronged.

But Mr. Brewster was very grave. "I am sorry, Mrs.

Kennedy," he said wiping his eyeglasses thoughtfully, "but what you propose is absolutely impossible."

"Do you mean to tell me," I spluttered, "that I can't give away some of the surplus of my income where and how I please?"

"I mean just that," he answered, "you may give it almost anywhere you wish, but never to your—shall I say ex-husband?"

"I—I—don't understand."

"Your uncle, Jackson Weatherford, was so incensed at the way you were treated by Mr. Kennedy that he specifically stipulated in his will that if at any time you spent one dollar on Gerald or in any way allowed him to be benefitted by Mr. Weatherford's money, the entire fortune would revert to his estate, a modest income to be settled on your mother during her lifetime, in order to secure for her economic independence in her old age, the rest to be distributed to charity according to a list which he drew up and added to the will."

"Why was I not told this in the beginning?"

"You were not to be told until and unless it was necessary."

I sat looking at him aghast. I had not known until this minute that much of the secret joy I had experienced in being the possessor of millions came from the feeling that now I could help Gerald, or shall I say, lord it over him? I tried to analyze my feelings. Did I really love him so much that I wanted genuinely to help him, or was I merely anxious to play the Lady Bountiful? I could not tell, but I was enraged to think how my uncle had tied my hands.

I went out from the office thoughtfully. Oh, well, Gerald had a faculty for landing on his feet. He'd get along somehow, and I knew it would never be possible for us to live together again. There was too much of the past between us now. I went back to my life of luxury and ease and comfort and travel. Friends and social pleasures, gowns and happy visits. Music and art and literature graced my life as I had dreamed it would when I was a girl. Surely no woman had a more lovely existence, so exquisitely perfumed a bed of roses.

But disquieting rumors came to me from time to time. My friends stopped talking sometimes when I came upon a group suddenly, and I heard Gerald's name on more than one tongue as I moved from throng to throng. The newspapers carried little squibs here and there. He had ceased to be a front page celebrity, but had descended to the police court records. He was in brawls. He was thrown out of cheap dance halls for not paying his entrance fee. He was in the Jefferson Market Night Court time and again. He was a common, drunken loafer, apparently waiting to die from the ghastly disease against which he no longer struggled. He had ceased to write, even the pot-boiler stories that had ruined his name as a literary artist. He was a bum in every sense of the word. No degradation could be more complete.

Sometimes as I thought of Gerald the delicate and delicious morsels of food at my table would choke me, and I would put my fork down, wondering with horror when he had eaten. Sometimes when I tossed among the silken draperies of my bed, I would arise, and walking to the window, look out upon the lordly Hudson that rolled beneath, wondering where Gerald had cast his weary limbs to rest. My life of luxury and ease was becoming a torture to me. I realized now that Gerald was the one love of my life, and that only in his life and love could I find the happiness of true fulfilment.

I was in my little sitting room, overlooking the rose garden early one evening, listening idly to the radio. The News of the Day was coming in, rattled off by a word Speed-King.

"And now friends, here comes one of the stories that illustrates life's little ironies. Gerald Kennedy, you all remember Gerald Kennedy, yesterday's idolized novelist and club-man, the author of more than one thrilling tale, tried to commit suicide this afternoon in a flop house on Second Avenue. Gerald has been running down for the past five years, and now it seems his degradation and misery are complete. He did not finish the job, but the doctors in the Miserercordia Hospital where he was taken say it would have better if he had. That's fame, isn't it?"

I did not stay to listen to anything else. It could not have been more than a half hour before my car drove up to the entrance to the hospital, but to me it seemed a half a day. The doctors and nurses were frankly skeptical at my claims of being Mrs. Kennedy, and allowed me in the ward with covert smiles of disbelief.

Gerald was weak almost to dissolution, but conscious. The brilliant light that leapt into his pallid face, the lambent flame of joy was payment in full measure for what I planned to do. In that instant it was revealed to me as in a blinding flash from Heaven that here was my work, my career, my entire life, no matter what sacrifice it involved, no matter what the world might think, no matter what the past had been. Some sort of like revelation, even in his pitiful weakness, came to Gerald too. For the first time in our lives words were unnecessary. A closer communion than had ever been possible before, drew us together within a sacred circle, and we both knew that our lives were inextricably bound together, come what may. I knelt by his side and laid my face gently on his hand. He had aimed the bullet at his heart, but his hand, weakly shaking from drink and lack of food, sent the bullet wide, and it had grazed his side and lodged in his back.

"If we can pull him through this terrible weakness," the doctor assured me, "rest and regular hours and care will help clear up the other trouble. But he must want to live."

"You do want to live, Gerald?" I asked him.

"If you will never leave me," he answered.

"I will never leave you," I promised him solemnly, "but you will have a poor woman for your wife."

"God be praised for that," he answered devoutly.

Mr. Brewster was disgusted with me when I told him my decision. "Women are past all comprehending," he said over and over, but somehow I fancied I caught a suppressed gleam of admiration in his eyes. "And what will a penniless woman do with an invalid husband?" he queried.

"Not exactly penniless, Mr. Brewster," I answered proudly, "I had saved a bit out of my salary the five years I was working, and I invested it wisely enough to get a fair return. That is a special fund still in a bank, untouched. That will be enough to take us west—and when Gerald is well and contented, he will write again and return to his old place in the literary world. And in the meanwhile," I smiled at Mr. Brewster, "Do you remember the other day you told me of the new development near the Que-Bar Ranch that was to be opened up, and said all it needed to make it go was a capable woman executive to hold the men in line."

Mr. Brewster stared at me without speaking.

"Well, here's an applicant for the job. I've had years of experience as an executive, I can give you first class reference, and I am ready to begin at once."

"Do you mean to tell me that you are willing to work for the estate that you once owned?"

"Why not?" I answered. I was happier at the prospect than I had been since our brief honeymoon eight years ago.

Gerald growing well and strong. Gerald beginning to write again in the little study of our tiny ranch-house near the Que-Bar Ranch. My duties as secretary of the development were not arduous, and the salary was flattering. Gerald and I had our long rides over the plains, our intimate camping parties, all the joy of companionship, the happiness of a new and deeper comradeship. When I thought of the luxuries I had given up I had a feeling as if a distasteful burden had dropped from my shoulders. In the happiness of our new love, the cloying luxuries of the east seemed pale and uninteresting. We talked of the days when his new novel—the best he had ever written—would bring him increased income; when our investments in the new work, which I had once owned, would bring us handsome returns, and I would stop work, and there would be children to ride on their little ponies at his side as he galloped across the plains.

These were wonderful dreams, and there was naught in the sky, not the tiniest fleck of a cloud to prevent their realization.

"May I tell you one thing, Gerald?" I said one evening, as we rode home over the sunset plains, and watched the glory of the sun as it sank behind the rose-colored snows of the mountains.

He waited silently. We reined in our horses and sat still, watching the ever wonderful panorama of the heavens.

"I have not been entirely guiltless—" I began.

He leaned over and took my hands in his. "Darling, I knew as soon as I came from Switzerland, and it was the realization that I, by my cruelty and callousness, had driven you to seek refuge in another man's arms—you the whitest of souls, the purest of women—it was the realization of that which drove me to wilder and wilder excesses. For I have always felt that *I* dragged *you* down and sullied your soul. Owens is dead—" I could not control a start of surprise at hearing this. "Once I thought I would kill him, but a wiser One than I took care of him. He could not stand the pace of his life, and died of a stroke, and you have washed away that sin by the supreme sacrifice of a sainted life. It was not your sin, but mine, and we have expiated it together."

"No sacrifice, darling," I answered, "but glorious happiness."

And the glory of the sunset covered us as our lips touched in a holy communion.

DRAMA
❧ ❧ ❧

THE AUTHOR'S
EVENING AT HOME*

SCENE—*Library. Weather—Ninety in the shade.*

> AUTHOR, *tired, nervous.*
> WIFE, *fidgety.*
> MOTHER
> SERVANT

WIFE *discovered lying on lounge.* AUTHOR *enters, and seats himself by her side.*

AUTHOR—Well, little girl, how are you?

WIFE—Oh, I am so sick!

AUTHOR—Let me go for a doctor.

WIFE—No, I don't need a doctor; I just have a headache.

AUTHOR—Well, lie quiet, dear.

WIFE—I don't want to lie quiet. *(Struggles to a sitting posture.)*

AUTHOR—Do you want to go out for a walk, dear? *(Kisses her.)*

WIFE *(crossly)*—No! *(Lies down again.)*

AUTHOR *(going to desk)*—Well, dear, I thought over that final chapter today, and I think I'll write it out.

WIFE—John!

AUTHOR—Yes, dear.

WIFE—You have kissed me only once.

AUTHOR *(dutifully rising and kissing her on her forehead)*— Poor little woman! *(Goes back to desk.)*

The Smart Set, September 1900, pp. 105–106.

WIFE—John!

AUTHOR—Yes, dear.

WIFE—If you only knew how my head aches!

AUTHOR *(seating himself again on lounge)*—I can imagine, dear.

WIFE—Why don't you do something to amuse me?

AUTHOR—I, dear? What can I do?

WIFE *(petulantly)*—What have you been doing to-day? You never tell me a thing.

AUTHOR—Well, I finished two chapters. Would you like to hear them, dear?

WIFE—Of course.

(AUTHOR *begins to read aloud.*)

WIFE—John!

AUTHOR—Yes, dear.

WIFE—Mrs. De Smythe was here to-day, and you have no idea how elegant she looked. She wore a gray satin suit trimmed with cut steel and gray chiffon, and her hat was a gray toque with violets.

AUTHOR—Have you finished, dear?

WIFE—Oh, yes; go on.

(AUTHOR *reads to end of chapter and looks to* WIFE *for approval.*)

WIFE—John!

AUTHOR—Yes, dear.

WIFE—Do you know that bald spot on your head has changed its form completely? Now it's almost a heart-shape.

(AUTHOR *says things under his breath and goes to his desk again.*)

WIFE *(pettishly)*—How cross you are!

(*Silence for thirty-three seconds.* AUTHOR *writes industriously.* WIFE *sits up and begins to embroider. Enter* SERVANT.)

SERVANT—I've come for the breakfast order, mum.

WIFE—Oh, yes. Well, Mary, we'll have—let me see—
John, would you like a mackerel to-morrow?

(AUTHOR *mutters unpublishable things and grunts for reply.*)

WIFE—All right. Well, Mary, we'll have broiled mackerel
and cakes, and—well, just anything.

SERVANT—Yes, mum. *(Exit.)*

*(Silence for twenty-six seconds. WIFE fidgets in her chair;
drops scissors; hums one of Sousa's marches.)*

WIFE—John!

AUTHOR—Well?

WIFE—John, if England whips the Boers, it will change
things about in Africa, won't it?

AUTHOR—Yes, I suppose so.

WIFE—John, where is the Boer country?

AUTHOR—Get an atlas and find out.

*(WIFE spends some noisy moments finding an atlas on the book
shelves, drops a book on her foot and cries out. AUTHOR groans.)*

WIFE—John!

AUTHOR—Well?

WIFE—Come and see the map; here it is.

(AUTHOR rises and seats himself beside her on the lounge.)

WIFE—I don't understand what the Orange Free State is.
Tell me.

*(AUTHOR explains tersely, shuts the atlas and goes back to his
desk. Enter MOTHER; sighs, and sits in an armchair.)*

MOTHER—Oh, my, how warm it is!

AUTHOR—Let me open the window. *(Rises and opens
window. WIFE resignedly puts on a shawl.)*

AUTHOR—Are you cold, dear?

WIFE—Oh, it makes no difference about *me*. (AUTHOR
*goes back to desk with lines deepening on his face. MOTHER and
WIFE converse in sibilant whispers.*)

AUTHOR—For heaven's sake!

WIFE—You're disturbing John, mother. *(Exit into next room, where she can be heard moving about and humming the Sousa march.)*

MOTHER—Are you busy, dear?

AUTHOR—Oh, no; just amusing myself, trying to make some bread and butter.

MOTHER—I'm sorry to disturb you, dear, but then, you know, I just like to be about and see you at work. Of course, I sha'n't bother you at all. You can go right on. I sha'n't make a bit of noise or be in your way. I don't disturb you, do I?

AUTHOR—Oh, no, mother, not at all.

MOTHER—I thought not. You see, it's just as I was saying to-day to Mrs. Blackwell; when John comes home in the evening, Bess and I love to sit in the library while he writes, and watch him and learn repose by keeping still.

(Enter WIFE on tiptoe; her shoes creak audibly. Goes to lounge, knocking against a chair on the way. Lies down with heavy sigh. Silence for three minutes, broken by the scratching of AUTHOR'S pen and alternate sighs from WIFE and MOTHER. Bell rings.)

WIFE—Mercy me, I hope it's no one to disturb John! *(Enter SERVANT.)*

SERVANT—Mr. and Mrs. Cartwright are in the parlor, mum, and Mrs. Cartwright says as how they've come over for a rubber of whist.

MOTHER—What a pity!

WIFE—Just as John was in such a good train of thought, too.

AUTHOR—Thank heavens!

MINE EYES HAVE SEEN *

A PLAY IN ONE ACT

(Rights of Reproduction reserved.)

CHARACTERS

DAN: *The Cripple.*
CHRIS: *The Younger Brother.*
LUCY: *The Sister.*
MRS. O'NEILL: *An Irish Neighbor.*
JAKE: *A Jewish Boy.*
JULIA: *Chris' Sweetheart.*
BILL HARVEY: *A Muleteer.*
CORNELIA LEWIS: *A Settlement Worker.*
Time: Now
Place: A manufacturing city in the
northern part of the United States.

SCENE   *Kitchen of a tenement. All details of furnishing empha-size sordidness—laundry tubs, range, table covered with oil cloth, pine chairs. Curtain discloses* DAN *in a rude imitation of a steamer chair, propped by faded pillows, his feet covered with a patch-work quilt. Practicable window at back.*

LUCY *is bustling about the range preparing a meal. During the conversation she moves from range to table, setting latter and making ready the noon-day meal.*

*The Crisis, 15, 1918, pp. 271–75.

DAN *is about thirty years old; face thin, pinched, bearing traces of suffering. His hair is prematurely gray; nose finely chiselled; eyes wide, as if seeing BEYOND. Complexion brown.*

LUCY *is slight, frail, brown-skinned, about twenty, with a pathetic face. She walks with a slight limp.*

DAN: Isn't it most time for him to come home, Lucy?

LUCY: It's hard to tell, Danny, dear; Chris doesn't come home on time any more. It's half-past twelve, and he ought to be here by the clock, but you can't tell any more—you can't tell.

DAN: Where does he go?

LUCY: I know where he doesn't go, Dan, but where he does, I can't say. He's not going to Julia's any more lately. I'm afraid, Dan, I'm afraid!

DAN: Of what, Little Sister?

LUCY: Of everything; oh, Dan, it's too big, too much for me—the world outside, the street—Chris going out and coming home nights moody-eyed; I don't understand.

DAN: And so you're afraid? That's been the trouble from the beginning of time—we're afraid because we don't understand.

LUCY: *(Coming down front, with a dish-cloth in her hand.)*
Oh, Dan, wasn't it better in the old days when we were back home—in the little house with the garden and you and father coming home nights and mother getting supper, and Chris and I studying lessons in the dining-room at the table—we didn't have to eat and live in the kitchen then, and—

DAN: *(Grimly.)*
—And the notices posted on the fence for us to leave town because niggers had no business having such a decent home.

LUCY: *(Unheeding the interruption.)*
—And Chris and I reading the wonderful books and laying our plans—

DAN: —To see them go up in the smoke of our burned home.

LUCY: *(Continuing, her back to* DAN, *her eyes lifted, as if seeing a vision of retrospect.)*

—And everyone petting me because I had hurt my foot when I was little, and father—

DAN: —Shot down like a dog for daring to defend his home—

LUCY: —Calling me "Little Brown Princess," and telling mother—

DAN: —Dead of pneumonia and heartbreak in this bleak climate.

LUCY: —That when you—

DAN: Maimed for life in a factory of hell! Useless—useless—broken on the wheel.

(His voice breaks in a dry sob.)

LUCY: *(Coming out of her trance, throws aside the dish-cloth, and running to* DAN, *lays her cheek against his and strokes his hair.)*

Poor Danny, poor Danny, forgive me, I'm selfish.

DAN: Not selfish, Little Sister, merely natural.

(Enter roughly and unceremoniously CHRIS. *He glances at the two with their arms about each other, shrugs his shoulders, hangs up his rough cap and mackinaw on a nail, then seats himself at the table, his shoulders hunched up; his face dropping on his hand.* LUCY *approaches him timidly.)*

LUCY: Tired, Chris?

CHRIS: No.

LUCY: Ready for dinner?

CHRIS: If it is ready for me.

LUCY: *(Busies herself bringing dishes to the table.)*

You're late to-day.

CHRIS: I have bad news. My number was posted today.

LUCY: Number? Posted?

(Pauses with a plate in her hand.)

CHRIS: I'm drafted.

LUCY: *(Drops plate with a crash.* DAN *leans forward tensely, his hands gripping the arms of his chair.)*

LUCY: Oh, it can't be! They won't take you from us! And shoot you down, too? What will Dan do?

DAN: Never mind about me, Sister. And you're drafted, boy?

CHRIS: Yes—yes—but—

(He rises and strikes the table heavily with his hand.)

I'm not going.

DAN: Your duty—

CHRIS: —Is here with you. I owe none elsewhere, I'll pay none.

LUCY: Chris! Treason! I'm afraid!

CHRIS: Yes, of course, you're afraid, Little Sister, why shouldn't you be? Haven't you had your soul shrivelled with fear since we were driven like dogs from our home? And for what? Because we were living like Christians. Must I go and fight for the nation that let my father's murder go unpunished? That killed my mother—that took away my chances for making a man out of myself? Look at us—you—Dan, a shell of a man—

DAN: Useless—useless—

LUCY: Hush, Chris!

CHRIS: —And me, with a fragment of an education, and no chance—only half a man. And you, poor Little Sister, there's no chance for you; what is there in life for you? No, if others want to fight, let them. I'll claim exemption.

DAN: On what grounds?

CHRIS: You—and Sister. I am all you have; I support you.

DAN: *(Half rising in his chair.)*

Hush! Have I come to this, that I should be the excuse, the woman's skirts for a slacker to hide behind?

CHRIS: *(Clenching his fists.)*

You call me that? You, whom I'd lay down my life for? I'm no slacker when I hear the real call of duty. Shall I desert the cause that needs me—you—Sister—home? For a fancied glory? Am I to take up the cause of a lot of kings and politicians who play with men's souls, as if they are cards—dealing them out, a hand here, in the Somme—a hand there, in Palestine—a hand there, in the Alps—a hand there, in Russia—and because the cards don't match well, call it a misdeal, gather them up, throw them in the discard, and call for a new deal of a million human, suffering souls? And must I be the Deuce of Spades?

(During the speech, the door opens slowly and JAKE lounges in. He is a slight, pale youth, Hebraic, thin-lipped, eager-eyed. His hands are in his pockets, his narrow shoulders drawn forward. At the end of CHRIS' speech he applauds softly.)

JAKE: Bravo! You've learned the patter well. Talk like the fellows at the Socialist meetings.

DAN: and LUCY: Socialist meetings!

CHRIS: *(Defiantly.)*

Well?

DAN: Oh, nothing; it explains. All right, go on—any more?

JAKE: Guess he's said all he's got breath for. I'll go; it's too muggy in here. What's the row?

CHRIS: I'm drafted.

JAKE: Get exempt. Easy—if you don't want to go. As for me—

(Door opens, and MRS. O'NEILL bustles in. She is in deep mourning, plump, Irish, shrewd-looking, bright-eyed.)

MRS. O'NEILL: Lucy, they do be sayin' as how down by the chain stores they be a raid on the potatoes, an' ef ye're wantin' some, ye'd better be after gittin' into yer things an' comin' wid me. I kin kape the crowd off yer game foot—an' what's the matter wid youse all?

LUCY: Oh, Mrs. O'Neill, Chris has got to go to war.

MRS. O'NEILL: An' ef he has, what of it? Ye'll starve, that's all.

DAN: Starve? Never! He'll go, we'll live.

(LUCY *wrings her hands impotently.* MRS. O'NEILL *drops a protecting arm about the girl's shoulder.*)

MRS. O'NEILL: An' it's hard it seems to yer? But they took me man from me year before last, an' he wint afore I came over here, an' it's a widder I am wid me five kiddies, an' I've niver a word to say but—

CHRIS: He went to fight for his own. What do they do for my people? They don't want us, except in extremity. They treat us like—like—like—

JAKE: Like Jews in Russia, eh?

(*He slouches forward, then his frame straightens itself electrically.*)

Like Jews in Russia, eh? Denied the right of honor in men, eh? Or the right of virtue in women, eh? There isn't a wrong you can name that your race has endured that mine has not suffered, too. But there's a future, Chris—a big one. We younger ones must be in that future—ready for it, ready for it—

(*His voice trails off, and he sinks despondently into a chair.*)

CHRIS: Future? Where? Not in this country? Where?

(*The door opens and* JULIA *rushes in impulsively. She is small, lightly built, eager-eyed, light-brown skin, wealth of black hair; full of sudden shyness.*)

JULIA: Oh, Chris, someone has just told me—I was passing by—one of the girls said your number was called. Oh, Chris, will you have to go?

(She puts her arms up to CHRIS' *neck; he removes them gently, and makes a slight gesture towards* DAN'S *chair.)*

JULIA: Oh, I forgot. Dan, excuse me. Lucy, it's terrible, isn't it?

CHRIS: I'm not going, Julia.

MRS. O'NEILL: Not going!

DAN: Our men have always gone, Chris. They went in 1776.

CHRIS: Yes, as slaves. Promised a freedom they never got.

DAN: No, gladly, and saved the day, too, many a time. Ours was the first blood shed on the altar of National liberty. We went in 1812, on land and sea. Our men were through the struggles of 1861—

CHRIS: When the Nation was afraid not to call them. Didn't want 'em at first.

DAN: Never mind; they helped work out their own salvation. And they were there in 1898—

CHRIS: Only to have their valor disputed.

DAN: —And they were at Carrizal, my boy, and now—

MRS. O'NEILL: An' sure, wid a record like that—ah, 'tis me ould man who said at first 'twasn't his quarrel. His Oireland bled an' the work of thim divils to try to make him a traitor nearly broke his heart—but he said he'd go to do his bit—an' here I am.

(There is a sound of noise and bustle without, and with a loud laugh, BILL HARVEY *enters. He is big, muscular, rough, his voice thunderous. He emits cries of joy at seeing the group, shakes hands and claps* CHRIS *and* DAN *on their backs.)*

DAN: And so you weren't torpedoed?

HARVEY: No, I'm here for a while—to get more mules and carry them to the front to kick their bit.

MRS. O'NEILL: You've been—over there?

HARVEY: Yes, over the top, too. Mules, rough-necks, wires, mud, dead bodies, stench, terror!

JULIA *(horror-stricken):* Ah—Chris!

CHRIS: Never, mind, not for mine.

HARVEY: It's a great life—not. But I'm off again, first chance.

MRS. O'NEILL: They're brutes, eh?

HARVEY: Don't remind me.

MRS. O'NEILL *(whispering):* They maimed my man, before he died.

JULIA *(clinging to* CHRIS): Not you, oh, not you!

HARVEY: They crucified children.

DAN: Little children? They crucified little children.

CHRIS: Well, what's that to us? They're little white children. But here, our fellow-countrymen throw our little black babies in the flames—as did the worshippers of Moloch, only they haven't the excuse of a religious rite.

JAKE: *(Slouches out of his chair, in which he has been sitting brooding.)*

Say, don't you get tired sitting around grieving because you're colored? I'd be ashamed to be—

DAN: Stop! Who's ashamed of his race? Ours the glorious inheritance; ours the price of achievement. Ashamed! I'm PROUD. And you, too, Chris, smouldering in youthful wrath, you, too, are proud to be numbered with the darker ones, soon to come into their inheritance.

MRS. O'NEILL: Aye, but you've got to fight to keep yer

inheritance. Ye can't lay down when someone else has done the work, and expect it to go on. Ye've got to fight.

JAKE: If you're proud, show it. All of your people— well, look at us! Is there a greater race than ours? Have any people had more horrible persecutions—and yet—we're loyal always to the country where we live and serve.

MRS. O'NEILL: And us! Look at us!

DAN: *(Half tears himself from the chair, the upper part of his body writhing, while the lower part is inert, dead.)*

Oh, God! If I were but whole and strong! If I could only prove to a doubting world of what stuff my people are made!

JULIA: But why, Dan, it isn't our quarrel? What have we to do with their affairs? These white people, they hate us. Only today I was sneered at when I went to help with some of their relief work. Why should you, my Chris, go to help those who hate you?

(CHRIS clasps her in her arms, and they stand, defying the others.)

HARVEY: If you could have seen the babies and girls— and old women—if you could have—

(Covers his eyes with his hand.)

CHRIS: Well, it's good for things to be evened up somewhere.

DAN: Hush, Chris! It is not for us to visit retribution. Nor to wish hatred on others. Let us rather remember the good that has come to us. Love of humanity is above the small considerations of time or place or race or sect. Can't you be big enough to feel pity for the little crucified French children—for the ravished Polish girls, even as their mothers must have felt sorrow, if they had known, for OUR burned and maimed little ones? Oh, Mothers of Europe, we be of one blood, you and I!

(There is a tense silence. JULIA turns from CHRIS, and drops her hand. He moves slowly to the window and looks out. The door opens quietly, and CORNELIA LEWIS comes in. She stands still a moment, as if sensing a difficult situation.)

CORNELIA: I've heard about it, Chris, your country calls you.

(CHRIS turns from the window and waves hopeless hands at DAN and LUCY.)

Yes, I understand; they do need you, don't they?

DAN   *(fiercely):*   No!

LUCY: Yes, we do, Chris, we do need you, but your country needs you more. And, above that, your race is calling you to carry on its good name, and with that, the voice of humanity is calling to us all—we can manage without you, Chris.

CHRIS: You? Poor little crippled Sister. Poor Dan—

DAN: Don't pity me, pity your poor, weak self.

CHRIS: *(clenching his fist.)*

Brother, you've called me two names today that no man ought to have to take—a slacker and a weakling!

DAN: True. Aren't you both?

(Leans back and looks at CHRIS speculatively.)

CHRIS: *(Makes an angry lunge towards the chair, then flings his hands above his head in an impatient gesture.)*

Oh, God!

(Turns back to window.)

JULIA: Chris, it's wicked for them to taunt you so—but Chris—it IS our country—our race—

(Outside the strains of music from a passing band are heard. The music comes faintly, gradually growing louder and louder

until it reaches a crescendo. The tune is "The Battle Hymn of the Republic," played in stirring march time.)

DAN: *(singing softly.)*

"Mine eyes have seen the glory of the coming of the Lord!"

CHRIS: *(Turns from the window and straightens his shoulders.)*

And mine!

CORNELIA: "As He died to make men holy, let us die to make them free!"

MRS. O'NEILL: An' ye'll make the sacrifice, me boy, an' ye'll be the happier.

JAKE: Sacrifice! No sacrifice for him, it's those who stay behind. Ah, if they would only call me, and call me soon!

LUCY: We'll get on, never fear. I'm proud! PROUD!

(Her voice breaks a little, but her head is thrown back.)

(As the music draws nearer, the group breaks up, and the whole roomful rushes to the window and looks out. CHRIS remains in the center of the floor, rigidly at attention, a rapt look on his face. DAN strains at his chair, as if he would rise, then sinks back, his hand feebly beating time to the music, which swells to a martial crash.)

CURTAIN

GONE WHITE*

A PLAY IN THREE ACTS

CHARACTERS

ALLAN FRANKLIN CORDELL: *The Man*
ANNA MARTIN: *The Woman*
JOHN CHAMBERLAIN: *The Buffer*
BLANCHE PARKER: *The Aunt*
GRANNY WIMBISH: *The Grandmother*
HARRY BLAKE: *The Fool*
EMMA GORDON: *The Loyal One*
JIMMY DAVIS: *The Constant Lover*
EVAN MARTIN: *The Cripple*
Time: *The Present*
Place: *Anywhere in this country*

ACT I

SCENE: *Anna's Garden. A small plot of ground in a small city. One tree dominates the garden. Around it is a circular wooden seat. To the right a cottage door and window, practicable. To the left, a street, separated from the garden by wooden paling fence, with a gate, sagging on its hinges. A little garden with common flowers, bravely struggling to bloom. Geraniums in earthen pots are on the window sills of the cottage window, and cheap lace curtains flutter in and out in the breeze.*

It is sunset, and a stormy red suffuses the scene. Gradually it fades, darkens, and merges into a brilliant moonlight as the action progresses.

*Typescript.

250

A group of young people pass the garden on the outside of the palings, singing. Their song is of the lightest and most carefree, a popular tune. Emma and Jimmy detach themselves from the group, and enter the garden. They seat themselves, Emma swinging a little basket as she talks.

JIMMY: I wonder what's become of Anna?

EMMA: Probably singing a bedtime story to one of her charges.

JIMMY: That Evan is a pain. If I could get my hands on him once, I'd give him such a slap he'd get over his perennial peeve.

EMMA: But, Jimmy, you must remember Evan is crippled. Anna has had him since her sister died—

JIMMY: Some legacy—

EMMA: And she's been a slave to the child.

JIMMY: Not to mention her old Granny Wimbish— another pain.

EMMA: Sh, Jimmy! You're awful!

JIMMY: Well, she is and they are, both of them. Anna's too fine a girl to be a martyr. She's given up all her life, all her prospects of education and having the chance that other girls of her age and class have had. She'll never collect dividends on what she's put out in time and energy and love and devotion and sacrifice and—

EMMA: Catch your breath, Jimmy. When she marries Allan, she'll have happiness to spare. For if ever two people loved each other—

JIMMY: Yes, when.

EMMA: Jimmy, you don't mean, you can't think, you don't imagine—

JIMMY: I don't imagine anything, Emma. I know that Allan is ambitious. He's not making good now. He's not going to make good here. He's picked out a profession that no colored man can make good at, in this country—

(Harry Blake has gradually strolled down the street outside the fence. He leans on the gate, listening to the conversation. At the last word, he comes in and leans against the tree.)

HARRY: You're right there, old thing. What any colored man wants to be a civil engineer for in this dump I can't make out. About the only engineering he'll do is to fire the furnace in an office building.

EMMA: But you must give him credit, Harry, for his ambition.

HARRY: *(Snaps fingers, and lights cigarette)* Ambition! Old Stuff! 'T'aint going to buy no pork chops. As for me—

EMMA: *(Hotly)* Even if Allan didn't have pride, Anna's influence—

HARRY: Anna's influence! Anna's eyes! Fat chance Anna'll have of influencing him with a half-witted cripple hanging to her and a pesky grandmother nagging the heart out of her. Anna— *(jeers)* As for me and my house, it's the little old job that brings in the shekels for mine.

JIMMY: Hear! Hear!

EMMA: It's just like you men to be so sordid. I hate you all. I did think that YOU, Jimmy, —but— *(Chokes and flings herself out the gate. As she goes out, she collides with Allan Cordell. He is tall, slim, fair, light-haired. His shoulders droop with dejection, but he catches Emma by the arm as she falls against him. She looks up in his face, and speaks breathlessly.)*

EMMA: Oh, Allan, I'm so glad I met you. You do, you do love Anna, don't you?

ALLAN: More than my life, Emma.

EMMA: *(Triumphantly)* I knew it. *(She runs happily down the street.)*

ALLAN: Why the convocation, fellows?

JIMMY: Oh, nothing; just a question of values, that's all. Harry says the job's the thing. Emma says the ideal is the thing. I'm open-minded. What do you say?

ALLAN: I hope I may never come to the point where I have to choose. But I've always stuck to my ideals. I've got an ambition I want to realize for myself—and—for—Anna, and I'm going to fight it out with my back to the wall it may be, but fight I will.

HARRY: I always was the fool in the bunch, but I've got the money. When I run short of high palaver and ideals, I can always come to you two and get them. Contrariwise, when you run short of money, you'll find Harry's little old bank roll quite convenient.

(Jimmy laughs, and pushes Harry before him out the gate, and they pass down the street laughing. Allan sinks down on the seat and puts his head in his hands. A step is heard. Anna comes into the garden from the house door. Allan rises to greet her.)

ALLAN: Anna!

ANNA: Allan!

(Anna is young and slim, and brown and beautiful. Her manner is bit more sedate than Emma's, and her dress is almost severe in its simplicity. She is eagerly in love with Allan. Her hands caress his arm tenderly.)

ANNA: Something is wrong, dear. I saw you shake your head.

ALLAN: No, nothing more than usual. I'm disappointed. I wanted to set our wedding day—but—

ANNA: *(Catching her breath)* Yes, you can, Allan—yes. We could marry, and then you could go away and try for work somewhere else, and then send for me.

ALLAN: That's sneaky. I'm going to fight it out here. And why marry you and run away?

ANNA: You see, Allan. I—you MUST go away—you can't make good here.

ALLAN: *(Rising furiously)* Why can't I? I've got my diploma—my recommendations. I've been the best man in the university, none stood higher. Why—with all these big buildings going up—the contractors are crying for men. Here, now, is the big opportunity. I'll stay right here; color or no color. I know what you'll say—that my race is a bar. That's nothing but damnable propaganda to keep colored men from entering the profession. If you've got the goods you'll be able to make good. You're weak-kneed, like all the rest. Crying at your shadow—

(Anna shrinks against the tree, hiding her face in her hands. Allan sits by her and takes her in his arms.)

ALLAN: Forgive me darling. Of all women, you're the last anyone should ever call weak. But I've been nagged at everywhere until I'm sore, I guess. I WON'T run away. I'll stay right here, and with you to help me—

ANNA: And what little my love can do for you it shall do. Love may not be all, but it is my all. *(They open the garden gate and pass down the street, hand in hand. Granny Wimbish comes into the garden from the house, just as they go out the gate. She is withered, thin, yellow, a typical crone. She leans on her cane and shakes her head gloomily, as the lovers go down the street.)*

GRANNY: Humph! There they go. Lovers! SHE thinks they're lovers, but he'll not marry her. He's making a fool of her. No man as white as that is going to marry a brown girl. And if he does, there'll be misery! Misery! The world is full of nothing but misery!

(She croaks and croons on the last words, rocking to and from on the garden seat. Evan limps in the gate. He is little and elfish, with irons on his limps; a cruel limp and a weary scowl.)

EVAN: *(Shrilly)* I met 'em. I met 'em! They was going down to the river, and he was sayin' poetry. Silly! Silly! She thinks she's goin' to marry him, but I know better. *(He hops about in his elfish way.)*

GRANNY: Shut up, you brat! After she's worked her fingers to the bone, washin' and cooin' and sewin' for you, there you are makin' fun of her. What I tell you 'bout young folks? Don't care nothing for nobody but theirselves.

EVAN: Granny, ef Anna marries, she'll leave me an' you. *(Sniffs.)*

GRANNY: Anna ain't that kind. She's been all our 'pendence. And a mother to us both. Workin' at anything she could get. And never gettin' to graduate like the other girls, 'cause her poor no-count sister left her you to take keer of.

EVAN: *(Sullenly)* Well, I ain't no mo' burden den you. An' you don't want her to marry Allan needer. He ain't got a think for eeder of us to do.

(A masculine voice heard singing up the street, "Oh, Anna, dear Anna, my love to be!" Enter John Chamberlain, with a box of flowers. He is tall, dark, handsome. Older than Allan. He has the undisputed signs of well-being, well-doing, and an air of authority.)

JOHN: Good evening. Is Anna home?

GRANNY: No, she's gone out. *(Granny's manner is distinctly ingratiating.)*

EVAN: *(Chanting)* Down by the river-side, down by de river-side. With Allan. She ain't gwine study love no mo'.

(John looks annoyed. He turns to go, and Anna enters the gate alone.)

ANNA: John! *(She comes to him with outstretched hand.)*

JOHN: Anna! I brought you some flowers. Red roses. Like the red in your sweet lips. Like the red blood in your warm heart. Like the courage in your splendid soul.

EVAN: *(Aside)* Like the red light on the tail of a car! *(Limps out into the street.)*

GRANNY: *(Aside)* Like the red flag of a danger signal. *(Limps into the house.)*

JOHN: *(Still holding Anna's hands, oblivious of the others)* Anna, I won't wait any longer for my answer. Come to me. You know I love you—I—

ANNA: Stop, John, I can't—

JOHN: You only THINK you love Allan. But there can be no true happiness between you. Poverty. Struggle. The giving up—for you would have to give up Granny and Evan, after all your struggle to hold the home together. He hasn't a start yet. And I can care for all three of you.

(Anna's head droops. She is silent.)

JOHN: You've worked too hard, little girl. Be thoughtful of your own interests and come to me.

ANNA: Oh, John. You don't tempt me when you talk like that. You're only wasting breath.

JOHN: And, Anna, the time will come when Allan will look upon you as a handicap, as a drag. Children. Your own family. I will be patient. I will wait until you can care for me. Just a little. But think—think—before you say no again.

ANNA: Don't, John. I'm fond of you; I respect you, but this that you ask— *(She pushes him gently toward the gate. The postman pauses and gives Anna a letter.)* See, this letter has good fortune in it for me. *(John passes out into the street as Anna opens the letter.)*

ANNA: From Blanche Parker. Who is Blanche Parker? Oh, I know; it's Allan's Aunt Blanche he talks of so much. Why does she write me? Let's see.

"My dear Miss Martin: I am writing this to ask you to break off your affair with my nephew. He is trying to be loyal to his promise to you *(Anna's voice breaks as she reads)* but it is a foolish loyalty. He really owes something to me, his aunt, for I have done most to put him through college. Allan can make a career for himself, if he will step aside from his race, and he knows it. Only a stubborn and mistaken sense of gratitude and so-called race pride, is making him cling to the people, who have nothing but poverty to offer him. I feel that his engagement to you is making him still more determined to continue in this mistaken course. As a white man, and there is nothing about him to indicate color— he can rise in his chosen profession. As a colored man, he must compromise—and fail. I am sure you are too sensible to stand in his way. A girl of your complexion and class would be only a hindrance to him. If you love Allan, you will dismiss him from your life.

Sincerely yours, Blanche Parker."

(During the reading of this Anna has sobbed softly to herself. She crumples the letter in her hand.)

ANNA: Cruel. Bitter. Malicious. How could she! I hate her. I hate them all. "As a white man he could rise—" *(She sinks on the garden seat.)*

(Allan runs in the garden gate eagerly, a bunch of violets in his hands.)

ALLAN: Anna, see what I stopped to get you? Violets for your new dress to-morrow. Modest and fragrant, like you. Their sweetness hidden and lying close to the heart.

(Anna looks up indifferently, her eyes hard, as she lays the flowers on the seat without looking at them.)

ANNA: Allan, what are your prospects for getting taken on by the new firm?

ALLAN: *(Slowly)* Er—well, you see—I—er—

ANNA: *(Coldly)* In other words, they've refused you?

ALLAN: *(Slowly)* Yes—but I'm sure its only a tentative refusal. I am sure they will listen to the recommendation of Prof. Auerbach.

ANNA: And all the other places have refused you?

ALLAN: Well, but a man doesn't expect immediate big jobs.

ANNA: But didn't all the other men in your class get positions immediately at the Works?

ALLAN: Yes—but—

ANNA: And didn't you stand head of your class?

ALLAN: —Yes—but—

ANNA: Yet—when the positions were given out, you were overlooked?

ALLAN: But you see, Anna—

ANNA: Let's face facts, Allan. You're getting no work, because you're known to be colored?

ALLAN: Anna, it isn't fair—

ANNA: That being the case, since only white men are employed as engineers, if you want employment at your profession, you must "go white."

ALLAN: Never! I'll stick, until I compel them to admit that a Negro can be as good or better an engineer than a white man. I'll ram their damn prejudice down their throats. I'll— *(He stand excitedly, fists clenched.)*

ANNA: *(Stands also. Speaks coldly.)* All heroics, Allan. You'll starve or wind up your career hopping bells or being Pullman George.

ALLAN: What's come over you, Anna? You're cynical. That's a new role.

ANNA: *(Laughs bitterly)* Cynical? No, I'm not cynical. I'm disgusted. I can't see where we're getting anywhere. You'll never make good. I'm tired of waiting for you. And

Granny and Evan are dependent on me. You can't support yourself, much less three others.

ALLAN: *(Blustering)* Can't support myself?

ANNA: *(Wearily)* Oh, Allan, don't you suppose I know that your Aunt Blanche has been looking out for you? At least you owe her gratitude enough to try to make a living at the profession she gave you.

ALLAN: And so I will.

ANNA: But not with my help. I'm tired of being a step-ladder. Go on, Go white! Take your Nordic face out of my race!

ALLAN: Anna! Anna! Little Anna! *(They stand facing each other, tensely, like animals. Then a sudden gesture on Anna's part knocks down John's box of flowers from the seat. It falls open, disclosing the red roses.)*

ALLAN: Where'd those damn things come from?

ANNA: *(Stoops. Takes the flowers from the box and holds them against her breast.)* John Chamberlain brought them to me.

ALLAN: Humph! I see. Costly roses, John has money; a car. I see now why you're tired of waiting. No wonder you feel the burden of Granny and Evan. So I must be white, and get out of your way. You—you— *(Choking with rage, he seizes Anna's wrists.)*

ANNA: *(Slowly, as if the words were being cut out of her heart.)* You are right. It is—John Chamberlain. I shall marry him. He has money. I haven't the courage to face poverty with you. And you can be white. Be a great engineer. Have a career.

ALLAN: Damn careers! Damn you for a mercenary false thing. A prostitute sells her body for gold. You are worse; you'll sell your body, your soul and your lover to boot. Truth!

Vows! What is truth? There is none in woman and none in man! *(He tears the red roses from her arms, and rending them into the crushed bits, pitches the pieces in her face. Anna cows under the blows and the lash of his fury.)* Damn you. Hypocrites. Liars. All of you. White hypocrites, black liars. Lying women and thieving men. Damn you. All of you! *(He dashes out the gate and down the street. Anna sinks huddled on the seat, the rose petals clinging in her hair. Outside the gate, Emma and Jimmy pause and call to Anna. She raises her head dully.)*

EMMA: Jimmy and I have had a dispute. I want him to go on to school, and I'll wait for him until he graduates in law. But he's afraid I won't wait for him.

JIMMY: *(Sullenly)* Yes, while I am away grinding at law books, she'll be spending Harry Blake's money.

EMMA: Oh, Jimmy, just as Anna is true to Allan, and will wait for him—

ANNA: *(Interrupting)* You're wrong, Emma. I'm going to marry John Chamberlain. *(Droops her head against the tree.)*

JIMMY: Didn't I tell you? You women! You can't resist a dollar. Clothes. Good time. Cars. Fur coats. That's what you want. Why should a man scrimp and sacrifice to get a profession when a girl only wants money, and she doesn't care how the fellow gets it?

EMMA: You stop, Jimmy! If Anna is— *(But Jimmy slams the gate and goes out.)*

ANNA: Don't let him go away like that, Emma. Your happiness is slipping through your fingers. Call it back before it is too late.

EMMA: I'm not bothered about him. It's you, Anna. Why, dear—oh, I know you loved Allan. Why? Why? *(Granny comes from the house crooning, "Nobody knows the trouble I see.")*

GRANNY: No supper ready. Nothing done. Everybody talking, talking, talking. An' what does it amount to? Just words. No sense to them.

ANNA: God knows why, Emma. And He won't tell. They press us on every side. Bitter foes. And all we can say is—Courage! *(She sobs a bit on Emma's shoulder, then dries her eyes, straightens up, smiles bravely, and says, "Courage!")*

CURTAIN

ACT II

SCENE ONE   *By the riverside in a distant city. Twelve years have passed. A park by the side of the river. Benches face a walk which runs parallel to a wooded stream. The benches are set back in trees and shrubbery, which partly hide those who sit upon them. It is twilight. A heavy, scented, brooding dusky quiet.*

Anna enters, with slow dragging steps and sinks on one of the park benches. Even in the dusk, it is seen that she has grown visibly older. Her shoulders droop with weariness, and lines of pain and worry are carved in her face. Her dress is plain, shabby. She leans her chin in her hand, and gazes dispiritedly at the water.

ANNA: We used to sit by the riverside at home, just at this hour, and watch the lights come up one by one on the island. It was so much like this.

(In the distance a group of boys and girls sing. A stringed orchestra, apparently in a pavilion on the distant island, plays.)

ANNA: On such a night as this—oh, futile poetry of life!

(Voices heard approaching up the river walk. A group of white men appear, walking slowly. Allan Cordell is among them. They are all conventional and prosperous looking, in evening

clothes, with lighted cigars. They stroll down the path before the hidden bench.)

FIRST VOICE: I've seldom heard a better speech, Cordell, than the one you made this afternoon.

SECOND VOICE: Yes, he's got 'em all—the three P's of a good Rotarian—Pep, Punch, and Personality.

ALLAN: Am I to understand that I am another Babbitt?

THIRD VOICE: Not so bad as that; but you made us all feel that having you as our guest of honor at our annual luncheon, we were more than honoring ourselves!

ALLAN: *(Feigned modesty in his tone)* It was nothing but telling the truth—what I have done in the past twelve years.

FIRST VOICE: Yes, but few men have been able to do in two decades what you have done in one.

SECOND VOICE: And there's a good stretch before you yet. You have my contratulations.

THIRD VOICE: Just keep up the pace, and don't let your foot slip.

ALLAN: Thanks. I'll stop here, and finish this cigar, if you'll excuse me. This scene brings to my mind one that I knew in my earlier days. It—well—

FIRST VOICE: Not too successful to feel the urge for sentimental and romatic memories. Well, enjoy yourself.

(The three men laughing, pass down the walk. Allan seats himself on the bench, without seeing Anna, and relights his cigar. The flaring of the match shows him a dark, huddled form on the end of the bench.)

ALLAN: *(Starting)* I beg your pardon, I did not know anyone was on the bench. Will it annoy you if I rest here awhile?

ANNA: No, it's perfectly all right.

ALLAN: *(Under his breath)* That voice! Those rippling,

golden notes! *(He moves closer, and strikes a match. The light flares over Anna. She puts her hands over her face.)*

ALLAN: Anna! *(With a wild gesture, he seizes her, and crushes her in his arms. She resists, then sighs softly and relaxes in his embrace.)*

ALLAN: Twelve years! And you spurned me for another man. But I have found you, at last. Tell me, Anna, have you forgotten me?

ANNA: Never, for one instant. *(She sighs contentedly. They stand silent in a gripping embrace.)*

ALLAN: Anna, are you happy with him?

ANNA: You are successful, are you not, Allan?

ALLAN: Successful? Ye-es—

ANNA: Then I am content.

ALLAN: I hated you for years. I hate you this minute, when I think of the anguish you caused me. My loss of faith in women. The crushing blow to my pride—

ANNA: Your pride?

ALLAN: But underlying that hatred is a love that cries out in misery when it realizes what it has lost. I hated all women—

ANNA: But you married?

ALLAN: Expediency. The same old conventional story. Daughter of the employer, interested in the penniless youth, who sees chance for advancement by marrying into rich employer's family.

ANNA: That's a cynical way to put it.

ALLAN: Truth. Yet once I said there is no truth. God, how I suffered!

ANNA: Allan, listen. You have despised me for twelve years. Let me square myself with you. I was not the mercenary wretch you believed me when I sent you away. My heart ever since has been a dead thing squeezed dry of everything but anguish.

ALLAN: Yet, you sent me away—

ANNA: For your own good. You could not have made a success; you could never have even made good in a small way. I should have been nothing but a hindrance to you, in every way—my color and my poverty and my responsibilities. You could only succeed on the other side of the racial wall—I could not go there with you.

ALLAN: *(Seizing her by the arm)* Look at me. *(He strikes a match. The flare shows her face drooping, averted.)* Who put that fool notion in your head? I've often wondered. In one hour you swore to me that you would stand by me until death, and in the next hour you sent me packing, with some half baked reason, plus the cruelest thrust a woman can give a man.

ANNA: No one.

ALLAN: The truth, Anna. I believed that twelve years ago. I've had a chance to think it over. The truth. Who was it?

ANNA: *(Faltering)* Your—Aunt—Blanche—

ALLAN: Hm-m.

ANNA: She wrote me a letter.

ALLAN: And you let her impudent, infernal meddling wreck our lives?

ANNA: She was right. Your career has proved she was right.

ALLAN: Career? Career? But at what a sacrifice of manhood. Tell me about yourself.

ANNA: The short and simple annals of the poor. John went to war. His business failed. We have been very unfortunate. Granny's death came a year or two later. Evan lingered a bit longer. He was a great care. I have had to work hard. John was ill for a long while after he returned from overseas at the same time that Granny was. There was a baby, but it died when it was three months old. The war wrecked us. John has been in the veteran's hospital, but he's home now. I think he may come out all right, but it has been a long, hard pull. Were you in the war?

ALLAN: Exempt. Wife and three children, and building roads and bridges. I have made much money otherwise.

ANNA: So I heard. My sacrifice was not in vain. You are a success.

ALLAN: If money and the plaudits of the world is success.

ANNA: The white world. You are one of the supreme Nordics.

ALLAN: Yes, with a constant, nagging fear in my soul that my house of cards will tumble at any moment. I did not know that you lived in this city. If I had, I should probably not have accepted the invitation of the Rotary Club to address them.

ANNA: We don't live here now; we did before the war. But we are back in the old home town—for economy's sake. I came here today to look after some business of John's.

ALLAN: Ah! I do not wish to see anyone who knew me in the old days. The haunting dread of my life is that someone will arise one day, point a finger at me and yell, "Nigger!" And I should slink away like a spectre that is shot with a silver bullet. There would not be courage enough left in me to deny, or to brazen it out. My wife tells me of her childhood, but my lips are closed on my early days. She thinks it is because there were painful scenes in my early boyhood that I do not wish to recall. There are. They are the sweet days of my youth with the boys and girls of my own people. I do not go back to class reunions at the university. Someone might begin to piece together the name of Allan Cordell, the penniless Negro student, and Franklin Cordell, the successful engineer. I am not superstitious, yet the advent of each child filled me with dread. I dared not face a possible flare-back. I knew it was all silly poppycock—the things the propagandists tell us of atavism—but who knew what my fears and dread might have induced?

ANNA: Poor boy!

ALLAN: Poverty of the direst sort!

(Silence. The darkness has been lighted fitfully by flashes of light from boats passing on the river. A group of boys and girls go by singing and thrumming ukuleles.)

ALLAN: Anna. The past twelve years have been nothing but a horrible dream. Our love is the only reality. Let us forget it all. Come away with me. Let us start life over somewhere where we can forget all this past nightmare—just you and I—

ANNA: Don't. Hush! You must not.

ALLAN: We've paid our debt to the world, to our families, to convention. We owe it to ourselves to live—to live. Do you know what that means, Anna? To love each other, and to be to each other what God intended.

ANNA: You don't realize what you are saying.

ALLAN: Yes, I do. I do realize it. The hunger of my empty heart would tell me if I did not. I've found you, and I know now what life will mean to me should I lose you again. You can't send me away again.

ANNA: You are mad—

ALLAN: Yes, mad for love of you. Anna, you think I am impracticable, but I am not. I am rich. We can go away— to South America, to Europe, anywhere, just to be with you.

ANNA: You have forgotten—

ALLAN: My wife? She will weep a bit and then divorce me and marry again, and forget me. It was a tepid sort of love between us, easily forgotten.

ANNA: That is not all.

ALLAN: Your husband? The government will take care of him, and then—you never loved him, did you, Anna? Tell me, you never really loved him? Your silence is all the answer I want. Anna, my God, you will not wreck our happiness again, will you? I want you; you want me—Anna—Anna *(His voice breaks in sobs.)*

ANNA: Oh, Allan, Allan, I told you years ago that love is all.

ALLAN: Beloved!

ANNA: Beloved!

(A searchlight from a passing steamer finds them, and its beam of light rests on them. They are seated on the park bench, their forms clasped in a close embrace.)

CURTAIN

SCENE TWO   *The next morning. The same scene as in Scene One. A pitiless sunlight makes bare mockery all the romance of the night before.*

Harry and Jimmy enter from the left, and stroll up the walk. They are chatting and smoking. Just in front of the bench they pause, and face the river.

HARRY: Looks like the river front at home, doesn't it, Jim?

JIMMY: Enough to make me homesick.

HARRY: Homesick for that Main Street burg! The taste of some people!

JIMMY: Home is home.

HARRY: Yes, and a pig sty is a pig sty, and a barn is a barn. I imagine Farmer Brown would yearn for the haystack when he was in the bright lights of the big city.

JIMMY: Call me Rube. Doesn't hurt me. I'm homesick. Haven't seen the old place since before the war, when we went out together filled with zeal, patriotism, homesickness and an ineffable urge for the great adventure.

HARRY: And came back filled with bitterness, gloom, trench feet and no job. What became of Emma!

JIMMY: Threw me down. I said some bitter things when Anna turned down Allan Cordell for John Chamberlain, and Emma never forgave me. I thought she'd marry you.

HARRY: So did I. She thought otherwise. Wouldn't trust any man, and so on to the n'th degree of damfoolishness. So, it's the little old bachelor flat for mine, and a pipe and peace, and nary a skirt to disturb my bank roll.

JIMMY: So she didn't marry him, after all? *(Musingly to himself.)*

HARRY: Cordell made good on the other side.

JIMMY: Hm-m. Wonder how he likes it? I had some time connecting the two—but I pieced it all together, and doped out the great Cordell. Our old-time chum. Well, joy be with him.

HARRY: Yes. Pale face frau, 'n' everything. He's welcome to 'em. Never liked 'em too pale. All wishy-washy. Brown-a-tone suits me.

JIMMY: Success is all right. I'm glad he made good. But I wonder what price he pays for it? Dread of discovery. Shifting glance when a man looks at him too hard. Fear lest his wife discover his past. Skirting around the edges of places, lest he run into an old friend. There must be silences when his wife speaks of his past.

HARRY: If he doesn't love her, should think he'd relish some silences.

JIMMY: You can't turn your back on your own people without pulling down your flag of integrity.

HARRY: Flag of integrity is a mouthful of fine words, but it doesn't pay the little old landlord. And I've noticed that this integrity business doesn't command one half the respect that a good income tax receipt does.

JIMMY: Speaking of angels—

(Allan comes up the path from the right. Pauses awkwardly when he sees the two men in conversation. There are signs of recognition on the part of all three men, but half deprecatory nod from Allan meets no response from Jimmy or Harry. They move on down the path, right, their heads together, as if Allan did not exist.)

ALLAN: *(Looking after them)* Now how am I to interpret that? As a cut direct? As a tribute to my superior position? As a notice served that they will not betray me? Or as a disgusted desire not to acknowledge my existence? It's not the first time I've been slapped in the face this way. I've always wanted to do the cutting myself, but I've never been allowed the chance. They always see me and beat me to it.

(Enter Aunt Blanche breathlessly. She is a large domineering woman, fair of skin, white of hair, expensively gowned, flashing jewels.)

AUNT BLANCHE: As soon as I heard you were coming here to speak, I drove over. I'm glad you got my telegram to meet me here. I just wanted to congratulate you. It's been years since we've seen each other. But I've taken the greatest pride in your career.

ALLAN: *(Crossly)* Why couldn't you come to my hotel to see me?

AUNT BLANCHE: Because, my dear, there are too many

of the employees who know who I am. One cannot straighten the hair of half the colored girls in a county and not be known everywhere. They might wonder at your receiving a colored woman. One can't be too careful.

ALLAN: Oh careful!

AUNT BLANCHE: Yes, careful. A white man might have business calls or even social calls from colored people, and nothing would be thought of it, but a man whose antecedents are not mentioned must watch every step, and shun anyone who might be connected with the other race. He is under suspicion, and there are watchful eyes. Don't tear down in one hour what it has taken twelve years to build.

ALLAN: Rot! I must meet my relatives in the park like a servant girl.

AUNT BLANCHE: I am too proud of your success to do the least thing to militate against it.

ALLAN: Success! That's all you think of. You sacrificed my manhood on the altar of your ideal of success.

AUNT BLANCHE: I? Sacrificed you?

ALLAN: Yes, you sacrificed me. You wrote the only girl I ever loved a damnably plausible letter, and drove her into poverty and obscurity and misery with the man she didn't love, and sent me into the world a misanthrope and a coward.

AUNT BLANCHE: Puppy love! Sophomoric maunderings! What more do you want? There's hardly a man in the country more respected in his profession than you. You married a beautiful woman of family and wealth. You have everything the most exacting man could want.

ALLAN: All built up on a tissue of lies. I am sick of lies. I want the woman I love. And I'm going to have her.

AUNT BLANCHE: May I ask how?

ALLAN: For once in my life I'm going to have what I

want. I shall take her and fly to some country where a man can practice my profession without living a lie.

AUNT BLANCHE: More heroics. And your wife and children? Your position? Your property? Your place in the professional world? Your prospects? You are young. There are many years of honor yet for you. You are no schoolboy to throw aside material benefits for a fancied romance. Must all your struggles and sacrifices go for nothing now? Why, if you must love your race, glean what satisfaction you can out of the thought of the huge joke you're playing on the world.

ALLAN: *(Wavering)* But I love her, Aunt Blanche, I love her.

AUNT BLANCHE: Nobody objects to that. If she is as poor as you say she is, and loves you as much as you think she does, she might not object to your loving her.

ALLAN: Aunt Blanche! You are damnable!

AUNT BLANCHE: I think you'll find me damnably practical. Well, Good Luck to you. *(Exits.)*

(Allan nods indifferently. Lights a cigarette nervously. Paces up and down. Lights another. Tamps it out. Beats hands nervously together as he walks up and down. Enter Anna from left. She coughs slightly. In the daylight, her face shows even more drawn and haggard than at night.)

ANNA: I thought I should find you here. I felt that you, too, would want to see the sunlight on the river; feel the caress of spring on your check—with me.

ALLAN: *(Huskily)* Anna, all the world seems fairer since I have found you again.

ANNA: You never really lost me, dear. Just a pause, that's all.

ALLAN: A dreary interim, bounded by two golden epochs. *(They sit silent with clasped hands.)*

ALLAN: And now, dear, we must talk of our future.

ANNA: There is no future, Allan. A beautiful golden present. No more.

ALLAN: We love each other.

ANNA: Superfluous verbiage.

ALLAN: And there must be a future. I MUST have you; MUST possess you. I've starved for your warm beauty; for the tropical beauty and passion of your enduring love. When I was denied what I wanted as a boy, I whimpered and fled with bowed head; but I am a man now. I've been taking what I wanted with a ruthless hand. I want you, Darling. I must have you.

ANNA: Wait, dear.

ALLAN: I know what you will say—what you tried to say last night. You will tell me of your duty to John Chamberlain. I grant you that—you couldn't desert him.

(Anna starts, and looks at him searchingly.)

ALLAN: And I have a wife and childlren, and a position in the world, and responsibilities and a still more brilliant future. I know you would remind me of that.

ANNA: I had not mentioned those things—had not thought of them since last night you rejected them as having no further place in your life. Today, I remembered only that I had found you. Past and future alike merged into a mist of unreality. I was dazed with the happiness of the present.

ALLAN: *(Uneasily)* Yes, but one of us must think.

ANNA: You had thought it all out last night. I have let it rest there, until I can get my confused impressions in order.

ALLAN: *(Visibly embarrassed)* Anna, last night I was mad from the touch of your hands. I proposed impracticable things. Can we not love each other? What have we to do with conventions, man-made laws and all that?

ANNA: But you have just said that what you proposed last night is impracticable; that you cannot give up your family, your place in the world; that it is not right for me to leave John?

ALLAN: I know I did. But Anna, don't you understand? I want your love; I want YOU.

ANNA: *(Rising slowly)* Yes—I think I do understand. *(She leans on the bench, her hands gripping its back, until her knuckles are white. They face each other silently. Then Anna speaks through clenched teeth.)*

ANNA: Yes—I understand. You are offering me the position of your mistress. You are giving me the wonderful opportunity of having a secret liaison with you. You love me, but you love your position in the world of white men more. I don't blame you for that. The measure of the world's approbation does not go to the men who have stood by their ideals, but to those who have made a successful compromise with Necessity. But that you should come to me—No, don't interrupt. To me! Who had the courage to send you into another world! But you're running true to form. Your white blood and your white training and your imbibing of the Nordic ideals are showing up through your thin veil of decency. You would keep your white wife, and all that that means, for respectability's sake—but you would have a romance, a liaison with the brown woman whom you love, after dark. No Negro could stoop so low as to take on such degraded ideals of so-called racial purity. And this is the moral deterioration to which you have brought your whole race. White Man! Go on back to your white gods! Lowest and vilest of scum. White Man! Go Back!

(Allan stands with bowed head, lashed under the fury of her scorn. Anna stands still, trembling, then sinks sobbing, with her head on the back of the bench. Allan stands shamefacedly, looking

at her. He makes a gesture as if to touch her, pauses, shakes his head. The three men of the night before, come down the path, right, and looking up, hail him. Allan straightens his shoulders, and steps toward the river path.)

FIRST VOICE: I see you're enjoying the morning by our river?

SECOND VOICE: I hope you haven't been here all night. We left you here, and here we find you.

THIRD VOICE: That seems to be a woman in distress. Do you know anything about her trouble?

FIRST VOICE: Some poor colored woman she seems to be. Those people are so emotional aren't they?

ALLAN: *(Drawling)* Yes, it seems to be a racial characteristic. I would have spoken to her to see if I could help her, but she seemed to want to be alone.

SECOND VOICE: Well, this bracing air has given me an appetite! Shall we have luncheon together at the hotel?

(Exeunt down the river path.)

CURTAIN

ACT III

A few days later. Anna's garden. Same as in Act I, except that the gate has sagged more. It is spring. Blossoms struggle through the ground. The afternoon sun sends long shadows athwart the garden. Voices are heard singing in the distance, and young people pass and re-pass. Emma and Jimmy detach themselves from a group, as in Act I, and enter the garden.

JIMMY: But, Emma, twelve years of loneliness is a long and bitter punishment to inflict for a fancied wrong.

EMMA: Why fancied? Is it a fancied wrong when a woman hears a man blaspheme all women? Look at me. I'm an old maid because you taught me to distrust all men.

JIMMY: Look at me. I'm an old bachelor because you taught me to look down upon all women but you.

EMMA: Well, that's your hard luck. I'm sure it didn't make any difference to me whether you married or not.

JIMMY: But it made a difference to me, Emma. How could I put another woman in my heart after having known you? She would have rattled around like a dried up pea in a shell—

EMMA: You're accurately describing your heart. I congratulate you.

JIMMY: Oh, Emma, don't be so hard. You know what I mean. I see all these wasted years—

EMMA: Wasted words.

JIMMY: Emma, you quarrelled with me because—

EMMA: You flatter yourself. I did not quarrel with you.

JIMMY: You threw me over because—

EMMA: I did not throw you over. You walked off in a huff.

JIMMY: And why did I walk off? You sent me away—

EMMA: Well, that's an old story—

JIMMY: Emma, when I was wallowing in the mud and filth near the famous poppies of poetry, I had the chance to think through a lot of things that I've been waiting a chance to tell you. I'm lucky that I ran across you to-day, after all these years. Values are different. You were always the biggest thing in my life. And you stayed the biggest thing, while a lot of petty foolishness dropped away. It was a long wasted period that you let me in for, because you were taking on another's quarrels—

EMMA: I take on no one's quarrels. I simply had no room in my life for any man.

JIMMY: Maybe not. But how about love and a home and little ones, and all the real things—

EMMA: Sob stuffs!

JIMMY: Life is a grab bag, Emma, and you've pulled a cheap tin whistle out of it. You're blowing on it now, trying to kid yourself into thinking it's a golden trumpet.

(The door of the cottage opens and John Chamberlain comes wearily down the steps. He leans heavily on a cane. His hair is gray and his face seamed with pain. Emma runs to him with outstretched hands. He settles himself stiffly and awkwardly on the garden seat and sighs profoundly.)

JIMMY: *(With constraint)* How's things, old man?

JOHN: About the same. But I'll be all right in a few months, and then I can go about gathering up the loose ends of life. I'll come back, never fear. Only, it has been hard on Anna.

EMMA: She has been wonderful; hasn't she, John?

JOHN: *(Slowly)* She has. Devoted to Granny. Fine to Evan. And splendid to me. The more reverses came, the better she stuck. One woman in ten thousand. But life has played a cruel joke on us both, Emma.

(Jimmy has wandered down the garden, left, and leans on the fence, as if not interested in the conversation. He lights a cigarette, as if not hearing, but he listens keenly behind the smoke screen.)

EMMA: Why call it a joke, John?

JOHN: Wasn't it a joke on me when I married Anna to give her ease and comfort, though I knew she didn't love me—hoping the care and luxuries I lavished on her would win her love—and then went to war and lost it all? And then I came back broken, and she had to work harder than ever? We even had to come back to her poor little home, for I had no shelter to offer her. Wasn't it a joke on me when she married me, though she loved Cordell, to give ease and comfort to Granny and Evan, and they both died, and all her sacrifice for them was in vain?

EMMA: *(Slowly)* Are you sure she didn't love you?

JOHN: Sure? *(He laught bitterly.)* What woman can deceive the man who loves her? She gave her body to me, but her soul? It was an impregnable fortress, and my pitiful assaults upon it only threw me back upon myself. She has given me devotion and loyalty to the highest degree, but that precious ruby of her inner heart, she keeps secret, hidden, and I can only guess it is there. I have never really known her, much less possessed her.

EMMA: Poor John! Poor boy!

(Jimmy stirs uneasily, and looks out of the corner of his eye at the two.)

JOHN: I don't know why I am whining to you. I suppose physical weakness makes a man forget he is a man at times.

EMMA: Poor John. Poor Anna. Where is she? I wanted to talk to her.

JOHN: She went to my old home where the fragments of my business were left—to look after some matters for me. If all goes as I hope, I shall be on the way to a rehabilitation of our fortunes. I could not go myself—

EMMA: Anna is very efficient—

JOHN: Yes, too much so. It has laid burdens on her that no woman should carry. Efficiency in a woman is admirable, but it makes her too impersonal. It sets her in a class apart from the female herd—she becomes a celibate, married though she be.

(Jimmy snorts.)

EMMA: My heart bleeds for you and Anna. In a way you two are responsible for—responsible for—

(Jimmy's tense attitude and stillness attract Emma's attention, and she falters, while her eyes cling to his beseechingly.)

JOHN: Yes, for what?

EMMA: *(Desperately)* Jimmy and I parted from each other

because we quarrelled over Anna's marrying you instead of Allan Cordell. I was disappointed, frankly, but I trusted Anna to do the honorable thing. But Jimmy indulged in some cheap cynicism—and well—we parted, that's all.

JIMMY: *(Coming forward)* No, it isn't all—I was wrong, Emma, as I have told you before. Anna knew what she was doing, and if she didn't—

EMMA: It wasn't anyone's business.

JOHN: Life isn't so long that we can take time out for silly quarrels. Twelve years is quite a slice out of happiness, little as there is to go around.

JIMMY: That's what I've been trying to tell Emma.

EMMA: Allan Cordell isn't worth anyone of us thinking about.

JOHN: He's a very successful man. One of the big men in the country. He made fortune during the war that broke me. If he hadn't gone white, though, he'd probably have been by my side and been gassed with some of the same bombs that his father-in-law's factory produced.

(Anna comes slowly down the street, and stops outside the gate. She is dressed for traveling, and carries a handbag. When she sees the group in the garden, she pauses, straightens her shoulders, and enters with a light, quick step.)

ANNA: Emma! Jimmy! The old friends. It's good to see you again. *(She stoops and kisses John's cheek lightly.)* I have good news for you, dear.

(John clasps her hands and rises painfully. His eyes search her face hungrily.)

JOHN: To see you come back is good news enough for the present.

ANNA: *(Whispering)* Didn't you expect me back, when I had gone to look after your affairs?

JOHN: I don't know. I should have, I suppose. But somehow, you always seem to be going out of my life, and I should not be surprised some day to find you gone. What's the news?

ANNA: The best in the world. Mercer will finance the business. We can start anew and build up again. He predicts that with good management, we can be back to our old status in less than five years.

JOHN: Wonderful woman!

ANNA: Not wonderful, not wonderful, John. Weak, foolish. *(She grips him by the shoulders.)* Look at me. I'm not going to make any confession to you. When I tell you that I saw Allan Cordell and talked to him—you will know.

JOHN: You love him still?

ANNA: Not now.

JOHN: Thank God! I prayed, oh, how I prayed, that some day you'd see this man, this sleek, well-fed, smug hypocrite of a near-white man, with his veneer of superiority, and his soul clogged in the fat of compromise and cowardice, and seeing him, the years would drop from your life, and the scales from your eyes, and you would know that you could never take pride in him, and you would be proud of your clean-washed soul again—

ANNA: And proud of you, John. You because you have been clean, and honest, and when you have lost, you have lost like a good sport. Because you have never compromised— even though you lost the material things of the world. Yes, I'm proud of you, John—and that means life to me.

(During this conversation, Emma and Jimmy have drifted toward the lower end of the garden, not hearing the other two. Their hands have gradually found each other.)

(A long whistle heard from the street. Harry Blake comes

briskly to the gate, leans on the top of the gate, from without, and surveys the two couples within.)

HARRY: Some love-nest; all billing and cooing, and all the rest of it.

JIMMY: Congratulate me, old man.

HARRY: So I do, though I'd rather you'd be congratulating me. But Emma's taller than I am; she'd probably throw things at me anyway. So you're going to leave this dump, Anna, and you and John going back to God's country, and the little old business again, eh? Time, says I.

ANNA: *(Smiling at him and turning to John)* Yes, we'll leave it all here, youthful romance, ashes of the past, the restless spirit of poor, tortured Evan, the lonely soul of Granny, the poor baby who smiled at us for so brief a time, your illness, our poverty, my blindness, all—all—and we'll start life anew. A new life, with no rose-colored cobwebs of the past to distort it—and who knows what the future may have in store for us?

(As John takes her in his arms, Jimmy does the same to Emma, and Harry Blake, in the mock attitude of a preacher, bestows a blessing on the two couples.)

CURTAIN

LOVE'S DISGUISE*

SYNOPSIS

Agnes has a dual face, one side being beautiful, the other side paralyzed and disfigured. Wherever she goes to secure work, her services are at once refused because of her frightful appearance. At last she secures work in a restaurant, opening oysters and doing mean chores. Her employer, seeing an opportunity to hire a servant for the price of a marriage fee, offers to marry her, telling her that such a fright as she will never have another offer. When she refuses him, he turns her out.

One day Agnes faints on the street, and is taken to a charity hospital. Later, when she is convalescent and is one day sitting with the madonna-like side of her face toward the window, Dr. Weaver, passing by, is attracted by her beauty. Coming in the room to speak with the nurse, he is startled to see the disfigured side of the profile. Many times later he thinks with interest of the strange face. One day he asks Agnes if she would like to be an attendant to his blind mother. She eagerly consents. After giving her case much study, Dr. Weaver asks her to allow him to experiment. She consents; and after an operation and patient effort, he restores her face to a normal condition. Agnes rewards him by marrying him.

CHARACTERS

AGNES, *beautiful and ugly*
ANDY LAYFIELD

*A typescript film scenario by "A. M. Dunbar, 916 French Street, Wilmington, Del.," probably 1909–1916.

281

Dr. Weaver
Mrs. Weaver, *his mother*
 Proprietor store
 Kitchen employees
 Nurse
 Mother
 Little boy

SCENARIO

1————Bedroom————
Agnes looks at herself in the mirror, first at the beautiful side of her face, then at the ugly side—dons hat—exit—

2————Exterior mansion————
Agnes approaches—ascends steps—rings—maid admits her—

3————Living room————
Mother reads to little boy—maid admits Agnes—Agnes explains—

Leader————"YOU ADVERTISED FOR A NURSE GIRL."

————Back to scene————
Little boy cries at sight of Agnes—hangs on to mother in fright—mother declines services of Agnes—rings—exit Agnes with maid—

4————Interior store————
Enter Agnes—approaches proprietor—explains—

Leader————"YOU ADVERTISED FOR A CLERK."

————Back to scene————
Proprietor regards her as curiosity—refuses her services—exit Agnes—

Leader————AT LAST————

    5————Interior restaurant————

Enter Agnes—approaches proprietor—offers her services—Layfield finally accepts her—motions her to follow him—they exeunt into—

    6————Kitchen————

Layfield puts her to work opening oysters and doing mean chores—he smiles at her coarsely—

Leader————ONE NIGHT————

    7————Kitchen————as 6————

Agnes drudges—Layfield approaches—smiles—tries to embrace her—

Leader————"SUPPOSE WE GET MARRIED. YOU CAN WORK HERE JUST THE SAME."

————Back to scene————

Agnes shrinks away from him—refuses him—he sneers—

Leader————"IT'S THE ONLY CHANCE YOU'LL EVER GET—A FRIGHT LIKE YOU!"

————Back to scene————

He proceeds to embrace her—she struggles to be free—he becomes angry—pushes her out the door—

Leader————ONE DAY————

    8————Street—

Agnes walks wearily along street—suddenly faints—people rush to her aid—

    9————Room in hospital————

Agnes lies ill—nurse bends over her—

Leader————ONE DAY————

  10————Room in hospital————

Agnes, with disfigured side of face turned toward nurse, sits sewing at window—

11———Exterior room in hospital———
Dr. Weaver, passing by, is attracted by the beauty of face at window—

12———Room in hospital———back to 10———
Dr. Weaver enters—talks to nurse—looks at disfigured side of Agnes' face—is startled and interested—slowly exit—

Leader———THAT NIGHT———

13———Living room———
Dr. Weaver talks to blind mother—speaks of Agnes—(vision of beautiful side of face)—(vision of disfigured side of face)—mother is interested—

Leader———THE NEXT DAY———

14———Room in hospital———as 9, 10, 12———
Nurse is reading to Agnes—enter Dr. Weaver—approaches Agnes—talks—

Leader———"MY MOTHER, BEING BLIND, NEEDS AN ATTENDANT. WOULD YOU LIKE TO SERVE HER?"

———Back to scene———
Agnes expresses her eagerness—

Leader———LATER———

15———Park———
Agnes guides Mrs. Weaver's steps—

Leader———ONE NIGHT———

16———Living room———
Agnes reads to Mrs. Weaver—enter Dr. Weaver—he sits near Agnes—shows her some medical books—

Leader———"I'VE STUDIED YOUR CASE UNTIRINGLY FOR MONTHS. WILL YOU LET

ME PERFORM AN OPERATION ON
YOUR FACE?"
————Back to scene————
Agnes hesitates—then consents—
Leader————ONE GLAD DAY————
17————Living room————as 13, 16————
Dr. Weaver removes bandage from Agnes'
face, revealing it to be normal—looking into
a mirror he hands her, she becomes radiant
with joy—when he embraces her, she looks at
him with grateful, loving eyes.

AAN-3478